# Learning through Supervision and Mentorship to Support the Development of Infants, Toddlers and their Families: a source book

Edited by EMILY FENICHEL

 ZERO TO THREE: National Center for Infants, Toddlers and Families

Copyright © 1992 **ZERO TO THREE**
Second printing October, 1997
Third printing March, 1999

ZERO TO THREE
734 15th Street, N.W., Suite 1000
Washington, D.C. 20005-1013
(202) 638-1144 - Phone
(202) 638-0851 - Fax

For publications ordering information, call **ZERO TO THREE** toll free 1-800-899-4301.

ISBN 0-943657-19-9
Library of Congress Catalog Card Number 92-085451
Design: Susan Lehmann

Chapters 5,7,10,11,12,13,14,16,17, and 18 appeared previously in *Zero to Three*, bulletin of the **ZERO TO THREE**.

Please note that ZERO TO THREE: National Center for Clinical Infant Programs changed its name in 1996 to ZERO TO THREE: National Center for Infants, Toddlers and Families.

This publication was developed with support from the Center for the Future of Children, The David and Lucile Packard Foundation.

**ZERO TO THREE's** mission is to promote the healthy development of America's babies and young children. We are the nation's leading resource on the first three years of life and work to strengthen the critical roles of professionals, policymakers and parents in giving all of our children the best possible start.

We focus on the first three years of life because this is the time of greatest human growth and development. It is also the time when caring adults have the greatest opportunity to shape a child's future.

## Work Group on Supervision and Mentorship of ZERO TO THREE

*Judith Bertacchi*, District Administrator, the Virginia Frank Child Development Center of the Jewish Family and Community Service, Chicago, Illinois

*Barbara Fields*, private practice, New York, New York

*Linda Gilkerson*, Co-director, Infant Studies Program, Erikson Institute, Chicago, Illinois

*Judith Pekarsky*, Senior Staff Psychologist, Infant-Parent Program, San Francisco General Hospital, University of California, San Francisco

*Kyle Pruett*, Clinical Professor of Psychiatry and Coordinator of Training, Child Development Unit, Yale Child Study Center, New Haven, Connecticut

*Madie Robinson*, Vice President/Deputy Director, Healthy Start, Florence, South Carolina

*Rebecca Shahmoon Shanok*, Director, Therapeutic Nursery Group Program, Child Development Center, Jewish Board of Family and Children's Services, New York, New York

*Eva Thorp*, Associate Professor, Department of Curriculum and Instruction, George Mason University, Fairfax, Virginia

*Marcy Whitebook*, Executive Director, Child Care Employee Project, Oakland, California

*Carol Lou Young-Holt*, Director, Training and Technical Assistance, Center for Child and Family Studies, Far West Laboratory for Educational Research and Development, Sausalito, California

*Staff to* **ZERO TO THREE's** *Project on Learning through Supervision and Mentorship*

*Emily Fenichel* (Director), Associate Director **ZERO TO THREE**

*Linda Eggbeer* (Assistant Director), Program Associate for Training, **ZERO TO THREE**

# Contents

5   Acknowledgments

7   Findings and Recommendations of ZERO TO THREE/National Center for Clinical Infant Programs' Work Group on Supervision and Mentorship

9   1. Learning through supervision and mentorship to support the development of infants, toddlers, and their families

18   2. Overcoming obstacles to reflective supervision and mentorship

27   3. Improving training of infant/family practitioners through supervision and mentorship: An action agenda

## 35  Supervision and Mentorship of Students

37   4. The supervisory relationship: Integrator, resource and guide—*Rebecca Shahmoon Shanok*

42   5. Individualizing training for early intervention practitioners—*Carole W. Brown and Eva K. Thorp*

49   6. A supervisor and student reflect on their relationship—*Kelley Bateman and Eva K. Thorp*

53   7. Scenes from supervision—*Judith Pekarsky*

56   8. A review of infant/toddler issues in supervision and mentorship based on instruction of the mentor teacher class—*Jane Perry*

61   9. A clinical approach to the training of supervisors: The model of co-supervision—*Kyle D. Pruett*

## 65  Supervision and Mentorship of Infant/Family Practitioners

67   10. The professionalization of early motherhood—*William M. Schafer*

76   11. Supervision as a catalyst in the evolution of an integrated infant mental health/developmental intervention program—*Barbara Ivins and Nancy Sweet*

84  12. The professional use of self in prevention—*Judith Bertacchi and Julie Coplon*

91  13. Lay home visiting programs: Strengths, tensions and challenges—*Mary Larner and Robert Halpern*

100  14. A developmental/relationship in-service training model—*Serena Wieder, Robert Drachman, and Tippie DeLeo*

## 111 Issues for Supervisors and Program Directors

113  15. Supervision and the management of programs serving infants, toddlers, and their families—*Linda Gilkerson and Carol Lou Young-Holt*

120  16. Management in the South Carolina Resource Mothers' Program: The importance of supervision—*Madie A. Robinson*

125  17. Toward tenacity of commitment: Understanding and modifying institutional practices and individual responses that impede work with multi-problem families—*Barbara Fields*

132  18. A seminar for supervisors in infant/family programs: Growing versus paying more for staying the same—*Judith Bertacchi and Frances M. Stott*

## 141 Appendixes

143  A. Supervision and mentorship: A qualitative study of early intervention practitioners, child care professionals, and public agency supervisors in Maryland—*EDK Associates*

154  B. A list of selected readings on supervision and mentorship

## 157 Contributors

# Acknowledgments

This *Sourcebook* is a product of the 1991-92 Learning through Supervision and Mentorship Project of **ZERO TO THREE**/National Center for Clinical Infant Programs, supported by the Center for the Future of Children of the David and Lucile Packard Foundation. The goals of the project have been:

- to improve understanding of supervision and mentorship as critical elements in the training of practitioners who work to support the development of infants, toddlers, and their families; and

- to suggest strategies for incorporating supervision and mentorship into training and practice institutions and systems.

To accomplish these tasks, **ZERO TO THREE** convened a multidisciplinary work group of 10 individuals who represent a range of training and practice settings. They have met as a group to exchange perspectives, have worked collaboratively with each other and with project staff to develop material, and have individually spent many hours writing, reviewing, and commenting on the ideas collected here. Our heartfelt thanks go to Judith Bertacchi, Barbara Fields, Linda Gilkerson, Judith Pekarsky, Kyle Pruett, Madie Robinson, Rebecca Shahmoon Shanok, Eva Thorp, Marcy Whitebook, and Carol Lou Young-Holt. Special appreciation goes to Deanna S. Gomby, Director of Research and Grants, Child Development, Center for the Future of Children, whose insight and support stimulated and encouraged our group throughout its work.

Our work group discovered early on that experienced administrators, trainers, and practitioners seem to agree that reflection, collaboration, and regularity are the essential features of effective supervision and mentorship in the infant/family field. We also learned that few publications either make a compelling case for the importance of reflective supervision and mentorship in infant/family work or offer concrete examples of how these features can be integrated into the diverse settings that characterize our field. Our work group decided, therefore, to publish not simply a report, with findings and recommendations, but rather this *Sourcebook*, which includes detailed descriptions of supervision and mentorship, as seen from the perspectives of students, teachers, front-line practitioners, supervisors, mentors, and administrators. We thank all who have contributed their hard-won expertise to this volume, as chapter authors, as interviewees, and as participants in focus group research.

As always, we are grateful for the extraordinary assistance of the Board of Directors and staff of **ZERO TO THREE**/National Center for Clinical Infant Programs. On their behalf, we invite all readers of this volume to join with us as we learn together to support the development of infants, toddlers, and their families.

Emily Fenichel and Linda Eggbeer
July, 1992

# Findings and Recommendations of ZERO TO THREE/National Center for Clinical Infant Programs' Work Group on Supervision and Mentorship

The three chapters of this section represent the collective thinking of **ZERO TO THREE**/National Center for Clinical Infant Programs' Work Group on Supervision and Mentorship. We conceptualize and describe supervision and mentorship as relationships for learning, characterized by reflection, collaboration, and regularity. We identify obstacles—practical and attitudinal—to reflective supervision and mentorship. Finally we suggest ways to overcome these obstacles, including five strategies for collaborative action to improve the training of infant/family practitioners through supervision and mentorship.

# 1

*Learning through Supervision and Mentorship To Support the Development of Infants, Toddlers and Their Families*

**Emily Fenichel,** with the
**ZERO TO THREE/National Center For Clinical Infant Programs' Work Group on Supervision and Mentorship**

Supervision and mentorship are relationships for learning. In the world of professional practice with infants, toddlers and their families, supervision and mentorship provide regular opportunities for individuals and groups, less experienced and more experienced, in training and service settings, to reflect together about their hands-on work.

Just as services to support the development of infants, toddlers and their families take many forms, so do the supervision and mentorship arrangements designed to support the development of practitioners in this field. Indeed, the terms "supervision" and "mentorship" themselves are understood very differently across the disciplines and service systems that work with young children and their families.

In 1991-92, a multidisciplinary work group convened by ZERO TO THREE/National Center for Clinical Infant Programs and supported by the Center for the Future of Children of the David and Lucile Packard Foundation, examined supervision and mentorship in the context of the range of practice with infants, toddlers and their families. As we tried to describe and demystify supervision and mentorship, we looked at both differences and similarities across disciplines and settings. We have discovered that experienced administrators, trainers, and practitioners seem to agree on the essential features of effective supervision and mentorship in this field. These are:

- reflection;
- collaboration; and
- regularity.

In this essay, we describe and discuss reflection, and the collaboration and regularity that support reflection, as essential features of supervision and mentorship in infant/family training and practice. Before doing so, however, we address the special characteristics of infant/family practice that make supervision and mentorship essential for delivery of high quality services and that make these relationships particularly appropriate vehicles for teaching and learning in this field.

> To use one's individual talents fully in work with infants, toddlers and their families is no easy task. Such work engages the emotions as fully as the intellect.

## The special characteristics of infant/family practice

Work with infants, toddlers and their families takes many forms in this country. These forms are constantly evolving. The health care system touches virtually all infants and mothers, however fleetingly. Some form of out-of-home child care is part of the experience of a majority of infants, toddlers, and families. Early intervention services for very young children with special needs and their families are becoming increasingly widespread. Formal and informal family resource programs, of widely varying size, scope, and sponsorship, flourish in many communities. Infant mental health services are provided by private practitioners, free-standing or institutionally based clinics, or consultants to other service settings. Community planners, federal and state administrators, and private foundations are experimenting with service system changes designed to address effectively the multiple, often complex needs of families with young children. One consequence of this diversity is that people who work with infants, toddlers and their families come from a range of professional and non-professional backgrounds, may or may not have been trained specifically to work with young children and/or families, and are certain, in the course of their careers, to encounter novel challenges.

During the last half-decade, a consensus has been developing around principles that lead to quality in infant/family programs. Such principles are reflected, among other places, in accreditation standards for service programs and for professionals, in fieldbased program evaluation and longitudinal research, and in the specifications of requests for proposals issued by federal and state agencies serving diverse populations of infants, toddlers, and their families. Thoughtful front-line practitioners and administrators in the field are likely to agree that:

- Services for infants, toddlers and their families must be specially designed for this population in order to be developmentally appropriate. They cannot be scaled-down versions of programs for older children.

- Infants and toddlers must be understood and served within the context of their families.

- Families are the constants in a child's life; the job of the professional is to assist families in supporting the child's development.

- Services to infants, toddlers and their families must be individualized to respect and build on unique constitutional, developmental, and cultural characteristics.

- Service coordination should be available to ease families' access to the range of services they require.

- Policy and practice should recognize and build on the capacities, resilience, and resourcefulness of children and families.

The extent to which such principles are actually applied in a service program or institution depends to a large extent on the competence of staff. Competence, in turn, depends on the skill, commitment, and personal qualities of front-line practitioners. It also depends on the ability of program designers, administrators, and managers to enable front-line practitioners to use their individual talents fully and to work effectively together.

To use one's individual talents fully in work with infants, toddlers and their families is no easy task. Such work engages the emotions as fully as the intellect. Very young children stir powerful feelings in adults (the species is programmed that way). Moreover, parents and parent-child interaction evoke complex responses in professionals that are often difficult to sort out and respond to in ways that support the parent, the child, and the relationships between them. The practitioner must learn to take advantage of her* individual skills and gifts. She must

---

*We have chosen to use the female pronoun when referring to practitioners and supervisors since the overwhelming majority of infant/family professionals is female. Unless otherwise stated, however, points apply equally well to male practitioners and supervisors.

also become more aware of aspects of her work that are troublesome—including areas she is prone to overlook. She must come to terms with the realization that no single individual can possibly meet all the professional demands she is likely to encounter in working with children from birth to three and their families.

The infant/family practitioner is likely to encounter large caseloads, physical demands, paperwork, inadequate resources within and beyond her work setting, and expectable tensions among colleagues. She will have to find ways to cope with these current realities of infant/family practice, or ways to change them.

The very words and phrases that we have used to describe responses to the challenges of work with infants, toddlers and their families—"sort out," "become aware," "cope," "realize"—suggest that reflective practice is a key element of "best" practice in our field. We suggest further that the job of enabling students and practitioners to become reflective professionals can be accomplished, in large part, by collaborative, regular supervision and mentorship.

## Supervision and mentorship: More than temporary relief from distress

Efforts to implement principles of best practice in work with infants, toddlers, and their families yield a host of daily, emotionally charged dilemmas for service providers and administrators. Comments around the coffee pot or copy machine are revealing:

*"I went to school to learn to work with children—not babies, and not parents."*

*"I'm the only 'baby person' here."*

*"I have so many families to see that I can't be really helpful to any of them."*

*"I couldn't say anything about the baby's language development, the way I had planned to in this month's home visit, because Mrs. P. never stopped talking about Mr. P."*

*"When Mr. and Mrs. P. were finally ready to take Joey for an assessment at Mercy, their so-called team of experts talked down to the P's and acted as if I were invisible. I'd like to murder the whole 'multidisciplinary' crew."*

*"I have so much stuff to enter into the computer that I can't see my families."*

*"I just got back from the Q's house. How could a human being let a baby suffer so? I don't see how I can go back there."*

"Copy machine commiseration" may offer temporary relief from discomfort caused by limitations in professional training, changing job demands, and the inevitable stresses of working with people. In contrast to casual "support," supervision and mentorship offer ongoing opportunities to recognize, understand, and cope successfully with the challenges of becoming an infant/family practitioner—just as practitioners offer opportunities for support and growth to parents, and parents to children. Supervisory and mentorship relationships embody what some call the golden rule of supervision: "Do unto others as you would have them do unto others."

Supervisory and mentoring relationships provide opportunities for the individual participant to:

- Deepen and broaden knowledge;

- Reflect regularly, in a safe environment, on the full range of reactions to the experience of practice;

- Discuss individual goals and measure progress toward them;

- Develop and refine one's professional use of self and individual style, through increased self-understanding.

- Examine the philosophy that underlies an approach to infants, toddlers and their families, as it is expressed in the policies and practices of a professional discipline or service setting; and

- Learn from a more experienced practitioner who describes why and how she works as she does—and discusses both successes and failures in the course of her own professional development.

Supervisory and mentorship relationships provide opportunities for educators and administrators to:

- Model a mutually respectful, collaborative approach to monitoring performance and maintaining an acceptable level of service to children and families;

- Model a mutually respectful, collaborative relationship that parallels the supervisee/family relationship;

- Offer information and instruction that are relevant to the individual learner's level of professional development and immediate practice needs;

- Support individual practitioners, particularly as they deal with the stressful aspects of work with infants, toddlers and their families; and

- Create and maintain an overall climate of intellectual inquiry, open communication, empathy with staff concerns, and support for the long-term professional development of staff.

A note of caution must be sounded here. People who have had satisfying experiences as a supervisee or supervisor, protegee or mentor, value these relationships highly. One seasoned administrator of a large, multiservice agency calls supervision "the greatest gift I can give my staff." A student reflects that supervision by a mentor teacher helped her to "take on experience in a manageable chunk." But people who have not had positive personal experience with reflective, collaborative, regular supervisory or mentoring relationships often, quite literally, "don't know what they are missing." They may think of supervision as, at worst, "checking up on," and, at best, measuring the adequacy of performance against some fixed list of competencies.

In addition, people who work with infants and toddlers are often victims of the myth that working with babies should "come naturally"—at least to women. This idea may account for the belief that extensive training is unnecessary for effective practice with infants, toddlers and their families. It may explain the sense, common among infant/family practitioners, that they should dismiss or be ashamed of feelings toward infants or parents that reflect anything other than a wish to help. It may mean that when a supervisor encourages a trainee to explore new ways of responding to a baby or family, this encouragement is seen as a judgment that the worker lacks some expectable skill or information, and as a threat to the supervisee's basic self-esteem and sense of security.

Simply to label as "misperceptions" such widely and deeply held beliefs about supervision is not likely to diminish their influence upon either practice or policy. An alternative way of perceiving the supervisory or mentoring experience and relationship must be offered. We hope that our effort to identify core features of supervision and mentorship as they occur in the specific context of work with infants, toddlers and their families will be a first step in such an approach.

## Essential features of supervision and mentorship in infant/family training and practice

The knowledge and skills of many professional disciplines find a place in the wide range of settings that serve infants, toddlers and their families. Similarly, different traditions of supervision and mentorship are being adapted for use in training and practice in our multidisciplinary field. It is important to recognize that a variety of supervisory and mentoring models may offer similar opportunities to staff for learning and reflection. At the same time, identical terms—including "supervision" and "mentorship" themselves—may have quite different meanings, depending on discipline and setting.

In the midst of all this diversity, many experienced administrators, trainers, and practitioners seem to agree that reflection, collaboration, and regularity are the essential features of effective supervision and mentorship in infant/family training and practice.

## Reflection

Reflection can be thought of as both the means and the end of the process of supervision. Reflection involves stepping back from the immediate, intense experience of hands-on work. Depending on the "contract" she establishes with her supervisors, the supervisee provides material for mutual consideration—written process notes from a meeting with a child and family, an oral narrative, a curriculum or treatment plan, behavior recorded on audiotape or videotape or observed directly by the supervisor. The supervisor or mentor offers an enlarged perspective, another pair of eyes, a mirror. From the dialogue between supervisee and supervisor emerges, one hopes, a clearer vision of the work in progress.

Reflection means continuing conceptualization of what one is observing and doing.

It is required of the supervisor or mentor as well as of the student or less experienced practitioner. "What were you thinking about when you did that?" is a question that either partner in a supervisory or monitoring relationship can ask the other, and that the experienced practitioner continually asks herself. Consequently, the first step in learning to be a supervisor often involves articulating the principles underlying one's own practice—for example, why does one set up the physical environment this way? What are the advantages and disadvantages of visiting weekly instead of monthly (or monthly instead of weekly)? What is one looking for and wondering about as one seems (to the trainee) to be saying or doing so little? Why does one learn from paying attention to one's emotional responses to working with individual children and families? The more supervisors or mentors are able to conceptualize their own practice, the better prepared they are to help trainees understand principles and formulate possible solutions to the challenges at hand.

Sometimes, of course, reflection fails to yield clarity. Experienced supervisors often say that one of the chief benefits of supervision is an increased tolerance for ambiguity, even for helplessness. People who are drawn to work with infants, toddlers and their families want to help if not to heal—to do something. Virtually all trainees underestimate the value of the relationship itself, of "being there" for and with a child and family. It is the supervisor or mentor who listens to the frustrated trainee and can say, "This is really complicated. I'm not sure what I would do in these circumstances. It will get clearer as you continue with the familiy. We do know that you are an important presence in their life." Because supervision and mentorship are processes and relationships, not sequences or courses of instruction, such difficult messages, and others, can be delivered repeatedly, as "teachable moments" present themselves—and as supervisors and mentors "are there" for students and workers.

Reflection in the course of supervision and mentorship helps the trainee come to terms with what it means to go beyond doing what "comes naturally" to help babies or parents—to become a professional who works with infants, toddlers and their families. Part of the process of developing a professional identity involves recognizing the need to enlarge one's own knowledge, skills, and sensitivity. Supervisors and mentors can direct the trainee to relevant materials and demonstrate, or even role play specific techniques. They can help supervisees develop skills in observing infants, toddlers, and their families and in using their observations in responsive, reflective practice. The diverse demands of infant/family work make experiences with supervisors and mentors from a range of disciplines and traditions particularly useful for the trainee. Indeed, transdisciplinary practice in early intervention requries that colleagues be able to teach their perspectives and skills to each other.

It is important to remember, however, that many students and practitioners find it much easier to ask for information or technical advice than to reflect on the

> Reflection can be thought of as both the means and the end of the process of supervision.

> Supervisors and mentors need to resolve their own conflicts about exercising authority before they can establish clear expectations for their students or employees.

feelings they experience as they work with babies and families. Supervisors and mentors can reinforce (or introduce) the idea that emotions are the basic stuff of parents' and children's relationships. By attending to her own affective experience, the worker may be able to learn more about what children and families are feeling. As the supervisee's own emotional responses are acknowledged and respected, she may become increasingly able to to acknowledge, respect, and respond sensitively to the emotional experiences and expressions of infants, toddlers, families and colleagues.

Reflecting on professional identity also involves examining values. The complexities of daily practice may bring the student or worker face to face with conflicts between competing priorities, clashes between traditional and innovative approaches, policies that seem to disregard or undermine the well-being of young children or families, and evidence that her own work is not valued. In the words of one veteran administrator, "In this field, you have to fight so hard to do what you love, and the world out there isn't even sure what you're doing." Supervisors and mentors can help trainees shape questions with which to probe and ponder their own behavior, beliefs, and values, as well as those of the programs, institutions, and service systems in which they are working. Such discussions, of course, may prompt supervisors and mentors to thoughtful reflection and change as well. One area involving behaviors, beliefs and values that represents a source of conflict for many supervisors and administrators—especially women—concerns the exercise of authority. Supervisors and mentors need to resolve their own conflicts about exercising authority before they can establish clear expectations for their students or employees.

It takes time to feel comfortable with a professional identity, just as it takes time to "become" a student, a colleague, a parent or a spouse. Supervisors and mentors can provide a relationship and an environment in which the trainee's professional identity can emerge gradually, until what once seemed "tacked on" becomes a core part of the trainee's sense of self.

How does one learn to reflect? Some educators suggest preparing students early on to use the experience of supervision or mentorship. In the classroom, teachers can encourage students to question conventional wisdom and their own thinking and decision making. In supervised practice or internships, supervisors and mentors can take time to discover what each trainee brings to this hands-on training, in order to guide and support the supervisee's reflection. Program managers and administrators encourage reflection in the work setting not only by providing opportunities for individual supervision but also by encouraging thoughtful, open communication in daily activity. As the experienced practitioner acquires and values the habit of reflection, the process comes full circle—the reflective practitioner prepares to observe the supervisor or mentor.

## Collaboration

The experience of supervision or mentorship in work with infants, toddlers and their families has been described as like "having a friend on a difficult journey." As practitioners who work in a wide range of settings talk about the "rich and troubling" intellectual and emotional challenges they face, they speak of their field as a "frontier." No one knows for sure what lies ahead; new information pours in, but may be unreliable; the strategies of early pioneers may or may not be appropriate for those who wish to establish permanent settlements. One doesn't want to travel through uncharted territory alone.

Supervision has also been described as offering "the occasional bliss of the collaborative state." While we believe that the development of close professional relationships may be one of the most rewarding aspects of working in our new and challenging field, we must admit that "bliss" is likely to be only "occasional" in any human relationship. But nourishing, enduring, rewarding, "good enough" collaborative supervisory and mentoring relationships can become established parts of any training or work environment—if we recognize the foundations upon which such relationships are built. These elements, which are not unique to infant/family work, are power, mutual expectations, and communication.

**Power** in a collaborative relationship is shared power. In supervisory and mentorship relationships in the infant/family field, power derives from knowledge, not just experience or conviction. Just as a parent is the expert on his or her own child, so the supervisee is the authority on her own work experience. In addition, the supervisee or protegee brings to a relationship his or her life experience as child and perhaps as parent, as a participant in at least one culture and perhaps as an observer of others, and as a member of racial and gender groups. Not uncommonly, the supervisee or protegee will have academic or clinical expertise that is directly relevant to work with infants, toddlers and their families and that surpasses that of the supervisor or mentor in at least some areas. This will certainly be the case in peer supervision arrangements, which depend in large part on the pooling of expertise and the contribution of different perspectives to common understanding.

Power can be held mutually without being shared equally. Supervisors of students are likely to be responsible for evaluating the supervisee's performance and growth; supervisors in service settings may have specific responsibility within the organization for assuring the quality of services provided to children and families. But when the evaluative function is shared, however, the process of reflection encourages ongoing self-evaluation by the supervisee. Periodic formal evaluations become occasions for a systematic review of what have been continuing conversations between supervisor and supervisee. Again, as in family life or a therapeutic relationship, one hopes to see shifts in the balance of power over time. With experience comes movement from greater dependence on authority to fuller autonomy (although "interdependence" rather than an illusory "independence" should be the lifelong goal of the infant/family professional).

**Clear mutual expectations** seem to be critical to the success of a collaborative supervisory or mentoring relationship. The supervisory "contract" clarifies the boundaries and responsibilities of each participant in this unique relationship. Participants need to agree on the logistics of their arrangement—where and when they will meet. They need to agree on the content that they will look at together—this might include on-the-job performance, directly observed; written notes of interactions with children and families; an oral account of the trainee's experience with children, families, colleagues; reflection on the supervisory relationship itself.

Some disciplines use a model of regular, formal cycles in which supervisor and supervisee together negotiate planning, observation, analysis, and critique of performance. In other models, the supervisor tries informally to learn as much as she can about the supervisee early in the relationship, and freely discloses her own clinical experience. Mutual candor and trust are expected to facilitate the kind of highly interactive discussion that makes supervision or mentorship "not a course, but a process." Observations, ideas, feelings, connections, questions, and recurring themes are all welcomed as part of an unfolding, deeply meaningful, and mutually built conversation. Even (or, perhaps, especially) in this type of supervisory relationship, there must be clear mutual understanding about the boundaries and distinctions between supervision and friendship, and supervision and therapy. And the supervisory "contract" may need to be re-negotiated perodically.

In some circumstances, expectations must be clarified among three parties. In the context of a student practicum or internship,

> **Collaborative supervisory and mentoring relationships involve shared power, clear mutual expectations, and open communication.**

> **There is no getting around it. To be worthy of the name, supervision or mentorship must occur regularly.**

for example, roles and responsibilities must be established for the student intern, the field supervisor, and the faculty member or academic program director. Field supervisors and faculty members need support and opportunities to expand their roles as much as students do. As the range and variety of infant/family practice expands, "multi-level" supervisory and mentorship models increase as well. For example, a state-level training and technical assistance agency may match mentors and protegees from different service programs, or leaders of a multi-site research and demonstration project may use their periodic site visits to help project staff at various levels reflect on their work.

The kind of **communication** that occurs within a collaborative supervisory or mentoring relationship in the field of infant/family practice may be the element that contributes most often to "occasional bliss." Such communication flows freely in both directions. It is open between participants, yet protected from outsiders. This kind of communication is highly suited to its specific task of examining professional work with infants, toddlers and their families. For such work is itself designed to foster communication, establish trust on a bedrock of confidentiality, and strengthen human relationships. One may use the term "parallel process" or speak of "doing unto others as you would have them do unto others," but the meaning remains the same. Open communication between supervisor and supervisee can be seen as a model for communication between professionals and parents, and between parents and children.

### *Regularity*

Time is a scarce resource in programs that serve infants, toddlers, and their families. Daily demands are immediate and unrelenting, with little if any "down" time for staff. Funding patterns create pressure to spend as much time as possible in direct service; at the same time, reporting requirements consume hours of effort. The rapid pace of development during the first three years adds an extra sense of urgency to infant/family work: timing is critical, and missed opportunities for preventive intervention can be costly to child and family. Finally, the awareness of unmet need haunts every thoughtful practitioner in the field.

There is no getting around it, however. To be worthy of the name, supervision or mentorship must occur regularly. Time must be allocated for these relationships, and this time must be protected. It takes time to reflect, time to collaborate, and above all time to establish trust in the reliable nature of the relationship itself. The parallels with parent/infant and parent/professional relationships are clear.

Although they may argue eloquently for the importance of investing in very young children and their families, practitioners and administrators who work with this population are often reluctant to invest in the professional development of their staff members or themselves. Administrators may resist allocating time and staff for regular supervision or mentorship on the grounds that staff should "already know" how to do their jobs; or because basic services to as many children as possible must take precedence over improving, or even maintaining, the quality of planning or performance.

Infant/family training and service programs vary enormously in the amount of time they allocate to supervision or mentorship, but the importance of regularity is universally emphasized. If scheduling regular supervision by the calendar seems extraordinary difficult, it may nevertheless be possible to build collaborative reflection into an already regularly occurring process. The beginning of a program year or the entrance of a new child or family into an ongoing service program could be used as occasions for staff reflection, as an integral part of assessment and planning.

### In sum...

While supervision and mentorship take many forms and build on many traditions in work with infants, toddlers, and their families, reflection, collaboration, and regularity seem to characterize virtually all effective supervisory and mentorship relationships in this diverse field. Resources are more likely to be scarce than abundant in any setting that serves very young children, but trainers and administrators who are convinced of the value of supervision or mentorship find endlessly creative ways to offer these experiences to their students and staff.

# Overcoming Obstacles to Reflective Supervision and Mentorship

**Emily Fenichel and Linda Eggbeer,** with the
**ZERO TO THREE/National Center For Clinical Infant Programs' Work Group on Supervision and Mentorship**

For their invaluable contributions to this chapter (and to the field of infant/family training and supervision), the authors wish to thank Ann Adalist-Estrin, Annette Axtmann, Victor Bernstein, Barbara Bodner-Johnson, Dan Couet, Mary Ann Doud, Sarah Gardner, Freddie Herbert, Joan Luby, Bernadette MacLellan, Mary McLean, Judy Nebrig, Sandra Petersen, James Redmon, and Deborah Weatherston. Also Ethel Klein of EDK Associates, the Board of INTERACT, and the dedicated infant/family practitioners of Maryland whose participation in focus groups taught us so much.

*"A lot of times I'm going to my director asking her questions: 'What about this? What about that?' but she can't always answer my questions so I have stopped asking. Now I'm just trying to figure things out between myself and a co-worker and we just kind of come up with something that works for us. We don't even ask anymore."*—Senior staff teacher, child care center, toddler room

*"It's painful to think that there are times when you could have delivered better service. It may not be your fault that you did not get good supervision, but you still feel helpless and responsible, like the agent of the damage. Our mistakes could be death sentences for some of our kids."*—Masters' level social worker, therapeutic nursery

*"If you're not providing direct service to a child, you're not working."*—Experienced early interventionist, characterizing the attitude of third-party payers

*"I see as a priority the people that we are serving, and the people we are serving are the children ... I guess better supervision is important, but it just seems so far away, so far removed."*—Experienced early interventionist

The ZERO TO THREE/National Center For Clinical Infant Programs' Work Group on Supervision and Mentorship believes that reflection, collaboration, and regularity are the three essential features of effective supervision and mentorship in the infant/family field. We believe that reflective supervision, supported by collaboration and regularity, is demanded by the complexities of working with families and their infants. All infant/family practitioners must be able to step back from fast-paced, emotionally intense assessment or intervention; to question the meaning of their experience and interactions; and to resolve problems within relationships formed on behalf of the baby. These skills are necessary to ensure quality services. These are skills that make a significant difference in daily work with families with very young children. They affect the longevity of the practitioner's commitment and enthusiasm to the work as a whole. These are skills that grow within reflective, collaborative, and regular supervisory and mentorship relationships.

How widely shared are the work group's convictions within the diverse field of infant/family training and practice? What do supervision and mentorship look like as they occur among different training institutions, and service settings? To learn more about our colleagues' experiences of supervision and mentorship and their attitudes toward these relationships, work group staff conducted telephone interviews with approximately 20 supervisors, educators and administrators who were self-identified or referred to us because of their interest in these issues. We met with the INTERACT Committee of veteran early intervention professionals to hear their 20-year perspective on supervision and mentorship. Finally, in November, 1991, with the assistance of EDK Associates, we used the open, unstructured format of focus groups to explore ideas and attitudes about supervision and mentorship among early intervention practitioners, infant/toddler child care professionals, and public agency supervisors of employees working with multirisk families.

This chapter describes what we learned, with particular emphasis on objective and attitudinal obstacles to reflective supervision and on strategies to overcome these obstacles.

## Attitudes about supervision and mentorship: "Yes, but ..."

Not surprisingly, colleagues in ZERO TO THREE's extended network tend to value supervision and mentorship in infant/family practice highly. In extensive telephone interviews and written communications, they told us that supervision protects the quality of service to children and families, as well as providing opportunities for professional growth for practitioners. The supervisors, educators, and administrators with whom we talked know first hand the difficulty of finding—and protecting—resources for reflective supervision. Some of them had begun infant/family programs without including a supervision or mentorship component. Others had seen budget cuts or, more typically, narrow reimbursement regulations, erode their capacity to supervise staff well. These administrators reported that staff members felt keenly the lack, or the loss, of good supervision. Even with limited resources, many of these managers and direct service staff were determined to provide opportunities for regular, collaborative reflection. Their strategies are described later in this chapter.

Participants in our focus groups, who are possibly more representative of infant/family practitioners in general, had a somewhat different perspective on supervision and mentorship issues. We recruited:

- Early intervention practitioners working in programs for infants and toddlers with disabilities or at risk of developmental problems (two groups);

- Infant/toddler child care professionals—lead teachers working in licensed child care centers; and

- Administrative supervisors of public agency employees working with multi-risk families.

All groups were recruited in Maryland, to assure that the social and political contexts were held constant. The average group size was eight participants. In considering what participants told us, it is important to remember that the purpose of the focus group study was to explore the meaning and value of supervision and mentorship to these front-line practitioners and supervisors. We were interested in hearing about their past and current experiences of supervision and mentorship, to be sure, but our chief goal was to learn about attitudes, opinions, and beliefs.

When they were asked to describe good supervisors in their own words, participants in all of the groups used terms that included dimensions of:

- reflection (sensitivity, good listening skills, "someone who explains things");

- collaboration (mutual respect; giving staff autonomy; constructive handling of conflict, "someone willing to work along side of you"); and, to a lesser degree,

- regularity (availability).

As they explored these concepts further, participants placed the highest value on collaboration in a supervisory relationship.

They expressed a desire for reciprocity, recognition, and respect. Participants described reflection as a time for self assessment and "an opportunity to think about what you are doing." Public agency supervisors, however, did not easily associate reflection with supervision, and the group of child care providers paused for some time before they offered that reflection "lets you work through something" and increases one's ability "to pick things apart." Regularity in supervision, as distinct from a supervisor's general availability, did not seem as important to focus group participants as the other two elements identified by the ZERO TO THREE work group.

Across disciplines and settings, participants in the focus groups acknowledged that supervision was important, especially in a "frontier" field where so little is known for certain and so much learning comes through experience. They described working with infants and their families as rewarding, but stressful. Cultural and value divisions between practitioners and families exacerbate tension. A special educator noted:

*You have to get rid of your own value system and listen to what the parents are saying and what the kids are saying, and it gets very difficult... That's when you need to go back and tell everyone what your thoughts are and get the support, not only in what to do with the child but what to do with the parents and what to do with yourself.*

When they were asked what happens when there is no supervision or inadequate supervision, early intervention practitioners and child care providers described a troubling prevalence of "chaos" and "panic." People told stories of past experiences with inadequate supervision. They described feeling "floundering," "insecure," and in some cases so frustrated that they began to look for different jobs.

The focus group moderator found it remarkable that most participants' answers to the question, "What are the consequences of inadequate supervision?" had to do with the consequences for the professional—how it was harder for them to do their work. When the moderator probed further, asking, "Who suffers when there is bad supervision?" the initial reaction tended to be "everyone," and then, after some silence, "the client" or "the kids." Ultimately, with considerable discomfort, group members acknowledged that working with inadequate supervision means, at best, not doing a good job and, at worst, doing real harm.

It is important to keep in mind that the focus group approach explores how people approach issues and problems. Thus the difficulty that infant/family practitioners demonstrated in confronting the issue of inadequate supervision sends a loud signal. Was it hard for focus group participants (who had already expressed their strong sense of responsibility for children and families) to acknowledge that real harm can come about from inadequate supervision? Did a perception that inadequate supervision is pervasive (and unlikely to change) lead them to minimize, rather than confront, its consequences? Do they lack enough firsthand experience with reflective supervision to believe it can affect practice? Anyone hoping to mobilize practitioner dissatisfaction with existing opportunities for supervision needs to explore these questions further.

In this respect, the answers of focus group participants to the "bottom line" question—"How would you spend a gift of $50,000 to your program?"—were revealing. Even though they had acknowledged the importance of supervision, these infant/family practitioners and supervisors were not ready to allocate scarce resources to improving supervision. Their first priority for new money was more services ("...the value is in the program, and let's try to beef it up"); their second priority was hiring more frontline personnel. Child care providers were ready to spend money on "training" but saw supervision (which none of these providers had at present) as a luxury.

How are these responses of focus group participants best interpreted? Ethel Klein, designer of the focus group protocol, suggests that:

*The most salient challenge to "selling" supervision is the lack of entitlement many of these practitioners feel. They see supervision as something for them, rather than their clients, and they are not as important as the people they serve. In order to really institutionalize good supervision and mentorship programs... education (will be needed) on how supervision translates to better care for the clients, so that practitioners feel entitled to ask for this help.* (EDK Associates, 1991, appendix to this volume)

Another explanation for focus group participants' apparent reluctance to use (even hypothetical) resources for supervision or mentorship may involve the ambivalence that everyone feels about supervising and being supervised—even when supervision is designed to be reflective, collaboratively planned, and occurring regularly in an atmosphere of trust and respect. At some level, many practitioners wonder, "If I need supervision to do a good job, does that make me a 'bad' professional?" Other practitioners may be concerned not only about revealing professional ineptitude, but also about disclosing a complexity of responses evoked by work with infants and parents that may touch on aspects of their own personal history and emotional life. Reflection may be essential to an individual's professional growth and development and to the integrity of a service program. But reflection is rarely easy, or comfortable. It takes skill to be able to encourage reflection and not to withdraw from it when difficult material emerges.

*Is supervision important to front-line infant/family practitioners and supervisors? Yes, but . . .*

## Starting where the program is

As Linda Gilkerson and Carol Lou Young-Holt suggest (this volume), reflective supervision becomes an important part of a program's shared culture only when it is valued and protected by management. The program director is responsible for making sure that reflective supervision for individual staff members and for teams is incorporated fully into the service setting. This is equally true of training programs, where the director of training must use his or her authority to protect and value reflective supervision as integral to the development of students' professional competence and identity. Graduates of training programs in which supervision is embedded within a cohesive philosophy of reflective practice tend to seek out work settings that provide good supervision or make an effort to find the supervisors and mentors they need on their own.

Ideally, the director of an infant/family program has the authority to allocate resources so that all services are provided by well-supervised staff. Managers of Hawaii's Healthy Start/Family Support program paint a clear picture when they talk to state legislators responsible for appropriations: Their model of community-based home visiting/family support services has virtually eliminated child abuse among project families. Their supervisory ratio is one professional to five paraprofessionals. It is their model, in its entirety, that produces the outcome. Anything less will not get the results (Breakey & Pratt, 1991).

There are many training and service settings in which reflective supervision is a valued, integral, and established component of daily work and learning. But all too frequently, with many misgivings, infant/family administrators and practitioners do the best they can with inadequate resources to meet the needs of program participants or staff. In all too many universities, the faculty reward system does not encourage spending time on supervision of students, and supervision is assigned to adjunct faculty.

The image of the impoverished mother diluting infant formula with water may be an apt one here. In some agencies, program directors tend to take on supervision in addition to administrative responsibilities. They may have an "open door" policy for staff, but never be able to offer the regular, uninterrupted "closed door" time needed for screening out distractions and competing demands, needed for the quality of attention that reflective supervision requires. Moreover, program directors who have excellent managerial skills may not have the ability to supervise clinical work. In other service settings, supervisors may be assigned more direct service work than they can handle and still make reflective supervision a priority. When caseloads are too high, crisis management is likely to replace reflection. If services are not being used fully and funding is threatened, pressures to increase quickly the numbers of families served may impair the ability of staff to analyze the reasons underlying a poor fit between the program and its target population. As with formula dilution, the result of inadequate supervision may not be starvation, but failure to thrive. As one rural program director told us, her responsible, intelligent staff can "get by" with minimal supervision. But they won't grow. And they won't become supervisors and mentors of the next generation of practitioners.

If managers and direct service providers are committed to doing so, they can create, collaboratively, some regular opportunities for reflection. These can become a foundation for more specialized supervisory and/or mentoring relationships. The strategies suggested in our telephone interviews, like those described by many contributors to this volume, include using existing program elements in new ways and taking advantage of available outside resources.

## Using existing program elements to encourage reflection

Every setting that serves infants, toddlers, and their families has its own climate or culture, has some mechanism for staff to meet together, and has participants. Each of these elements can be used to encourage reflective practice.

### *A climate of respect, trust, and inquiry*

Watch. Ask. Adapt. The basic guidelines for responsive caregiving, articulated and demonstrated in print and video training by the Program for Infant/Toddler Caregivers (1991) stress observation, inquiry, and reflection about the meaning of children's behavior from birth onwards. But all kinds of pressures can push parents and professionals alike toward reflexive, "get through the day" coping. And in the educational experiences of many practitioners, only the "right" answer was rewarded, not the good question. Leaders who model respectful, reflective behavior can create an institutional climate safe enough for reflection by everyone. For example:

• A required course in the Merrill-Palmer Institute Interdisciplinary Graduate Certificate Program in Infant Mental Health involves observing a family through the last weeks of pregnancy, the newborn period, and the baby's first year. There is no "reason for referral," "identified client," or "treatment plan." The goal is to give the student a chance to learn about "entering gently into a relationship," and to practice "being respectful, careful, sensitive, attentive, nonintrusive, and consistent." (Weatherston interview)

• Senior public health department leadership, assisted by an outside trainer, helped community nurses use case conferences as an opportunity to focus on conceptualization and process, rather than "treatment planning" narrowly conceived. Case conference discussion explored the process of engagement with families, possible differences between families' perceptions and those of the nurses, nurses' feelings as indicators of families' experiences, and mutual expectations. The goal was to enable professionals to shift perspective, returning to families with renewed energy and, at times, redefined goals. (Wieder, Drachman & DeLeo, this volume).

• In the Developmental Program of Illinois' Ounce of Prevention Fund, Victor Bernstein and Candice Percansky make a point of offering paraprofessional staff the same kind of relationship-building experiences in supervision and training that they are being asked to facilitate with adolescent mothers (Bernstein, Hans & Percansky, 1991). Training and supervision are designed to help staff themselves find answers and discover skills within themselves. Reflection on important positive relationships in their own lives, observation of parent-infant interaction, and participant-centered discussion "combine into a powerful experience for the staff leading to personal growth and more effective job performance once they understand that their role is one of enriching relationships" (p.35).

## Staff meetings as a starting place for reflection

Routine staff meetings are unlikely to head anyone's list of settings most likely to encourage reflective discussion. They can be a starting place, however, especially when we remember that isolation from colleagues constitutes a serious occupational hazard in work with infants, toddlers, and their families. Lay home visitors, who often work with highly stressed families in communities with few resources, and who typically have less professional training than other infant/family practitioners, do their work alone for much of the time. Child care providers for infants and toddlers, even in center settings, may spend most of their working day as the only adult in a group of very young children.

Staff meetings for home visitors and child care providers are not an adequate substitute for individualized supervision. The evaluation of the North of Market Homebased Program to support Southeast Asian families in San Francisco noted, for example:

*Supervision, which is an essential component to any homebased service, was not built into the original grant proposal. A once a week staffing was thought to be sufficient in the beginning of the program, and it was discovered that it was totally insufficient... (Currently) supervision of the homebased workers requires about half of the director's work week (Knox, 1991).*

Staff meetings are, however, a place to begin building a foundation for reflective practice. As Mary Ann Doud, an early intervention state coordinator from southeastern Pennsylvania told us, mandatory weekly meetings of home based providers in early intervention offered a place to share emotions, a powerful antidote to the "overwhelming nature of being alone."

An experienced child care consultant said:

*There are very few problems with kids that can't be solved if things are going well among staff... Sharing information in a group makes all the difference in the way a person can use her knowledge. You discover your options, your flexibility. You find you have far more capacity than you thought to effect change. (Petersen, interview).*

But child care providers in our focus group study reported that the only staff meetings in their newly established corporate child care center were scheduled for the evenings. Staff members who worked the 7 a.m. to 3 p.m. shift faced a double commute on meeting days—long commutes, since housing affordable for child care providers tends to be some distance from corporate headquarters.

Suppose that staff meetings are scheduled regularly. How can they become collaborative undertakings that support reflection? Gilkerson and Young-Holt (this volume) suggest that unless they are firmly circumscribed, administrative issues tend to take over any meeting. An effective solution to the problem, used by staff of the Kennedy Family Center in Baltimore, Maryland, is to schedule team/staff meetings every week for one and one-half hours. One week, the discussion will center on clinical issues; the next, on administrative questions with "big" implications for program design. (Staff trying this approach may want to appoint a gatekeeper to make sure that the designated focus of each meeting is maintained.)

## What about peer supervision?

Collegial support is an essential ingredient in promoting and maintaining the competence of practitioners who work with infants, toddlers, and their families. Practitioners offer and receive timely support from co-workers, and they share specific knowledge and skills. The relationships established through these exchanges are so rich that Gilkerson describes many staff groups as "program families." But do these activities constitute "peer supervision"? Where does peer supervision belong in an infant/family service setting?

The concepts of reflection, collaboration, and regularity may prove useful in analyzing the role and effectiveness of peer supervision in a given infant/family setting. For example, as the first quotation at the beginning of this chapter illustrates, several participants in our focus group study rely on peers as "supervisors of last resort." For a variety of reasons, they do not feel that their official supervisors are available to help them master the challenges of their daily work with infants, toddlers, and their families. Committed to serving children and parents as well as possible, these resourceful practitioners turn to each other. They do collaborate to solve problems. But their contacts tend to be ad hoc, and reflection—the chance to stop and think about what one is doing, why, and with whom—is not on the agenda.

In contrast, in some settings, particularly new, small programs, peer supervision may quite adequately provide reflection, collaboration, and regularity. Barbara Ivins and Nancy Sweet (this volume) describe an intentionally collegial supervisory model that worked well in the early days of an infant mental health/developmental intervention program. The multidisciplinary staff were by no means interchangeable, but they were truly peers, pooling their expertise and insights to create and implement a new way of working with infants and families. As the program grew, however, the need for a more differentiated model of supervision emerged, and was addressed over time.

### *Parents as a resource*

In family support and education programs, and in family-centered care in general, parents participate as designers and shapers of service systems as well as of services for their own families. In these roles, and in interaction with individual staff members or trainees, parent participants can encourage reflective practice. Parent/professional collaboration on the mission statement of a service program and periodic review of program practice in the light of the statement can help staff and families alike stay on track, or consider changes in program direction. Parents and faculty can together develop criteria for rating preservice students' competence in establishing relationships with family members and involving families in assessment and treatment planning.

Parents may also participate in the evaluation of individual students or workers. For example, questionnaires filled out by parents of the infants and toddlers in her care are an important part of the assessment of a candidate for the national Child Development Associate credential. As student and supervisor, Kelley Bateman and Eva Thorp (this volume) reviewed videotapes of Bateman's home visits with the parent involved. One question for the mother was, "At that moment, did she do what you needed to have done?"

Once again, collaboration and regularity must support reflection. Ongoing interaction with a parent policy council and regular evaluation of participants' experiences with program services are more valuable than one-time surveys. Similarly, parents who are hired as paid, regular consultants to training programs for professionals are able to offer increasingly rich and valuable feedback to students and faculty.

### Using resources beyond the program

Few if any service programs in the infant/family field will be able to meet fully the supervisory needs of all staff members. Junior staff may need supervision from a professional in their discipline in order to improve discipline-specific skills and to achieve full professional credentials. Senior practitioners may need outside supervision as they integrate a new perspective—mental health, for example—into their intervention repertoire. Program directors, "alone at the top," can use outside supervision or consultation as they develop and consolidate managerial skills.

Sometimes assistance can be found close to home, at little or no cost. For example, a community-based service program that is part of a larger umbrella agency or interagency consortium may be able to call on a staff member from the parent agency or a collaborating institution to facilitate reflective staff meetings, case conferences, or retreats. The outside facilitator may bring expertise in a specific content area, such as mental health, or may be valuable chiefly as a disinterested observer and facilitator of the group's reflective process itself. In Virginia's system of early intervention for infants and toddlers with disabilities and their families, an investment is being made in a "mentorship model" of technical assistance to coordinators of local interagency councils. Contractual arrangements are made with qualified consultants to work with local coordinators in the five administrative regions of the state, facilitating the process of service delivery across all community agencies, monitoring and modeling the building of relationships on behalf of children and families.

In our "frontier" field, it may be necessary to cross geographical, as well as disciplinary and agency boundaries to provide appropriate supervision. A group of staff members from one early intervention program drove to supervisory sessions an hour away once a week for nine months. The program paid for staff time; the program and the individual staff members contributed toward the outside supervisor's fees. In an ongoing arrangement, a clinician from Philadelphia flies to Boston once every six weeks for a six-hour supervisory session with a group of social workers in private practice. Since each practitioner's work is the focus of attention for one hour, the arrangement encourages development of both supervisory and clinical skills (see Pruett on co-supervision, this volume).

Planned mentoring relationships permit sharing of expertise across programs and disciplines. The mentorship program of Massachusetts' Continuing Education Consortium for Early Intervention Providers was conceived as a way to provide individual support and guidance to the whole range of staff in early intervention programs (Eggbeer, Latzko & Pratt, in press). A paid committee of eight clinicians representing a variety of disciplines and locations across the state oversees a growing mentorship program, now in its third year. Potential mentors submit applications and attend an orientation/interview session; they work under contract, compensated at $50/hour for their time. Mentees also have face-to-face interviews with a member of the committee before being accepted. After mentors and mentees are matched by the committee, one committee member is assigned to each pair for ongoing oversight and assistance. Mentors and mentees are required periodically to document the work accomplished and their level of satisfaction. Upon completion of the mentorship, they submit evaluations to the committee.

The Early Childhood Mentor Teacher Program of the Child Care Employee Project illustrates the use of outside resources to enhance training and career development in a service system under extreme stress. Begun as a pilot program in September, 1988 with funding from a consortium of foundations and in the process of expanding statewide in California, the program trains experienced child care teachers to become mentors to students in community college training programs for child care providers, creates a career ladder, rewards increased responsibilities with additional income, and provides an incentive to remain in the child care field. The program offers students the opportunity to observe model infant/toddler caregiving and to receive individualized supervision (Pemberton, 1990). Training for mentor teachers serving infants and toddlers was offered for the first time in October, 1991 (see Perry, this volume). A substantial portion of the available funding was used for scholarships that would pay for substitutes in centers whose experienced teachers were attending the one-week intensive course. All of the infant/toddler teachers attending said that the financial support granted to them contributed significantly to their ability to attend.

Outside resources that support reflective practice in infant/family programs may come in the form of expertise, funding, or both. The agenda for action in the next chapter suggests a number of potential initiatives that can be undertaken in individual communities, as multisite demonstrations, or in the context of system-wide planning for infant/family personnel development.

## Summary

In the course of learning about supervision and mentorship in the infant/family field, we have identified formidable obstacles—attitudinal as well as objective—to the establishment of reflective supervision as a core element of all efforts designed to support the development of infants, toddlers, and their families. But we have also identified steps that instructors and administrators, students, practitioners, and program participants are taking to introduce new opportunities for reflection into their training and service programs—and, more important, into their relationships with each other. Infants and toddlers teach us daily that taking one step at a time, climbing on one block piled on another, and taking advantage of all available support are effective ways to overcome obstacles.

## References

Bernstein, VJ, Hans, SL and Percansky, C. 1991. Advocating for the young child in need through strengthening the parent-child relationship. *Journal of Clinical Child Psychology.* Vol. 20, No. 1, 28-41.

Breakey, G and Pratt, B. 1991. Healthy Growth for Hawaii's "Healthy Start": Toward a Systematic Statewide Approach to the Prevention of Child Abuse and Neglect. *Zero to Three,* Vol. XI, No. 4, 16-22.

Eggbeer, L, Latzko, T and Pratt, B. In press. Establishing statewide systems of inservice training for infant/family personnel. *Infants and Young Children.*

Knox, JG. 1991. An Early Intervention Model for Southeast Asian Refugees with Infants: A Homebased Program Evaluation. San Francisco, CA: North of Market Child Development Center.

Pemberton, C. 1990. *Child Care Mentor Teacher Pilot Program: Final Report.* Oakland, CA: Child Care Employee Project.

The Program for Infant/Toddler Caregivers. 1991. Videos and curriculum guides. Sacramento, CA: California Department of Education.

# Improving the Training of Infant/Family Practitioners through Supervision and Mentorship: An Action Agenda

**Emily Fenichel,** with the
**ZERO TO THREE/National Center For Clinical Infant Programs' Work Group on Supervision and Mentorship**

ZERO TO THREE's 1991-92 project on Learning Through Supervision and Mentorship has described key elements of supervisory and mentoring relationships that increase and maintain competence among infant/family professionals from a variety of disciplines and service settings. We have also identified promising approaches that leaders in professional education and service delivery are using to overcome very real obstacles to the widespread establishment of reflective supervision and mentorship throughout the field. The action agenda that follows offers a number of coordinated strategies to:

- incorporate effective supervision and mentorship into existing service systems and institutions across the country;

- build supervision and mentorship into the infrastructure of infant/family programs and service systems that are in the process of creation; and

- increase our understanding of the mechanisms and impacts of supervision and mentorship.

The strategies for promoting more and better supervision and mentorship for infant/family practitioners that are described below invite—indeed, require—collaboration among individuals, training and service programs, sponsoring institutions, and funders with a range of capacities and interests. The need for collaboration around supervision and mentorship represents a challenge, but also an opportunity to build or strengthen precisely the kinds of collaborative relationships that serve children and families well.

## Strategy 1: Training and ongoing support for supervisors and program directors

Through the Learning through Supervision and Mentorship Project, we have learned that supervisors in infant/family programs tend to be promoted to, rather than prepared for, their roles as supervisors. Because training and ongoing support for supervisors are sparse, most report that they have learned to be supervisors by "trial and error." Consequently, the first item on our action agenda is a two-pronged approach to expanding training opportunities for supervisors in the field of infant/family practice and reinforcing training with ongoing support for supervisors and program directors.

a) *National Intensive Seminar on Supervision*

The first element of this approach would be an intensive three-day seminar in supervision, open to individuals from around the country who are preparing to be supervisors or who are relatively new at their jobs. The seminar should be under the auspices of or in collaboration with an educational institution, to give participants the option of receiving academic credit for the seminar.

The curriculum for such a seminar should elaborate upon the principles of effective supervision—reflection, collaboration and regularity. It should address both clinical and management issues and include experiential learning. The seminar should incorporate extensive case material, drawn from the full range of infant/family practice, in order to illustrate common issues that arise in work with very young children and families across disciplines and settings, and to help supervisors to be more effective interdisciplinary and interagency collaborators. This *Sourcebook* might be used as a text for the seminar. The curriculum should be designed to be flexible enough to be adapted for future replication in regional and local settings. The curriculum could also be adapted to prepare preservice faculty to move toward more reflective models of supervising students.

The process of developing the curriculum and of planning, convening and evaluating the seminar could take place over an 18-month to two-year period.

b) *Ongoing Seminars for Supervisors and Program Directors*

Supervisors and program directors in the field of infant/family practice need ongoing opportunities for guidance from more experienced supervisors and for consultation and support from peers. One way of addressing this need would be adaptation and replication, in several sites across the country, of a seminar for supervisors and program directors pioneered by the Erikson Institute in Chicago (Bertacchi & Stott, this volume). This model of a nine-session seminar provides a mechanism for program directors and supervisors to receive guidance on the content and process of effective staff supervision and program administration. It also offers supervisors and directors a much-needed opportunity to consult with peers, and reflect together upon the challenges that emerge in the course of their daily supervisory and administrative experiences.

A project to replicate this model could identify and train two seminar co-leaders from each of up to ten localities that have infant/family programs sufficient in number to supply a pool of seminar participants among supervisors or program directors. After training, these leaders would convene 9-session seminars in their locales to help supervisors or program directors integrate principles of effective supervision into their daily practice. During this process, the team leaders themselves would continue to be supported by ongoing telephone consultation, and perhaps an interim meeting. The project should be evaluated in order to assess the impact of this approach on supervisory and administrative practice in infant/family programs and its potential for modification and further replication by others in the field.

A two-year period should be sufficient to develop, oversee, and evaluate such a project. This would include a 6-7 month recruitment period, training for seminar leaders, a 9-month period in which local seminars are held, and an evaluation period. This project lends itself to participation by multiple funders, especially community-based foundations or corporations in the localities where seminars will be held.

## Strategy 2: Developing an instructional videotape on the supervision process

Individualized supervision as a vehicle for learning and reflection is not part of most infant/family programs and preservice training traditions. In focus group interviews and at presentations before national conferences of infant/family professionals about its Supervision and Mentorship Project findings, work group staff encountered overwhelmingly positive reactions on the part of front-line practitioners and program directors who wished to learn more about this promising "hands on" approach to improving their own practice and that of their staff. Infant/family personnel have expressed strong interest in receiving more detailed instructions on how to incorporate individualized supervision as an ongoing component of their own service programs. At the most basic level, individuals who have been accustomed to other models of supervision want to know what a reflective, collaborative supervisory relationship "looks like."

This need could be addressed readily by a videotape that demonstrates uses of the supervisory and mentorship processes as vehicles for strengthening and supporting efforts to promote the health and development of young children and their families. Such a tape should be designed for educators and their students at the preservice level, and for program directors and their staffs at the community service level. In addition to explaining the rationale, functions and characteristics of the supervisory/mentorship relationship, the videotape should illustrate promising models of supervision and mentorship that are appropriate and feasible for use in the widely diverse training and practice settings that constitute the infant/family field. The tape should also incorporate discussion of clinical case material within a supervisory relationship, to illustrate how supervision helps front-line workers address the intellectual and emotional challenges that arise in work with children and families with diverse backgrounds and needs. The tape should be accompanied by a users' guide, to facilitate its use in workshop and classroom settings.

Development of the videotape, users' guide, and a plan for dissemination could take place during an 18-month period. The tape should be developed in collaboration with a group of nationally recognized experts in the design and implementation of supervision and mentorship experiences for students and practitioners

## Strategy 3: Developing models for supervision across distances

One of the greatest challenges faced by program directors, practitioners and policy makers who seek to deliver high quality services to infants and families is that of how to translate current expertise on infant/family health and development—which is largely concentrated in selected research and clinical centers of excellence—into "best practices" in programs across the country. For too many community-based programs in the infant/family field, lack of time for interaction with more experienced colleagues and physical distance from sources of expertise are formidable barriers to adequate supervisory/training experiences, and thus, to more effective professional practice. For example:

● In order to be more accessible to families, many service programs consist of small satellite offices or have practitioners spending most of their time making home visits throughout a large geographic area;

● Part-time work schedules may make scheduling of ongoing supervision difficult;

● The design of interdisciplinary programs may result in practitioners in smaller programs being supervised by people outside their own professional discipline;

● In larger institutions, workers may be supervised by someone from their discipline who has no experience in working with infants and families;

● The rapid evolution of knowledge and best practice throughout the field of infant/family practice may mean that recently trained practitioners may be more knowledgeable than their official supervisors.

Training needs of isolated community-based programs may be addressed by identifying and supporting the development of innovative approaches to supervision that use telecommunications technologies to: (1) surmount distance barriers by connecting infant/family service providers in rural or other geographically separated settings with sources of expert guidance on best practice in work with infants, toddlers, and their families; and (2) overcome time barriers by providing supervisors and supervisees with opportunities for regular reflection, learning, and collaboration that do not depend on frequent face-to-face contact.

Resourceful people are piloting a variety of promising strategies that might be developed further to meet these criteria. Student teachers fax lesson plans to their supervisors, who fax comments back. Colleagues who have different work schedules or live in different time zones may communicate using voice mail or electronic mail systems. An expert trainer in one state receives videotapes of home visits made by workers in another state and comments on these in regularly scheduled group supervision via conference call. Audiotapes are not uncommonly used as documentation of the supervisee's work. They might also be used to record a supervisor's comments and questions, particularly in programs where workers can listen to tapes as they drive long distances to make home visits. In a similar fashion, audiotapes of supervisory sessions can be reviewed and commented on by off-site consultants to train and support supervisors.

In order to allow sufficient time for further development of these innovative models, full implementation in the field, and evaluation and dissemination, a four-year project seems appropriate. The sponsoring institution would:

- Draft and disseminate a request for proposals to begin or replicate projects that use telecommunications to facilitate supervision and mentorship;

- Select demonstration projects to be funded for two years each;

- Convene participants in all projects for initial face-to-face orientation and relationship building;

- Provide opportunities for ongoing interchange, feedback and technical assistance to participating projects during the two-year period of project implementation;

- Evaluate project outcomes; and

- Produce for national dissemination a document describing the supervisory mechanisms used and their impact on supervisees' job satisfaction and performance, associated impacts on participating agencies, and cost considerations.

## Strategy 4: Incorporating supervision and mentorship into the infrastructure of emerging state and national personnel development systems

Recent federal legislation, major private funders, and professional associations are encouraging the establishment of statewide systems of training for people who work with young children in a variety of capacities. Most prominent are the areas of early childhood care and education, services to young children with disabilities, and family support. Nevertheless, little has been done to implement recommendations related to training.

For example, despite "policy alerts" warning of the length of time it takes to establish an adequate system of personnel preparation, most states involved in planning for Part H of the Individuals with Disabilities Education Act have focused on the immediate issues of establishing eligibility or setting standards for personnel, rather than addressing training needs in any comprehensive or systematic way. It is probably accurate to say that issues of supervision and mentorship are not even on the agenda of most Part H personnel development planners. In one of the relatively small number of states that is in the full implementation phase of Part H, for example, the Comprehensive System of Personnel Development sets out a timeline by which practitioners need to achieve "suitable qualifications" to work with infants, toddlers and their families. However, the plan assumes that "competencies" will be acquired through coursework and "contact hours" of inservice or continuing education. There is no acknowledgement of the role of supervision in creating and sustaining competence, and hence neither a requirement for ongoing supervision, nor a recognition that supervised practice might constitute "contact hours." In a neighboring state, however, the Comprehensive System of Personnel Development includes mentoring and contracted supervision, as opportunities to increase skills and as flexible ways to demonstrate competence.

Findings of the Learning through Supervision and Mentorship Project suggest that supervision and mentorship should be key components of any comprehensive, state-sponsored training system for infant/family practitioners, for several reasons:

- Quality assurance is an accountability issue, not only a "best practices" issue, in publicly funded programs;

- Supervision and mentorship offer opportunities for career development that keep talented practitioners close to infants and families, as compared to administrative jobs that take them farther and farther away from delivery of services.

- Individualized supervision and mentorship are likely to be cost-effective investments when evaluated in terms of improved staff performance.

Before the need for supervision and mentorship in state systems of personnel development can be met, it may be essential to address the need for consciousness raising and education about supervision and mentorship. We found that individuals who are involved in "personnel preparation" committees at the state level are responsive to ideas about supervision and mentorship. However, when practitioners, program directors, and state policymakers are faced with competing demands on scarce resources, those who lack experience with models of reflective supervision are unlikely to protect, much less introduce, supervision and mentorship opportunities for staff. They are likely to want to spend any new resources on more staff—the training and supports that staff need to do a good job are not considered.

It is not difficult to list the elements of a reasonable approach to bring about improved supervision and mentorship for infant/family practitioners within state systems, since these elements would be the same as those that are being used by other efforts to change state human services systems. These elements would include:

- Identifying sources of power;

- Identifying potential change agents;

- Establishing effective relationships with change agents in order to educate sources of power;

- Collaborative planning towards an initiative that addresses perceived state needs and is on a scale that can be supported over the long term with local funding;

- Garnering support for a proposed initiative;

- Implementation and evaluation of an initiative;

- Refinement and replication of promising approaches;

- Dissemination of findings.

What is difficult to anticipate is the time necessary to accomplish the sequence or even a single step within it—especially since changes in political leadership or economic conditions can send all players back to square one. One would like to be able to maintain a kind of supervision/mentorship "ready alert" status, prepared to respond to any signal that a committee or task force or administrator was interested in learning more about supervision and mentorship or exploring implementation possibilities.

A "piggy-backing" approach might make sense. This would involve grant-makers that are supporting major state systems-change projects or new multi-site community-based efforts; groups like the Council of Governors' Policy Advisors that work regularly with states on systems change; and providers of technical assistance. All of these players would be encouraged to engage with the ideas and products of the Learning Through

Supervision and Mentorship Project. If staff of these organizations become persuaded that supervision and mentorship are important ingredients of quality infant/family programs, they can take on the "ready alert" function themselves, prepared to refer "ripe" state policymakers to sources of expertise.

Especially if the first three strategies described above are implemented, it is not unreasonable to envision a technical assistance project driven by demand. For example, the readers of this *Sourcebook* are likely to be people in states or communities who are interested in the ideas of the Learning through Supervision and Mentorship Project. They can arrange for individualized training, consultation, or technical assistance through contact with individual contributors to the *Sourcebook* or **ZERO TO THREE/** National Center for Clinical Infant Programs. Moreover, if the strategies described above are implemented, states and communities can also send people to the basic training course in supervision, send teams of supervisors to be trained to lead seminars for supervisors, and respond to the request for proposals that address time and distance issues. States and communities that have positive experiences at these levels may then choose to redirect some of their own training funds toward supervision and mentorship activities or to make the in-kind commitments necessary to attract outside funding.

## Strategy 5: Evaluating the impact of supervision and mentorship—and of their absence

Experienced practitioners, educators, and administrators in the infant/family field are sufficiently convinced of the value of reflective supervision and mentorship to warrant implementation of any or all of the strategies outline above, which are designed to increase supervision and mentorship opportunities. All of these strategies, whether replications of earlier successful demonstrations or novel approaches to overcoming barriers, should include meticulous process evaluations. The multi-site design of several of the proposed initiatives may reveal factors which are key to success, as well as frequently encountered obstacles.

Although many practitioners and administrators themselves are convinced that good supervision and mentorship of program staff result, ultimately, in positive impact on children's development, such an effect is almost impossible to demonstrate. A more immediate question is whether the resources invested in supervision by a service program yield a measureable benefit to the program itself. For example, one program director has anecdotal data to suggest that an increase in good supervision leads to an increase in appointments kept by program participants, which results in increased third-party reimbursement. The experience of another administrator has persuaded her that offering good supervision has allowed her to attract highly qualified staff even with low pay scales. A third director believes that individual supervision is actually a less expensive training approach than group in-service workshops if cost is measured in relation to demonstrated more skillful intervention by trainees.

Do these impressions stand up under scrutiny? What other financial measures of benefit might be meaningful and capable of being tracked?

A service to the field might be rendered by identifying a researcher respected for his or her expertise in cost-benefit analysis and working with him or her to produce a protocol that program administrators could use to gather and analyze cost-benefit data related to the presence or absence of supervision in their own settings. One would hope that the same protocol could also be used or adapted by researchers in a multi-site comparison study. Individuals and organizations in the field could do a fair amount toward briefing an experienced researcher about the context of infant/family programs in general, but the researcher would probably also have to interview program managers at length and make some site visits to be sure that variables were meaningful.

(For example, reduction in staff turnover might seem like a cost rather than a benefit to managers who rely on the use of low-paid junior staff to keep personnel costs down.)

Recent analyses of effective service programs, combined with a conceptual model of the mechanisms through which service programs achieve their impact, suggest some further avenues of inquiry. In *Investing in Children: A Strategy to Change At-Risk Lives* (June, 1991), the Task Force on Children at Risk of United Way of America used findings of an Urban Institute study and the work of Lisbeth B. Schorr, Charles Bruner, and Olivia Golden to create a list of 10 common attributes of programs with documented success in improving outcomes for disadvantaged children and families. Among these attributes are: comprehensive, responsive services, intensive efforts to meet the needs of the most disadvantaged; collaboration with families, rather than imposition of a defined program; relationships of trust and respect among staff, children, and families; staff who are highly skilled, well-trained, well-supported, and sensitive; and a welcoming climate.

If one believes 1) in the model of "parallel process" in service programs—that, consciously or unconsciously, directly or sympolically, people treat each other as they have been treated; and 2) that supervision and mentorship are respectful, collaborative, and nurturing relationships for staff development, then one would expect to find supervision and mentorship as significant elements of the infrastructure of effective infant/family programs. (Indeed, this is hinted at by the United Way study's use of the term "well-supported" in describing staff characteristics.) Similarly, one would expect that expanding opportunities for reflective, collaborative, and regular supervision and mentorship would increase programs' ratings with respect to some or many of the "attributes of effectiveness." Since programs with these attributes have documented their positive impact on child and family development over the long term—some participants have been followed for decades—the attributes themselves seem reasonable markers to use in program evaluation when longitudinal prospective research is not an option.

The Council on Accreditation of Services for Families and Children, Inc. has established standards concerning the supervision that member agencies must provide in order to become and remain accredited by the Council. Designed for mental health and human services agencies, these standards might be adapted to evaluate supervision in early intervention settings and other programs serving infants, toddlers, and their families.

A number of research initiatives, of varying scope, could increase our understanding of the mechanisms through which supervision and mentorship influences individual staff performance; overall program climate; and children and families' experiences of program participation. Some options follow:

• A review of accounts of infant/family programs with documented positive impact to identify quantitative evidence of supervision or mentorship and qualitative factors (reflection, collaboration). A second level of analysis would involve a review of the same accounts, looking for mention of regular opportunities for reflection (case conferences, retreats) that might not fit traditional descriptions of supervision or mentorship.

• An examination of data from multi-site studies (e.g., the Infant Health and Development Program, the Child Care Staffing Study, the Early Intervention Collaborative Study) to determine the range of supervision and mentorship opportunities among programs within each study and to look for correlations between supervision and mentorship and other relevant study findings, such as staff turnover, ease of interdisciplinary collaboration, and consumer satisfaction.

• A task force of researchers, practitioners, and consumers to devise a set of indicators or measures likely to capture the impact of supervision/mentorship (or lack thereof) on program effectiveness—e.g., staff turnover, "no show" rate, capacity to serve most challenging children and families, and overall program ratings by funding agencies.

• Use of indicators/measures in prospective studies. A prospective study could be part of a planned demonstration project directly addressing supervision and mentorship, such as the strategies listed above. A prospective study might also take advantage of opportunities for "natural experiments." Where infant/family programs are expanding (as in the Head Start Parent and Child Center Program or in Part H implementation), researchers could study the opportunities for supervision and mentorship that are built into new programs, and their impact. Where states and communities are reducing the resources available to infant/family programs, one can study the extent to which existing supervision and mentorship are protected, as well as the impact of reduction in opportunities.

## Conclusion

In outlining the five strategies above, we have described expected outcomes, tasks to be accomplished, and timelines. The language may resemble the terminology found in grantmakers' funding priorities and government agencies' requests for proposals. This is no accident. The **ZERO TO THREE** Work Group on Supervision and Mentorship believes that it is time for funders of services for infants, toddlers, and their families to make a substantial investment in supervision and mentorship initiatives. We believe that the strategies in this action agenda build on a solid enough foundation of demonstrated effectiveness to warrant such investment.

We by no means wish to suggest, however, that only multi-site or multi-year initiatives to improve supervision and mentorship merit support. As the chapters that make up the next three sections of this *Sourcebook* illustrate, small innovations can, over time and given resources, lead to significantly more reflective, collaborative, and regular supervision and mentorship opportunities for students and practitioners. They can build stronger relationships for learning. They can achieve more effective support for the development of infants, toddlers and their families.

## References

The Task Force on Children at Risk. June, 1991. *Investing in Children: A Strategy to Change At-Risk Lives.* Alexandria, VA: United Way Strategic Institute.

# Supervision and Mentorship of Students

The habit of reflective practice begins in preservice training, nurtured by mutually respectful relationships with instructors, fieldwork supervisors, and mentors. The chapters in this section describe the supervision of students who are preparing to work in a variety of roles with infants, toddlers, and their families; also included are approaches to training practitioners for supervisory and mentoring roles. These chapters emphasize the importance of using supervision and mentorship to individualize training experiences.

# 4

# The Supervisory Relationship: Integrator, Resource and Guide

## Rebecca Shahmoon Shanok

The best supervisors I've had—and there need to be many over the course of a career—listened intently, found something to value, and then recast what I told them, embellishing it with something of their own. The experience of good supervision is like finding a fellow-traveler on a challenging journey, a companion worthy of trust who has visited similar destinations. This fellow-traveler knows many routes to our goal but is open to discovering a different path, a path we walk together, often with me in the lead, except when I miss the flowers to smell, or when I stumble or can't find my way. Then the supervisor is there to guide, even to prod a little, to bolster my courage, and to help me regain my footing and focus, to help me find my strength.

When it's going well, supervision is a holding environment, a place to feel secure enough to expose insecurities, mistakes, questions, and differences. Supervision parallels good work with families, the place for parents and children to feel safe enough to recognize the worst and best of their feelings and capabilities with a partner who helps them get where they need to go.

Good supervision makes the supervisee long for more. She feels, "If only I could tell my supervisor every single thing that happened in the interaction, I would feel more secure and know what to do." Of course, this is never possible, and, in fact, reminds us of the frustration that is an integral part of "good enough" mothering. "Good enough" supervision cannot review everything that *has* happened, nor can it anticipate everything that *might* happen.

The supervisory relationship represents an investment on both sides, a cooperative enterprise, a comradeship. To understand its power and value, it is useful to look at what the supervisee and supervisor each bring to the relationship, and at the ways learning takes place within it.

### The supervisee

In her daily work with infants, toddlers, and their families, the supervisee is on the spot. She must make a multitude of moves in the given situation. "Out there" in the situation, she learns by doing; in supervision, she learns by reflection.

Initially, the supervisee focuses on and reports behaviors and actions. She may give verbal summaries to her supervisor, basing her reports on memory, notes written after a treatment session, or notes written during a session. She may use process recording, a method of attempting, after a session, to record every nuance of both the client's behavior and apparent feeling state, her own, and the interaction between them. Both approaches encourage the supervisee to become more adept at reporting, a skill which is fundamental to the ability to reflect on process and, eventually, to introspect about it. Moreover, with the help of animated yet gentle inquiry by the supervisor, the supervisee increasingly observes and reports on her functioning in relation to feelings, and

**Supervisor:** *"Tell me what you did, and how you felt about what you did."*

*Rebecca Shahmoon Shanok, Early Childhood Group Therapy Program, Child Development Center, Jewish Board of Family and Children's Services, New York, New York*

**Supervisor:** *"What I think that I hear, Jean, is that whenever the Mom begins to talk about her feelings of being trapped by having such a needy child, you tend to move away. Let me tell you what that suggests to me and then you can think it over and see what occurs to you. Okay?"*

gradually in relationship to complex feeling states as they are responsive to her patients ... and as her patients may be reacting to hers. She becomes able to consider thematic connections between patterns in her own key life relationships and the evolving relationships with her clients (Greenspan & Wieder, 1984). She comes to know herself in the work, to recognize herself as an instrument, learning which vibrations are likely to be emanating from the patient and which, though stimulated by the patient, are in fact refrains from her own inner melodies.

Front line work with very young children and families is an intense experience—always challenging, sometimes joyful, many times humbling. To metabolize these experiences fully, the practitioner requires a confidante—someone with whom to focus, investigate, and brainstorm; someone with whom to share the experiences and the reactions; someone to be a model and to mirror the emerging professional self. Every practitioner has had uniquely painful experiences, and each tends to keep some things hidden. How much a given supervisee feels she has to keep hidden and how much she lets the supervisor see depends greatly on her sense of being partnered, her sense of safety in the supervisory relationship. In a good one, the supervisee feels understood, recognized and respected. As she comes to convey more and more of the whole story, even those aspects which hurt, confuse, or humiliate her, her supervisor's empathy and clarifications boost her ability to accept, even make use of, that which had previously felt unacceptable. She is thus able to feel enabled, rather than undermined, when the supervisor raises questions and concerns or offers information. The supervisee feels that the supervisor, knowing not only her strengths but also her vulnerabilities, is on her team.

## The supervisor

The supervisor is an expert because she was a front line worker. She was there. She saw it, felt it. By now, the supervisor can also bring a conceptual framework, experience, and a process of inquiry to the task of finding a way of working with a particular family and child. With supervisees, she hunts for strengths to support and cultivates a sense of optimism about the supervisee and about the work. She plays midwife to the emergence of the trainee's own strength and style.

The supervisor is a teacher who fosters the integration of process and content learning. But unlike classroom instruction, which can be planned systematically in terms of content and objectives, supervision is more like a life-space, spontaneous interview. In this context, the supervisor may relate theory to practice, teach a theoretical point, make a connection, appreciate what the supervisee did, tell a story to illustrate a point, share an experience or feeling, ask questions, point out a pattern, or raise a concern (Sheafor & Jenkins, 1982); or she may simply listen, validating, even cherishing the supervisee's experiences. She also helps the supervisee to maintain continuity of attention, so that concerns and strands of interest are developed rather than lost.

The supervisor models openness and good practice. She is willing to say, you can relax here and let the picture build. But here where there is danger, we must decide on an intervention. And here where there is opportunity, let us move forward.

Like any other good clinician, a supervisor develops a sixth sense about how others are feeling. She has an ability, often preconscious, to place herself in another's space, to imagine how he feels. But every once in awhile she checks it out: "I think you are letting me know that .... tell me, did I catch it correctly?" Thus she shares what she sees/feels, enlisting the supervisee as co-adventurer, indeed as expert on her dawning self-recognition. And within such colleagueship, self-recognition, plus knowledge, plus skill equals self-as-instrument, self-as-observer, self-as-assessor, self-as-intervenor, self-as-clinician.

The supervisor is open to honest feedback from students and workers and is willing to be led by them when appropriate. Supervising democratically means knowing when and where to ask for help. Like a "good enough" mother, the supervisor needs to figure out what she needs to avoid becoming overwhelmed—companionship, peers to talk with, time to think.

## The supervisory relationship

A supervisor and a supervisee are not unlike Sherlock Holmes and Dr. Watson, the senior partner more a thinker and the junior more a doer, but each essential to the other. Curious and motivated to solve a problem, they hunt for clues to guide their understanding of how best to offer services to a distinctive family and their unique child. Through their exchanges, supervisor and supervisee develop a mutual formulation as they strive to understand what is going on with children and families in their care. Neither one could do the work alone.

Each keeps the balance of the other. For example, work with children and families often involves going beyond our personal comfort zone in the making of relationships. Making relationships across classes and cultures, or with people who have been wounded and who cannot join reciprocally, who cannot give us the feedback that would let us know that we are doing all right, requires the insight, courage, and resilience born of collaboration.

The supervisory relationship is about power, but it does not need to be about dominance or control. Any supervisee recognizes her supervisor as someone with power over her. The greater the felt power, the greater will be the supervisee's anxiety. As much as possible, then, the power needs to be transferred. In the relationship model described here, the power is shared (which is a great relief not only to the supervisee but also to the supervisor!). The supervisor facilitates the articulation of a contract, even as she helps supervisees make explicit their contracts with families. The supervisee needs to have the right to:

- participate in developing the learning structure to which she is being exposed;
- develop a contract or an agenda defining reciprocal expectations;
- take first responsibility in analyzing her own work; and
- contribute meaningfully to her own evaluation.

In doing these things, the student/supervisee develops her capacities for reflection, analysis, and planfulness. She becomes more responsible and is better able to think and contribute creatively to her own learning when she has had a stake in developing the terrain to be covered, when the qualities of the learning are explicit, and when the supervisory relationship features openness (Manis, 1979).

For her part, the supervisor depends on the supervisee's ability to observe, interact, and report. She acknowledges—even respects—the supervisee's style and choices. The "good enough" supervisor recognizes that there are many roads to Rome and that her supervisee will come up with a novel, yet authentic and meaningful response in a given situation. The supervisor seeks and supports that which is facilitative in the supervisee's work. She also raises questions about those areas of the supervisee's interactions and functioning which reflect either blind spots, limited knowledge, or lack of experience, confidence, or awareness. The supportive supervisor violates the supervisee's negative expectations, just as the supervisee will try over and over again to violate the negative expectations of those families too wounded by past experience to enter the therapeutic relationship with optimism. People learn and grow when they feel understood, supported, and, when appropriate, even appreciated. There is an exquisitely delicate relationship between the experience of positive regard, self-esteem, and the ability to be effective.

Thoughtful supervision is a process through which the supervisee comes to recognize the decision points in a given case and the basis upon which to make decisions. But "decisions" are not to be seen as

**Supervisor:** (Earnestly) *"If we realize that you were only at the center for two hours last week, it's easy to see why your observations are so sketchy at this point. It's just not possible to do an adequate job in such a short time. You'll recall that the application materials state that ten hours per week at the Center is required. What else are you trying to juggle?"*

"answers" (or worse, *the* answer). Rather, decisions represent a forward position, a choice of direction along a path that will yield further useful information and another decision point. In-depth supervision looks beyond decisions and beneath manifest details of behavior, interactions and learning styles. The trust and safety of the process encourage peering below the surface to latent ideas and *feelings* of clients, of the supervisee, and, at times, even of the supervisor. By recognizing and engaging with the supervisee around the emotions they are experiencing, the supervisor models the use of empathy and the recognition and use of emotional experience in professional situations.

To understand feelings, it is important to attend to the history and context of *each* individual involved; people get to know each other in supervision that is going well. (Attention to what lies beneath the surface should not distract us, however, from appreciating what might be taken for granted. Sally Provence has talked about using common opportunities to facilitate learning, and how supervision can assist a practitioner in recognizing the value of her daily work. People do not always appreciate the tremendous power of concentrated listening, for example, or the importance of "merely" playing with a baby, helping a baby be aware of you and the exchange when doing something as mundane as changing a diaper.)

Monitoring and evaluation are part of the supervisory relationship, but because the monitoring or evaluative aspects are built in, the supervisee always knows where she stands. Strengths are emphasized while vulnerabilities are partnered. Depending on the styles of both the supervisor and supervisee, the relationship may be informal or relatively formal. There is always, however, a fostering of deep respect for observation of others and of self. Such painstaking observation sponsors the capacity for introspection. To teach introspection requires that the supervisor use an appropriate level of self disclosure to alleviate unproductive anxiety of the supervisee and model, as well, thoughtful self-evaluation.

## Special issues in supervising work with infants, toddlers and their families

Supervision in infant-toddler-family practice is particularly challenging because so much of what we sense and of what we communicate occurs without words, most obviously with the children. While we tend to think of supervision as a verbal medium, it is worth dwelling for a moment on the non-verbal aspects of the process. Expressive and gestural communication, patterns of mutual gazing and turn-taking, and body language convey much. When patients do not yet use words, supervisees are challenged to notice and to report on behaviors and expressive nuances that they take in through the range of their own senses (good practice even for work with highly verbal people). As Stanley Greenspan (1989) notes, "the basic emotional messages of life, safety and security versus danger, acceptance versus rejection, approval versus disapproval, are all communicated through facial expressions, body posture, movement patterns, and vocal tone and rhythm. Words enhance these most basic communications, but ... we all form split-second judgments (about) a new person ... before the conversation even gets started." It is worth asking what, without the use of words, will help a particular individual feel accepted, safe, and understood in supervision; so, too, in treatment.

Another challenge in working with infants, toddlers, and their families involves the "continuum of identifications from baby to parent" (Bertacchi & Coplon, 1989, and this volume) represented by the very different professions that work with this population. Reflecting on the differences in training emphasis in, say, social work or early childhood education (to say nothing of the different personal experiences and proclivities which incline an individual to select one or the other field in the first place), one can see how one professional may more easily identify with the parent, the other more easily with the child. Supervision can be the place to recognize such positions and to motivate change toward the ability to mix identifications, see from many perspectives at once, and plan interventions that will work for *families*, rather than only for an individual parent or child. As Bertacchi and Coplon point out, the internal shifts necessary for good dyadic and family work do not diminish the unique insights and talents that individual professionals use themselves and share with team members. Similarly, the great value of receiving supervision from individuals trained in other disciplines complements, but does not replace, the importance to one's professional identification and maturation of enjoying the supervision and leadership of someone trained in one's own discipline.

As we think of supervision in the overall context of training people to work effectively with infants, toddlers, and their families, it is worth pondering about how adults develop, change, and grow. Let us reflect on our own histories and present experiences as learners and as leaders. The intertwining of theory and practice implies a process. We are deeply aware of the tension between the process-oriented approach to training, which seems to take close to forever, and a didactic "cookbook" approach, which obviously cannot do the job. The analogies and parallels between training and practice in the infant/family field provide us with fortunate synchronicity and coherence among what we know, what we believe, what we value, and what we do.

But there is also an unfortunate side, because our training approaches cannot be mass produced. Relationship is a very special subset of experiential learning. When we recall the enormous contributions to education of John Dewey, father of experiential learning, or the long history across cultures and fields, of apprenticeship, or in fact, when we remember how babies learn to become mothers or fathers, we recognize that student workers fully need activity and reflection to become integrated; they need to be "brought up" in their fields and in the zero to three concentration. Jeree Pawl has said, "Supervision is a safe place, where the generosity which is shared with a supervisee can then be passed on to families and to children." It is an oasis where new practitioners can stumble and can stride, be refueled, and then go off to do their work once again. The supervisee moves forward carrying within herself self-respect, a sense of responsibility, and knowledge internalized through meaningful relationship.

Experiential learning and relationships demand risk-taking. They foster coping, adaptation, and mastery. Through the myriad transactions of supervisory relationships, the supervisee changes and grows. Her new capacities move from what has been called "the domain of the new and 'tacked-on' to the domain of the familiar and indispensable" (Pine, 1985). Change occurs in self-image, in behavior, and the way she is viewed by others. The supervisee develops an expanded and more resourceful sense of self, including self as observer, self as intervener, self as committed to zero-to-threes and their families, self as not necessarily knowing the answers, but as being able to figure out the next step—*collaboratively*.

**Supervisor:**
(Smiles) *"Okay. It's time for us to do your formal evaluation. I'll just sum up what we've been talking about all along. Here's what I see as your strengths ... And these are the areas to work on ... Tell me what you think of what I've said, and if it makes sense to you, how do **you** think we could work on those areas?"*

## References

Bertacchi, J and Coplon, J. 1989. The professional use of self in prevention. *Zero to Three*, Vol. IX, No. 4, p. 6.

Greenspan, SI. 1989. *The Development of the Ego*. Madison, CT: International Universities Press, p. 132.

Greenspan, SI and Wieder, S. 1984. Dimensions and levels of the therapeutic process. *Psychotherapy* Vol. 21, No. 1.

Manis, F. 1979. *Openness in Social Work Field Instruction*. Goleta, CA: Kimberly Press, Inc.

Pine, F. 1985. *Developmental Theory and Clinical Process*. New Haven, CT: Yale University Press, p. 120.

Sheafor, B and Jenkins, L. 1982 *Quality Field Instruction in Social Work*. NY: Longman, p. 64.

# 5

# *Individualizing Training for Early Intervention Practitioners*

## Carole W. Brown and Eva K. Thorp

**The unique blend of skills and personal experiences that each individual brings to training forms the context for supervision.**

Individuals pursuing pre-service or in-service training in early intervention services come to the training experience with a number of strengths. Not the least among these strengths is the fact that their enrollment in a training program is a sign of their willingness to learn and change. However, change does not always come easily. For a variety of reasons, students may be unprepared to apply family-centered principles in their work with families. Often these individuals come from previous training programs that have prepared them to work with children, but not the families of these children. Their sole exposure to a family focus may have been reading about the "stages of grief." They may or may not have had personal experiences that allow them to be introspective and demonstrate self-knowledge. They may or may not have had experiences which would enable them to understand the daily routine and challenge of parenthood. They may or may not have had direct positive experiences with handicapped individuals in their family or peer group or neighborhood.

The unique blend of skills and personal experiences that each individual brings to training forms the context for supervision. Composite descriptions of some students, whose strengths and vulnerabilities are based on the students we have worked with, in several settings, will be used to illustrate the importance of individualizing educational experiences.

### The young student

Alice is a 22-year-old who has recently graduated from an undergraduate training program in special education. She has demonstrated great skill in her coursework and has now decided to proceed to graduate school to obtain advanced training in working with high risk and handicapped infants and their families. Alice is from a rural area and grew up in a supportive, middle-class, two-parent family. She has had a great deal of paid and volunteer experience with children with handicaps. She has, however, had no experience with their parents: she has never done a home visit and is unsure of what she would do on one, she has no knowledge of the social service web which often surrounds families with multiple problems.

### The child advocate

Susanne is a 30-year-old who has been employed for several years as a parent-infant educator. She has an undergraduate degree in child development but feels the need for further training and skills in order to work effectively under PL 99-457 guidelines. She is highly skilled at developing individualized learning plans for the children with whom she works. She has done homebased service delivery and sometimes develops strong friendships with families. She has very strong feelings about helping children with special needs. At the same time, she feels that it is not relevant to attempt to under-

*Carole W. Brown*, George Washington University

*Eva K. Thorp*, George Mason University

stand the emotional climate of the families with whom she is working. She especially feels that it is completely unnecessary to systematically explore her feelings about her own family and about the families with whom she is working in the process of carrying out her work.

## The experienced professional

Lindsey is a 45-year-old speech pathologist who has worked for the past 15 years in a variety of public and private settings. Just recently she has taken a position with an early intervention program. Up to this time she has provided direct therapy to children and has occasionally developed behavioral training programs for parents to carry out with their children. She believes that one of the major barriers to successful outcomes for the children with whom she works is lack of commitment and follow-through on the part of families, particularly those whom she perceives to be "lower functioning".

## The families to be served

Each of these students must be prepared to work with a variety of families, including those whose multiple problems typically confound community agencies and providers. Amelia's story is of one such family.

Amelia is 21 and the mother of two children under five years of age, both of whom have some degree of developmental delay. She is married, but her husband has been in and out of their home. Mary, her oldest child, aged 30 months, was in foster care for three months when she was an infant but is now living with her mother. She often appears unkempt and sad. She almost never vocalizes, although she seems to understand simple requests. Amelia's younger child is a son, Jack, aged 15 months. He seems quite happy and seems to enjoy a lot of attention from his mother. However, he also vocalizes infrequently, and there is an emerging suspicion of delay. Amelia often appears uninterested in her surroundings, and rarely initiates conversations with other adults or with her children. She receives public assistance, is monitored by social services, and receives home and center-based services for both of her children from a local parent-infant program. Although she typically looks sad and unresponsive, Amelia clearly enjoys any activity that involves music. She has indicated a concern that her daughter is not talking, and she has further indicated that she knows that her daughter seems happier with other people than when she is with Amelia.

What training strategies will be necessary to enable each of the potentially competent professionals above to function in optimally supportive positions vis-a-vis Amelia? What will enable them to identify and support the natural strengths that they bring to the intervention process? What will enable them to explore the meanings that each of her children may have for Amelia? What will enable them to construct intervention environments in which they can support Amelia in her interactions with each of her children? In one student's case there may be a need for a broadened experiential base; in another a need for opportunities for safe self-exploration; in a third, the need for attitude change. What common content combined with what individualized clinical experiences must a training program provide in order to respond to the issues each of these individuals bring to the training process?

## The role of a family-centered philosophy

The training materials and media which enable the infant/family practitioner to work effectively with families are by nature eclectic and derived from many disciplines. No one discipline uniquely possesses the knowledge necessary to accomplish this task. Thus, training experiences must integrate in sensible fashion key information from the many disciplines which contribute to parent-infant service delivery. A clearly articulated set of principles, based in theory and acknowledged best practice, about how to facilitate child development and family functioning may be the most appropriate vehicle for integrating this disparate information.

The task for pre-service and in-service training programs is to further explicate a philosophical base that can guide decision-making, intervention, and the development of one's own theories about infants and families (Odom, 1987).

The provisions of PL 99-457, the 1986 Amendments to the Education of the Handicapped Act, support a philosophical basis for training early intervention services providers. The legislation is based upon assumptions about how families are viewed and what it means for services to be family-centered, about the nature of high risk and handicapped children and how they learn, and about the process of professional interaction across disciplines.

In addition, statements of integrative principles and philosophy to guide family-focused intervention are emerging in the field. Johnson, McGonigel and Kaufmann (1989) have identified conceptual guidelines for best practice in the development of the Individualized Family Service Plan, which is central to the implementation of PL 99-457. Dunst, Trivette, and Deal (1988) have identified intervention principles derived from a family empowerment perspective. McCollum, Thors and Rowan (1988) have developed integrative philosophy statements to guide training of early intervention specialists.

How might these sets of principles assist our typical students as they begin to interact with families? Alice possesses a firm grounding in intervention with children but has no experience with families. These principles give her a standard to guide her in new situations. When confronted with an issue in her interaction with families, Alice learns to evaluate her actions for their compatibility with the philosophy. She becomes able to say, "If I believe this to be true about families, what potential strategies are available to me at this juncture? What potential actions would be incompatible with the philosophy?"

In contrast, Lindsey has had "too much" experience. In the absence of a philosophical perspective on the nature and needs of families, she has come to see families as a major barrier to accomplishing her goals for children. Family-centered principles enable her to come back to a more hopeful view of families. They serve as a continuous reminder to look for resourcefulness in families and to listen to what families tell her they want for their children. These become the basis for collaboration.

## The role of instructional content

An information base is also required to guide professionals in working more effectively with parents. An understanding of the attachment process and of potential barriers to attachment, for example, will enable Alice, Susanne, and Lindsey alike to examine a parent's behavior in new ways and to develop hypotheses about the nature of the parent's relationships with his or her children. Learning about interaction-focused intervention strategies will enable Alice and Susanne to see that intervention does not require choosing between a focus on only the child or only the parent. They will learn how to extend what they have already learned about structuring child interventions to parent-infant interventions. Learning about collaborative goal setting and problem solving will enable them to support Amelia in the IFSP process and to assist her in identifying the outcomes she desires from intervention. Further, learning about the role descriptions and disciplinary scope of each of their fellow teammates will enable whichever one of them is functioning in the case management role to enlist the assistance of the others and will assist all team members in coming to recognize the limits of their own expertise. Finally, when these professionals in training learn about the network of social service agencies in their community, they will acquire a better understanding of the larger context of Amelia's daily life into which they must embed their interventions. It is this latter knowledge that brings a young professional such as Alice to understand that advocacy efforts on behalf of adequate shelter and nutrition for families are appropriately within the scope of early intervention.

## The integrative role of individualized clinical experiences

Ultimately it is through systematic and repeated exposure to children and families that professionals come to see themselves as competent infant/family practitioners. It is in these real-life, conflict-ridden situations that students acquire the strategic knowledge of decision making and problem solving necessary in early intervention (Bailey, 1989). It is in these practice settings where students acquire the clinical skills of really listening to all the actors in the family, including the voiceless ones; of generating hypotheses about behavior; and of responding thoughtfully and respectfully (Trout, 1988).

Field experiences should ensure students access to a diversity of families, to a richness of cultural backgrounds, and to a broad range of child and family needs. Such experiences may be acquired at the pre-service level through a practicum, or at the in-service level through the implementation of systematic supervised case review and problem solving with experienced professionals. One of the best ways to acquire this knowledge is through exposure to experienced parents of children with special needs in the classroom or through personal interaction.

## The supervision process

The work of the clinical supervisor is central to the learning process in the practicum, where students are being prepared for a task which is ultimately interpersonal in nature. Through the relationship she establishes with the student, the supervisor models and calls attention to key aspects of this task. Each professional-in-training will require different strategies of the supervisor, as the supervisor must keep in mind two questions. First, what will it take for this individual to integrate her understanding of infants and families and to apply a family-focused approach to planning and intervention? Second, and perhaps more importantly, what will it take to enable this student to sufficiently explore her own family experience in order to experience empathy for the most difficult of families, thus becoming able to work collaboratively with them? The supervisor must also note the issues that surface in the interactions between the supervisor and the student. These issues often parallel the interactions of the student with family members. By paying attention to these parallel process issues and modifying her own behavior, the supervisor may influence the student's relationship with the parent. (Bertacchi and Coplon, 1989, and this volume).

## Alice: Understanding the parent's point of view

With Alice, the task of supervision is to find an avenue for empathy with the parenting role. Because Alice is energetic, playful and responsive, she is able to be very successful in her interventions with each of Amelia's children on an individual basis. But Alice's ability to actively involve Mary (the sad and withdrawn 30-month-old child) in vocal interaction makes Amelia acutely aware of her inability to engage Mary. Alice's ability to easily seduce Jack (the 15-month-old) only serves to alienate Amelia further from Alice.

Because she does not understand Amelia's experiences as a parent, Alice doesn't realize that she is alienating Amelia. The supervisor may use Alice's and Amelia's similarity in age as one avenue to encourage Alice to develop empathy for Amelia. Alice is asked to consider what it would be like to have two children, and also to consider ways in which Amelia's thinking and needs may be very similar to her own. Alice's youthfulness can be an asset if she is helped to form an alliance with Amelia, to offer friendship, and to share common experiences, such as Amelia's love of music.

With some young, immature students, this approach may backfire. Such students may find so little in common with a parent like Amelia or be threatened by such an identification, that they go to great lengths to differentiate themselves from the parent so that a relationship between the student and parent does not develop. Or the student may act out the role of child with the parent and reinforce immature parental responses.

A structured way to help inexperienced students learn to identify the strengths of a family whose deficits are obvious is to use family-centered principles as a guide. One family-focused principle that Alice is learning is, "Build on any interaction attempts between parent and child." While Alice's first impression is that "Amelia mostly ignores her kids," this principle alerts her to look for any signs of efforts by either the parent or child to elicit the other's attention. Following one supervision session, Alice is able to identify a mismatch in Amelia's and Mary's interaction efforts, noting that Amelia misses Mary's overtures to her and that Mary also misses Amelia's fleeting overtures to Mary.

Additionally, due to Alice's limited experiences, the supervisor models brainstorming techniques for forming hypotheses about and interpreting Amelia's interactions with her children. Alice is asked to consider, for example, how Amelia's apparent passivity toward her children might reflect the circumstances of her social environment and lack of social support. This mutual exploration and problem solving between supervisor and student becomes a model for mutual problem solving between a student and parent.

## Susanne: Acquiring self knowledge as a basis for work with families

Supervision with Susanne is more directly focused on affective issues. This is all the more challenging because Susanne is unsure about the importance of attending to either the mother's affect or to her own. Feelings of loss from her early experiences in her own family lead her to identify strongly with the very apparent vulnerability of Amelia's daughter, Mary, and even with Amelia. She is able to begin to form an alliance with Amelia. However, this alliance is shaky, as Susanne's unresolved conflicts frequently interfere with her full awareness, and interactions become unclear and communications somewhat convoluted. For example, when things otherwise appear to be going well, Amelia withholds some critical information about Mary's foster placement from Susanne. Susanne's response is to become angry and resistant to working with Amelia. To the supervisor, her response seems disproportionate to what actually had transpired between Amelia and Susanne. Susanne expresses feelings of betrayal; the supervisor suspects that such strong feelings may be remnants of Susanne's prior experience of loss and betrayal.

The task of supervision with Susanne is to support her so that she can learn to tolerate the powerful feelings that the problems of parents like Amelia trigger in her. The supervisor needs to call attention to Susanne's affect as well as Amelia's in different situations and begin to encourage Susanne to generate interpretations. She may further begin to explore the feelings that Amelia engenders in Susanne by identifying these in herself.

A potential trap in the supervision process with Susanne is the unanticipated power struggle with the supervisor in addition to those with the parent. Susanne becomes angry with the supervisor after the session in which she reveals that Amelia has misled her. She wishes that the supervisor had matched her with a truly resourceful parent and holds the supervisor responsible for teaching her a resourcefulness model for viewing families that she feels she cannot apply to Amelia.

In working with Susanne, the supervisor would do well to remember that Susanne's ability to be a competent and strong advocate of children is her area of strength. By creating a safe, supportive relationship, even in the face of challenge from Susanne, the supervisor can build on the fragile nature of that competence. Susanne is encouraged

> **Mutual exploration and problem solving between supervisor and student becomes a model for mutual problem solving between a student and parent.**

to "hang in there" with Amelia and when she learns that Amelia's withholding information is based on a very real fear that Mary again will be placed in a foster care home, she is able to see that Amelia needs protection just as her children do. Susanne becomes able to see herself as an advocate for the entire family.

## Lindsey: Recognizing the need to be a partner with parents

The task of supervision with Lindsey is in some ways even more formidable. She comes to the supervisory relationship with many strengths, both intellectual and experiential. Lindsey has been a successful parent. She sees Amelia as incompetent, and of course Amelia sees Lindsey as judgmental. This attitudinal set serves to make Amelia even less certain of herself as a parent, giving Lindsey fresh data to support her view that Amelia is emotionally a child and therefore not capable of responsible parent behavior.

Supervision focuses on the assumptions Lindsey makes about Amelia. Videotapes prove useful. Watching her own interventions with Mary and Amelia, Lindsey notices examples of Amelia responding to Mary, behavior that she had not picked up on as it occurred. She also sees herself missing opportunities to support these attempted interactions. The supervisor also challenges Lindsey's assumptions by asking her to examine case material and devise alternate scenarios that might potentially involve Amelia. In this exercise and in other conversations, the supervisor and student jointly identify strategies for avoiding judgments and identifying strengths.

Supervision for Lindsey should help her to direct her natural parenting strengths toward nurturing Amelia. It is important to focus on Lindsey's own parenting experience and the degree to which unresolved feelings or biases about how best to parent influence her work with other families; nurturing Amelia should not lead to a dependent relationship but to a partnership. Thus, in identifying her own parenting priorities, Lindsey is able to see that while a child's speech and language delay might be the most pressing problem that she would identify in her role as a speech pathologist, "this may not be the most important thing for the parent."

Trouble may arise if the supervisor is too directive toward Lindsey or allows Lindsey to be too directive towards the supervisor. Lindsey learns best when self-taught. The parallel process that the supervisor must model is of a partnership, allowing Lindsey to identify her own issues and points of change, while creating opportunities that challenge her less developed perceptions.

## Attending to self as supervisor

Supervisors face further challenge in training family-focused early intervention professionals. The supervisor must herself continue to monitor her own feelings and assumptions about families. She must continue to explore her own reactions to families and also to the students with whom she works. What are her own parenting issues? Only in so doing is she able to behave honestly with both clients and students and to model the attitude of self-reflection that underlies all the skills of early intervention (Trout, 1988).

## The successful trainee

It is through a complex of systematic interpersonal interactions and training structures that the varied professionals who enter the field of early intervention come to a common ground of empathy for and ability to collaborate with families like Amelia and her children. Alice, Susanne, and Lindsey are themselves in the midst of a developmental process. The supervision they receive in their interactions with Amelia provides the scaffolding for future encounters with families with diverse strengths and needs. Success for each of them must be evaluated individually and by the standard of how well each will be able to enhance the abilities of these families to meet the special needs of their children.

> **The parallel process that the supervisor must model is of a partnership.**

Once she becomes fully acquainted with the grim realities of the social system that Amelia encounters daily, Alice becomes a strong advocate of system change for Amelia and other families as well as a skilled observer and facilitator of parent-infant interaction. She begins to focus her energies on strategies to make the social environment better for Amelia. Susanne gradually shows more self insight and tolerance for her own feelings for families and children. Her advocacy for children is growing to encompass the family. Lindsey discovers theories that enable her to identify and restrain her own tendencies to "parent" Amelia when transacting with her on an "adult to adult" basis would be more appropriate.

All three students bring to the learning process a variety of skills and experiences and a motivation to change. All three bring attitudes that could create barriers to the forging of true partnerships with parents. But individualized training and supervision enable all three to acquire principles, concepts and skills to help them meet the new standard in early intervention in PL 99-457. All three can move closer to forging effective partnerships with parents, and to helping families enhance the development of their children.

## References

Bailey, DB. 1989. Issues and directions in preparing professionals to work with young handicapped children and their families. In JJ Gallagher, PL Trohanis, & RM Clifford (Eds.), *Policy implementation and PL 99-457* (pp. 133-146). Baltimore, MD: Paul Brookes.

Bertacchi, J & Coplon, J. 1989. The professional use of self in prevention *Zero to Three*, Vol. IX, No. 4.

Dunst, C, Trivette, C, & Deal, A. 1988. *Enabling and empowering families.* Cambridge, MA: Brookline Books.

Johnson, B, McGonigel, M and Kaufmann, R. 1989. *Guidelines and Recommended Practices for the Development of the Individualized Family Service Plan.* Washington, D.C.: Association for the Care of Children's Health.

McCollum, J, Thorp, E & Rowen, L. 1988. "Interdisciplinary Training for Early Intervention: A Philosophy Based Approach." DEC, National Early Childhood Conference on Children with Special Needs. November.

Odom, SL. 1987. The role of theory in the preparation of professionals in early childhood special education. *Topics in Early Childhood Special Education,* 7(3), 1-11.

Trout, M. 1988. Infant mental health: Monitoring our movement into the twenty-first century. *Infant Mental Health Jounral,* 9(3), 191-200.

# 6

# "Passing On the Process": Reflections of a Supervisee and a Supervisor

## Kelley Bateman and Eva K. Thorp

*Editor's note:* As a contribution to this *Sourcebook*, Kelley Bateman and Eva Thorp agreed to reflect jointly about the work they had done together when Kelley was preparing for her master's degree in early childhood special education. The following edited transcript of a telephone interview between Kelley and Eva describes and analyzes aspects of a semester-long internship, designed and carried out by Kelley and supervised by Eva. During their conversation, Kelley and Eva also reflect on the experiences that led Kelley to take on challenges beyond the minimum requirements of her degree program, and on workplace supports for (and barriers to) continuing learning through supervision.

### Coursework as a catalyst for reflective practice

Reflective professional practice does not begin with the student's internship or practicum. Basic courses communicate the philosophy of a profession (or, at a minimum, of a professor). Kelley's life experience and ongoing job responsibilities may have helped her to make immediate use of the concepts introduced in her first graduate courses.

**Eva:** *Kelley, when you began your master's program, you were already working with young children with disabilities. What was your philosophy about families at that time?*

**Kelley:** I had majored in special education as an undergraduate, but I hadn't learned how to work with parents. When I started my master's program I was teaching preschool children with disabilities. I felt frustrated with parents. I remember that I had to teach a little girl how to blow her nose properly, and I thought, "Why me? Why not the parents?" When I talked to another teacher, she said, "You can't let children suffer for what parents aren't able to do."

In my job, teachers were required to make home visits, but we weren't told what to do beyond "working on parent-child interaction." I had had enough experience with advice falling on deaf ears that I knew I didn't want to go into a home and give orders, or be a "give advice" person. But I **didn't** have the skills to go into homes and do anything more positive. That's how I ended up in your Family Intervention class.

**Eva:** *Did you have any particular feelings about "problem" families?*

**Kelley:** I thought they didn't have a right to their children. I was very judgmental. When mothers were described to me as "mentally ill" or "schizophrenic," it was impossible for me to see any virtue in their parenting. And this was with a whole range of parents—middle-class parents "in denial" were as difficult to deal with as low-income parents. I felt hopeless. The system said, "Go into homes and help parents," but we had no training or any systematic approach.

It was helpful to learn in the course that family development moves in stages, and that teachers need to fit in where families are.

**Eva:** *Can you reconstruct the process you went through in changing your judgmental view of families?*

**Kelley:** Learning about the family life cycle was helpful. As I learned, I could picture

*Kelley Bateman,* Manassas, Virginia

*Eva K. Thorp,* George Mason University, Fairfax, Virginia

myself in my own life cycle. I saw the changes I had gone through in 35 years, and I let go of some of my judgments about other parents. They were working with children in a certain way because of circumstances that weren't all their fault. There was "something there" in all families—I wanted to help families move along as other people had helped me move along.

As I started looking at one really involved mother (of a child I was teaching), I became less frustrated and angry. She was under "court guidelines" and had four children taken away, but I started looking for her competencies. She and I "clicked"; we never had the problems she had had with other teachers. Other teachers in the school avoided some parents who made them feel helpless, but this mother and I never "disengaged." I was seeing meaning in her behavior.

**Eva:** *What strategies did you use to communicate to your co-workers about parents they had given up on?*

**Kelley:** The principal of the school asked me, "How come this mother likes you?" (The mother had ragged on every other teacher her daughter had had.) I met this mother while I was in the Family Intervention class, and I started trying to find the good in her. I looked for what she did for her daughter. I noticed the new shoes (even though I saw the torn underwear, too).

This mother felt terrible about her "parenting skills." Most of the other staff used required home visits to work on "goals" with a child, one on one. Your course helped me see that this approach might actually make a parent feel **worse** about her own abilities, compared to the "professional." So when I worked with this mom, it was three of us—Mom, me, and the child. The mom led some activities. I was learning to look at her as competent, find her competencies, and point them out **to her**. She couldn't do that for herself—she had been told by so many people how incompetent she was.

Unfortunately, without training and support, staff aren't likely to use this approach with families.

## The supervised internship

In Kelley's state, students with previous experience in early childhood are not required to complete a supervised internship as a condition of certification. As Kelley noted, her decision to undertake an internship "had to do with finding a reason for it beyond a requirement."

**Eva:** *How did you decide what you wanted from the internship?*

**Kelley:** The new information (from coursework) about parent-child interaction had opened a door. I wanted to increase my skills. I wanted more from home visits.

**Eva:** *I remember that because you were already experienced you weren't really thrilled about doing an internship. I said that you could make some choices and set goals for yourself. The basic model was internship on a contract basis. All I did was say, "Kelley, this isn't something where I tell you what to do." The next time you came to see me, you had a project and a timeline figured out to meet your own goals.*

**Kelley:** I was at the end of my master's degree—intrigued, but tired. It's interesting that I picked home visits, my weakest area, to work on—not many people choose home visits; it's what they hate most. Of course, I was always challenging you: "I'm paying for tuition **and** a sitter. Make my time worthwhile."

There was a particular child in my classroom who I knew needed help in the home. He was autistic, with no language, and had total charge of the household. I kept wanting to ask the mother, "How can you let this little boy control your life?" but it wasn't possible to say to this mother, "Do this, do that." I had read that middle-class parents are more likely to change than some others, and I wondered if this was true. What actually happens?

This mother was probably the perfect parent for my project. She was desperate for help. I wanted the parents to get the best that they could get; I didn't want to be a bad model for that family. Christopher's disability wasn't something that was going away. I wanted them to feel less helpless, to feel that they could make decisions—impromptu or long-term—and that they could get good information to help make decisions.

**Eva:** *Can you describe what we did together?*

**Kelley:** I asked Nora, the mother, for permission for both of us to come into the home and help her interact with Christopher in a more developmentally challenging way. She was very open to this. We made five visits over a 10-week period and videotaped the visits. You and I had a debriefing (with food!) immediately after each visit. At first I thought they were corny, but they helped me retain my observations about the mother and gave me immediate feedback. Later we watched the videotapes together and discussed them.

I remember how slow I was to see and observe the mother's behaviors that supported Christopher's growth. It was easy for me to do things with Christopher, but harder for me to observe her helpful behaviors in their natural interaction, fix them in my mind, and then relate them back to her. I missed a lot, but later I could look at the videos several times and see more things each time. I could also use the videos to analyze a series of home visits and see patterns of behavior that I couldn't recognize at the moment.

Using video also removed the "criticism" factor. The tape was something concrete to work with.

**Eva:** *We had an interesting time fitting your goals for the internship and my goals for the internship into the format for home visits required by your job.*

**Kelley:** I had support for my graduate work from my job, but people said, "Remember, this is **theory**." When I made a home visit, I had to do a report with specific Individualized Educational Plan objectives and behavior counts. You helped me figure out which IEP objectives were addressed and how to write reports that showed that the mom was addressing the IEP objectives. But there wasn't any place on the form to show how I helped the mom work on the IEP.

**Eva:** *After each home visit, we would talk about what you observed the mother doing that related to the child making progress toward an IEP objective—like staying with a toy appropriately. We began talking about accomplishing developmental agendas while supporting the mother's interaction with the child. This fit into my own long-term training agenda—how to use natural environments to accomplish teaching objectives. Do you remember how you started to "supervise" Nora?*

## Passing on the process

**Eva (teacher):** I remember that in the Family Intervention class when I talked about supporting parent competence, you would challenge me, asking "What about the mom who refuses to get a job and just takes, takes, takes, and doesn't even get her kid off the bottle?" It was as if you were asking, "Does this mean I have to give up how I think about families?"

Then one evening all the family themes came out—that was the first time I heard that you were a single parent, working full-time and going to school. How could anybody be not-like-you? It was hard for you to deal with difference, to find the line between accepting differences and seeing what in a family might benefit from change. How could you support someone else's competence that didn't measure up to your own?

**Kelley (student):** I made a home visit not long ago and found a mom with her three-year-old snuggled in her lap with a bottle. The mom said, "Oh, you caught me, I'm guilty (of giving the child the bottle)." I joked, "You're right, but I bet his fussing was driving you crazy... You had to wake him up at the day care center to get him home in time for my visit."

The kid stayed snuggled against his mom's chest the whole time and did activities on his mom's lap. I didn't insist on "repositioning." I looked at the situation from the mom's perspective, and I could understand her choice. I used a little humor—asked her, "How is his cup drinking going, anyway?"

I wasn't angry or frustrated. But unless you've learned to put yourself in the mom's place and appreciate what the bottle and the snuggling meant, when both the mom and the kid were stressed out, you could spend the day worrying that one bottle-drinking incident will really set the kid's oral motor development back...

**Kelley:** I would show the tapes to her, and ask, "What do you notice about Christopher at this point?" Nora is a much better observer than she was a year ago. As I learned to observe her, she learned to observe Christopher more. She keeps the videotapes; they help her chart his progress. She's much more objective and introspective: She can say, "If I do this, Christopher will react this way." She thinks about the effect of her behavior on Christopher.

Looking at the videotapes together was very powerful for Nora. It was like passing on the process of what you and I had done together.

**Eva:** *The supervision process seems to have changed how you use questions.*

**Kelley:** I do a lot more thinking while I'm on home visits, but **not** about how to teach a certain thing to a child. On the way to the visit I think about what I want to know or have a family think about. I try to ask questions that lead a family to discovery—"How do you think babies learn?" "What do you think he's hearing now?" "How does he sound when he's excited?" I used to see myself as a giver of information, but now it's "Help me to see how you see it." If I ask, "Why does a parent do this this way?" it reduces my frustration. I don't have to fix everything.

**Eva:** *Formerly, you saw yourself as a fixer and giver of information. Now you are leading families to discovery.*

**Kelley:** There's still a picture in the back of my mind of what I would like this person to "go for" with her child, but I try to understand the picture in **her** mind for her child. There's a need to merge pictures.

## Maintaining and enhancing competence

Having earned her master's degree and become a teacher in a school based program for two- to five-year-old children with disabilities, Kelley finds that few, if any, of her colleagues in the county have had supervised internship experiences comparable to her own. She currently receives no clinical supervision or consultation.

**Eva:** *How is it going?*

**Kelley:** I've noticed a slacking off in my attention to parental interaction recently. I'm not sure why—increase in workload? There have been some permanent changes in the way I work as a result of my training, but the changes aren't across the board. I still use a "questioning" approach, but some of my home visits are routine now.

**Eva:** *Why do you think this is happening?*

**Kelley:** Maybe it's because I'm not required to focus on parent/infant interaction. The programs in the state that serve children from birth to their second birthday do seem to have a parent interaction focus, but in my situation (serving two to five-year-olds), parents are a priority in the state guidelines, but that's it. I don't have to think about parent interaction unless I want to. It's risky to encourage parents—easier to work with the child yourself.

Maybe it's because my skills aren't ingrained. The 10-week internship whetted my appetite and gave me information to try things, but I don't feel secure enough to use the new approach with everybody. After one experience, I'm not skilled enough to take the risk of making the kinds of comments I made to Nora to the parents of eight children who are all different.

Do I need more school?

**Eva:** *Well, what would give you the support you need? Skills can't be maintained indefinitely without support.*

**Kelley:** I need someone to be available—some initial contact, and then an awareness that someone is there until I don't need them any more. We have something called Technical Assistance Centers in Virginia, where teachers can call for consultation about a classroom situation; maybe this model could be adapted for working with families.

Intermittent visits with me to the families I work with would be helpful—want to come out with me on a home visit?

# 7

# Scenes from Supervision

## Judith Pekarsky

It is sometimes easiest to see the importance of supervision in rather intense, troubling situations where work with a young child and parents is clearly faltering. Such was the case when a trainee at our program walked into my office for supervision one day after several months of difficult meetings with a family, and announced firmly, "I'm not going back there." Her jaw was set, her tone challenging but resolute, and I believed her. I also recognized that this conscientious, dedicated woman must be feeling a great deal of distress to make such a pronouncement. I knew several other things, as well: that frustration and anger at families are common in this work, and that no one can do any kind of useful work with an infant, toddler, or parent while overwhelmingly in the grip of such strong negative feelings. I said to my supervisee that I was certainly not going to *make* her go back to see the family, that that could hardly do anyone any good, and then I asked her to tell me what was going on. We needed to understand this situation together and then we could figure out what needed to happen. The trainee was visibly relieved, sat down, and began talking. I listened.

This woman, Sheila, was a pre-doctoral student in clinical psychology who came to our infant mental health program for training in psychotherapy aimed at improving the relationship between infants or toddlers and their parents. The case we worked on together (she as therapist, I as supervisor) involved a little boy who had been removed from the care of his single mother at birth because of her history of serious emotional difficulties and acting out against an older child, now living with relatives. The little boy had returned to live with his mother at 23 months of age after relatively little contact with her. The reunification had not gone smoothly for mother or child, and while the mother did not physically hurt her toddler, she treated him in increasingly controlling and demeaning ways. During weekly home visits with mother and child, the trainee had witnessed many instances of such harsh treatment, but had rarely felt effective in her interventions with the mother. Her remarks, questions, and even her silence were frequently discounted.

As Sheila sat down to talk about why she was refusing to work with the family further, several issues in this complex situation became evident. Some of them we discussed; only a few will be noted here. Sheila explained she was sure that this mother could not be worked with, and she recounted the many exchanges in which her client had been unresponsive or dismissing of her efforts. We discussed how stymied she had felt, particularly when she watched the toddler being so badly treated. It was clear to me that Sheila's concern for and identification with this little boy, coupled with her frustrating inability to improve matters, had made her increasingly impatient with and angry at the mother. She had intensified attempts to explain the child's behavior to the mother and to suggest alternative ways of dealing with him. What had suffered in this process was her empathy with the mother's experience; efforts to understand her and the sources of her behavior had dwindled.

> I asked her to tell me what was going on. We needed to understand this situation together and then we could figure out what needed to happen.

*Judith Pekarsky*, Infant-Parent Program, San Francisco General Hospital, University of California, at San Francisco

> Taking time to think seriously about the status of the work regularly produces expanded understanding and new ideas.

While Sheila and I had discussed her frustration in numerous supervision sessions, this time I understood the situation differently. It seemed to me that I had never sufficiently recognized how awful it felt to Sheila to see this family. I had certainly listened to and acknowledged her concerns, but I always moved on to discussions of the mother and her feelings about her child, as well as ways to intervene around their interactions. Clearly, as I had pushed Sheila to empathize with her client, she had pushed the mother to empathize with her toddler. No one's feelings had been truly seen as important.

In the course of our conversation, I said to Sheila that I thought she had been telling me for some time how awful this case was and I had not really listened. Her tone shifted to one less challenging and more pensive. She began to talk about what had gone wrong in the intervention and why. She thought about the child, the reunification, and finally, about the mother. After an hour, we agreed to consider alternatives to Sheila's seeing the family, and Sheila volunteered that she would think further about the whole situation. For our next meeting, Sheila arrived looking more relaxed and composed, and calmly determined. She announced that she did want to try to work with this mother and child. She added how important it was that I had "respected her judgment that the mother could not be worked with" and had told her she "didn't have to". Later, she explained that she could then "be curious about what was going on." I had been fully prepared to discuss a plan for ending her work with the family and transferring the case to another therapist if the mother wished to do this; however, I was certainly supportive of Sheila's decision to continue, and we discussed what Sheila thought about future sessions.

The subsequent course of the work was not without difficulties, but a major shift occurred; the supervisee began to think about the mother's experience and could readily see things from her perspective. As this happened, Sheila stopped pushing her client toward particular ways of understanding and treating her son, and her client controlled the toddler much less demandingly and harshly. Months later, at the end of their work together, the mother thanked Sheila for her concern and for providing "just the thing we needed."

Most often the usefulness of supervision is embedded in quite ordinary exchanges between supervisee and supervisor. Discussions about what went on in a meeting with the family, who did and said what and in response to what, what did *not* happen, and possible reasons for all of this are the routine in supervisory sessions. Taking this time to think seriously about the status of the work regularly produces expanded understanding and new ideas about needed directions, as well as recognition of potentially troubling issues between clinician and family. What has been overlooked or incompletely understood by the clinician can be identified—whether by the supervisor, the supervisee, or mutually and interactively. This is what supports good work with young children and their families.

Recently a seasoned trainee in our program answered my query about why the report by the mother of a toddler's considerable distress in childcare had not been explored in a session; she said thoughtfully, "Well, I don't think I wanted to talk about Tina's behavior" with the mother. We both knew that this avoidance needed to be understood. My supervisee, Ellen, had been seeing this mother-child dyad for months. The family had come to the program because the child's response to even relatively brief separations from her mother had been inconsolable, prolonged high-pitched screaming. Ellen's assessment of the situation suggested that the difficulty around separation was related to the mother's complex reluctance to leave her child; this stemmed, generally, from her sense that only if she utterly sacrificed her own needs and wishes would she be a good mother.

Initial sessions had included discussions of the feelings mother and child experienced during separations and concrete ways to help both cope with these. The separation difficulty resolved, and the work then focused on other problems in the mother-child relationship and the mother's life, most of which were also reflections of her difficulty balancing her needs with those of others. After many months the mother was able to make a decision to resume her education by taking a few courses, which necessitated enrolling her daughter in partial-day childcare several times a week. Following the first week of school, the mother had spoken compellingly of her own experiences and concerns about classes, and in passing had mentioned her toddler's crying during mornings at childcare.

During our next supervision meeting Ellen had similarly been full of accounts of the changes in the mother's life and the reasons for and ramifications of these. A careful reporter, she also noted the little girl's response to childcare. Ellen and I spent some time discussing the mother, and no further mention was made of the problem Tina seemed to be having. I remained mindful of the initial mother-child difficulty and our efforts to support the child's functioning, however, and later in our supervision session, I inquired about the details of the toddler's upset in childcare. Startled, Ellen replied that she actually knew nothing about this. The mother had not volunteered anything, and she had not asked. It was at this point that Ellen stated she had not wanted to talk about Tina's behavior. She then began to reflect on her disinclination to pursue a discussion of the toddler's difficulties—explaining, "I guess I didn't want to make her mother feel more guilty." Ellen was readily able to see that she feared any focus on Tina's reaction would have exacerbated the mother's guilt at leaving her daughter in order to pursue her own wishes.

Together we decided that the mother's inattention to Tina's behavior already reflected discomfort with the decision she had made about school, and Ellen realized that she had joined the mother in avoiding the subject. I wondered whether the clinician's silence might have felt to the mother like a confirmation of her worst fears: that in leaving Tina, she had done something too bad to talk about. Ellen certainly did not feel this way, and she recognized that discussing the toddler's difficulties and the mother's feelings would in fact be helpful both in tempering the mother's guilt and in permitting her to help Tina with the separation. Whatever the possibly complex reasons for Tina's distress, the situation needed to be explored so as to arrive at ways to help the child. In the next session with mother and toddler, Ellen pursued the opportunities to discuss Tina's crying in childcare. This was an obvious relief to the mother, who quickly conceived an appropriate approach to the problem and went on to reflect further on her worry about doing things for herself. The clinician reiterated their conclusion of months before that she could do things both for herself and for Tina—though it was not always easy to balance these efforts—and therapist and client agreed to keep thinking about this issue.

**Later in our supervision session, I inquired about the details of the toddler's upset in childcare ... the situation needed to be explored so as to arrive at ways to help the child.**

# A Review of Infant/Toddler Issues in Supervision and Mentorship Based on Instruction of the Mentor Teacher Class

## Jane Perry

*Jane Perry, Child Care Employee Project, Early Childhood Mentor Teacher Program*

The Mentor Teacher class is a three-quarter unit course designed for experienced early childhood teachers in the field who are interested in supervising student teachers enrolled in a placement experience with their local community college. The Mentor Teacher class is the first step in a selection process leading to becoming a mentor teacher. The Mentor Teacher class highlights the dual nature of the mentorship role within an academic context: (1) to provide sensitive and appropriate guidance in the facilitation of the student's understanding of theoretical material related to child development and care, and (2) to continue to maintain developmentally appropriate standards in the child care setting. This dual nature to the mentorship role necessitates that the Mentor Teacher is both a representative of the community college and a local advocate. As a field instructor of the community college, the mentor will recommend a grade to the college instructor conducting the placement seminar. The mentor is also on her own professional path, and will participate in a monthly colloquium promoting her role as a leader and advocate in the field of early childhood through opportunities to speak in the community, participate in letter-writing campaigns and become active in local organizing efforts to upgrade child care careers.

## Expected outcomes and class activities

Five outcomes are expected for participants in the Mentor Teacher class. At the completion of the course, participants should be able to: (1) provide appropriate models, guidance and evaluation for student teachers; (2) recognize and support developmental stages of oneself and of the student teacher; (3) facilitate positive interactions between student teachers, children, parents and other staff; (4) maintain a safe and developmentally appropriate environment for young children while fostering growth of student teachers; and (5) understand the role of a mentor in leadership and advocacy in the field of early childhood education. Class activities include small group problem-solving sessions and role plays, field observations, reflective writing, whole class discussions and mini-lectures, guest speakers, audiovisual presentations and a final assessment of the quality of the teacher's own classroom linked to appropriate supervisory strategies for change involving both empowerment and advocacy.

## The feasibility of securing potential infant/toddler mentors

The Child Care Employee Project (CCEP) received funding to offer the Mentor Teacher Class to interested infant and toddler teachers in Alameda County, California (October, 1991). A significant portion of the funding was earmarked for scholarships that would pay for substitute time so the teacher could attend the class. The class was organized as a one-week intensive. Approximately twenty to thirty infant/toddler teachers initially expressed interest in the class. Ten infant/toddler teachers were able to attend. Of the ten infant/toddler teachers attending, all stated that the financial support granted to them significantly contributed to their ability to attend. Of those not able to attend, at least six who had the time to speak by telephone admitted that while they were very interested in becoming a mentor, they could not afford to take a week off without pay in order to participate. At the outset then, the feasibility of mentorship for infant/toddler student teachers involved compensation to potential mentors.

Three other factors were involved in the feasibility of securing potential infant/toddler mentors: (1) the availability of infant/toddler substitute teachers, (2) the issues of attachment and (3) interested teachers having had an experience of being supervised within their academic early childhood educational experience. Many center directors were willing to release teachers had there been substitutes available to cover the teacher's absence. Here again, the lack of a career ladder for infant/toddler care in the community directly affected a potential mentor's ability to initiate the process of mentorship.

A second factor influencing whether an infant/toddler teacher attended the Mentor Teacher Class involved a decision that participation in a one-week intensive would disrupt the process of attachment being established between the teacher and the infant and the teacher and the family. Feedback from teachers who did attend the class included the suggestion that in the future the class for infant/toddler teachers be scheduled to include some time during the week so that observations of other infant/toddler programs could be conducted, and switching other weekday class time to Saturdays both before and after the weekday sessions.

A third factor involved in the final determination of who attended the class concerned a recommended supervised field placement prerequisite to the class. Supported by NAEYC quality guidelines as well as NCCIP recommendations, CCEP felt that anyone interested in becoming a mentor needs to have already had the experience of being supervised in a college early childhood program before supervising others in such a program. In addition, the local community college Early Childhood Education (ECE) programs want those in positions of influence to have met the same prerequisites that students are being asked to meet. Many interested infant/toddler teachers, while currently practicing in supervisory positions and participating professionally in attending and/or conducting workshops, have never had a supervised practicum experience.

Based on written feedback from class participants, three important features of the Mentor Teacher Class content stood out for infant/toddler teachers: (1) the supervisory context, (2) a developmental perspective to supervision and (3) positive guidance strategies in problem situations.

## The supervisory context

The supervisory context included information about how the setting in which an infant/toddler teacher works affects her ability to supervise. Issues of empowerment and advocacy surfaced early in the class:

- "I already have a lot of turnover of staff as it is. I am hesitant about adding another new (student) face in the room."

- "Our staffing pattern is split between morning and afternoon shifts, and it is really difficult to get people together for a staff meeting. But we need to start dealing as a group with some problems in how we are caring for the babies."

- "I really want to be a mentor, but my co-teacher is acting so burned out, I'm afraid

> Three important features of the Mentor Teacher Class content stood out for infant/toddler teachers: (1) the supervisory context, (2) a developmental perspective to supervision and (3) positive guidance strategies in problem situations.

to even apply. I can't imagine trying to explain to the Mentor Selection Committee why she's changing diapers on the nap cots!"

• "My Head Teacher says I need to talk more to the toddler teacher, but whenever I try, she ignores me. From my side with the infants, I can see that the toddlers don't go outside enough, and I tell her this, but she says to mind my own babies. I know if I talked with the director, she would understand. She's Latino also."

• "Our ratio is too high. That's why sometimes our babies don't get outside enough. We have two stressful times during the day—mealtime and napping—they all crash at the same time. We could really use an extra hand to give individual attention."

It was helpful for the infant/toddler teachers to analyze critically the characteristics of their programs, and to appreciate that many of the obstacles to quality care and facilitative supervision, such as stability of the staff and staff stress and discord, have to do with the lack of support for infant care in their communities.

Other issues of the supervisory context involved the specific circumstances of care in the infant/toddler classroom. Issues of bonding, the variations of development among infants, the detailed and changing information regarding an infant's care, and the keen awareness of the safety issues for group care of infants all surfaced in class discussions about acclimating a new student teacher to an infant room.

• "My babies are quite young. I have some that are just three to five months old now. The relationship I am establishing with each baby and each family can really be thrown off by a new face. By the second semester, the babies will be OK with a new face, but then many will be into separation anxiety and another face will set them off crying again."

• "It takes up to ten weeks sometimes to establish a relationship with the infants. In a quarter system, the practicum class *ends* after ten weeks. Maybe placement for infants needs to be for two quarters."

• "Bonding needs to happen with the student teacher as well as with the infant. The student needs to see that she is establishing a primary bond in the child's life. A practicum of ten hours a week for a baby who has only been alive for 1000 hours is proportionately extremely significant."

• "Development really differs with infants. The student teacher may see me sit one three-month-old down on the floor without the support of pillows, and model that behavior with another chubby three-month-old who can't sit yet. The student teacher needs to learn *fast* to take cues from the baby rather than from the baby's size or age."

• There is so much changing information on my babies—what formula they are using, *how* they take the bottle, whether they are on solid foods and what specific foods their parents have already given them. The parents want to be the first to feed their baby a new food. I think I would have to remain in charge of all that information."

• "The student teacher needs to really *observe* to counter any safety concerns. She would need to know, for example, when to ask for help rather than leave two specific infants alone together after one has just thrown up all over himself. She would really need to be aware of safety issues such as biting, sucking, poking eyes and pulling hair as ways the infant merely explores."

## A developmental perspective to supervision

Teachers also found it useful to consider assessing both the mentor's and the student teacher's developmental characteristics and competencies early on in the supervisory relationship and again as problems arose. Much of the information for this part of the course was based on Joseph J. Caruso and M. Temple Fawcett's text, *Supervision in Early Childhood Education: A Developmental Perspective* (New York: Teachers' College Press, 1986). A developmental perspective to the mentor/student teacher relationship assumes that much of the dynamic in the supervisory relationship is based on:

- both the mentor's and the student teacher's life and family background experiences and beliefs (such as early childhood experiences with authority and assumptions about human nature and one's philosophy of learning);

- the student teacher's life stage and the implications for professional development (a student in her teens will respond quite differently to job expectations than someone married and her late forties);

- the mentor's stage of supervisory experience (Is the mentor just beginning and concerned with adapting to the role as the authority figure, or is she mature in her experience? Can she recognize the expertise of supervisees and be stimulated by solving problems?);

- the student teacher's capacity and/or inclination to analyze or abstract;

- both the mentor's and the student teacher's competencies and skills (in self-confidence, effective communication, understanding children and oneself, respecting others, deriving satisfaction and stimulation from professional growth, formulating a philosophy of learning, valuing good supervision and seeing the big picture); and

- both the mentor's and the student teacher's degree of job commitment.

Relevant information for the infant/toddler teachers surfaced in response to small group problem-solving or role play scenarios which highlighted supervising a colleague who had not had practicum experience, supervising a student teacher when racial and ethnic tensions existed amongst the staff, and supervising a student teacher with a significantly different philosophy of care than the mentor. Many of the infant/toddler teachers found that their own issues of authority, need for support, expectations of perfection, uncomfortableness with adult-adult communication and the pressure to juggle multiple responsibilities surfaced during small group work.

## Positive guidance strategies in problem situations

Additional information and experience were derived from small group role plays set up to offer the designated "mentor" both a challenging dilemma to learn from and specific feedback on the observed effects of the mentor's supervisory style. The role plays emphasized the ethical and safety issues of supporting a student teacher when developmentally appropriate classroom practice may be compromised. Purposes of the role play experience included: identifying ethical and safety limits in student teacher behavior; practice in asking questions; using active listening; silence and simple probing; communicating interest and support in the student teacher; encouraging the expression of feelings; using specific praise and providing specific information; reinforcing mutual respect, trust and a collaborative framework for conflict resolution; and practicing setting limits on inappropriate or unsafe practices of the student teacher. Questions which prompted critical and reflective responses from role play participants included:

- To the student teacher: How did you feel about your ability to express your position? What did you get out of the interchange? Were you able to communicate your needs as a learner? Why or why not?

- To the mentor: How did you feel about communicating your concerns to the student teacher? Did the meeting feel mutual to you? Why or why not?

- To the observers: What were your feelings as you watched the interaction? Where did your feelings come from? What specific communication skill did you identify the mentor using and what was the immediate effect on the student teacher?

In discussions following the role plays, teachers identified specific skills that would be fostered in a student teacher placed in an infant/toddler setting:

- Awareness of temperament differences in children (may include an awareness of the different tolerance levels of infants to new teachers);

• Self-awareness of one's response to the children and self-reflection on the reasons why certain children may be experienced more intensely (may include a decision *not* to participate in infant/toddler placement when the special stress of teething or a gassy baby who cannot be consoled is too draining for the student);

• Use of eye contact for bonding (suggesting that the infant needs to be physically very close to the student teacher, includes the awareness that when one's back is turned, one ceases to exist for the infant, and suggests that one would not leave an infant isolated even though they move around a lot);

• Awareness of the value of remaining quiet in order for the infant to take the student "in," reduction of stimuli versus providing overstimulation;

• Use of keen observation to take in the nonverbal communication provided by the infant (implies slowing down to be able to receive infants' nonverbal messages);

• Talking to infants because they do understand; and

• Appreciating the value of teamwork in the infant/toddler classroom (implies sensing the whole room, includes awareness of the "energy" of the room at any given time).

Teachers also noted five special supervision strategies relating to the issue of bonding in the infant/toddler classroom:

• Student teachers ideally would need to make placement arrangements for at least four consecutive days in order to insure continuity for both the infants and their families.

• Parents would need plenty of preparation prior to the student teacher's participating in the care of the infants.

• The mentor would need to attend to clearly designated areas of separate responsibility between herself and the student teacher (for example, some teachers felt it would be important for the process of bonding for the mentor to retain greeting rersponsibilities.)

• In order to promote bonding, mentors can use positive experiences for the individual infant (for example, going outside to swing) to balance the infant's stressful experience of not wanting to be near the student teacher.

• Trust between the mentor and student teacher is based on the student teacher's successful experience with infants and toddlers who are temperamentally easier to care for or with whom the student teacher feels more comfortable.

## Conclusion

The Mentor Teacher class is one part of the larger Early Childhood Mentor Teacher Program at CCEP. The Mentor Teacher Program involves all components of establishing mentor placement in community college ECE programs. The Program expanded from one site in its first two years of operation to five sites in the State as of May, 1990. The Program is scheduled to expand to 30 sites statewide over the next three years.

The Mentor Teacher Program is in its third year of operation. The Mentor Teacher class has been conducted in each of the three years, highlighting the infant/toddler teacher in the third year. CCEP will track all class participants as they encounter the next stage of the Program: the decision to apply to become a mentor. CCEP will also be tracking current mentors as they participate in the mentor role.

# A Clinical Approach to the Training of Supervisors: The Model of Co-Supervision

## Kyle D. Pruett

The process of co-supervision uses a relationship to teach a relationship. A co-supervision group that includes two practitioner/trainees, a supervisor-in-training, a social worker, and an experienced supervisor offers opportunities to learn not only the skills involved in direct assessment or intervention with very young children and families, but also the science and art of supervising such work. Co-supervision allows participants to witness, to study, and to practice an intricate, elusive, and important process. It bridges the transitional space between the roles of supervisee and supervisor.

Most people who supervise students or practitioners who work with infants, toddlers, and their families have had no formal training in supervision. They have had better or worse, greater or fewer, experiences of being supervised themselves. When they become supervisors, they try to incorporate their experience of "good" role models and to do a better job than the "bad" ones. But even those whose own experience of supervision has helped them to become better clinicians tend to remain largely unaware of the supervisory process itself. Like most parents, they, too, learn on the job. Co-supervision, however, allows the trainee to witness the process, as well as experience the result, of supervision.

The model of co-supervision that has evolved during the past 20 years at the Yale Child Study Center seems to meet the needs of trainees, supervisors-in-training, senior clinicians, and the training institution itself. Aspects of our approach may be adapted to both training and service settings.

## The evolution of our model

As a tertiary referral unit in a large medical center, the Yale Child Study Center trains advanced students (residents in child psychiatry or behavioral pediatrics; pre- and post-doctoral fellows in child psychology; doctoral-level students in early childhood education, social work, or nursing) in the diagnosis and treatment of young children with complex developmental problems. In their year-long course on evaluation, trainees work to begin mastering the considerable technical skills involved in administering standardized assessment instruments to, and playing diagnostically with, very young children. They also learn to evaluate the quality of a child's engagement with people and materials, interaction among the adults involved in the assessment, and their own emotional responses to the evaluation experience.

Our model of co-supervision was born from a transient shortage of supervisors. Traditionally, the supervisor, a staff or trainee social worker, and a child development trainee spent two hours on each diagnostic session, including half an hour for preparation; an hour's assessment by the trainee, observed by the supervisor behind a one-way mirror; and half an hour for debriefing. The co-supervision model

**Co-supervision allows participants to witness, to study, and to practice an intricate, elusive, and important process.**

*Kyle D. Pruett,* Clinical Professor of Psychiatry and Coordinator of Training Child Development Unit, Yale Child Study Center

allowed the supervisor to work with two students in three hours. The focus was exclusively diagnostic, as a previous parent interview by the social worker on the supervisory team had provided essential history and parent assessment. Each student spent 15 minutes preparing with the whole group. Then each student in turn conducted a 45-minute assessment with a child and family, joining the supervisor behind the mirror to observe her co-supervisee. Finally, the supervisor and trainees spent half an hour after each case debriefing together. This allowed one supervisor to observe and supervise two cases in three hours. Since the students found that they learned almost as much by watching their peers as by conducting an assessment themselves, their time was well spent also.

In recent years, we have expanded a small number of co-supervision groups to include a supervisor-in-training, or "associate supervisor." This is typically a clinician who has completed training and is establishing her own academic career or, more rarely, a clinical practice. Sharing supervisory responsibility with the senior clinician, the associate supervisor can hone her supervisory skills. She may go on to lead a co-supervision group in our center or to supervise in another setting. Perhaps equally important, the co-supervision group provides role modelling for the not-yet-established clinician who has been newly cut loose from the supports available to students.

## The experience of co-supervision

What do participants in a co-supervision group experience, as they observe behind the mirror and participate in debriefing sessions?

Sitting behind the mirror, the trainee is always aware that he will be next. The supervisor asks questions, encouraging the "on deck" trainee to make observations, including comments about the technical aspects of the evaluation in progress—how a test item is being presented, for example. But knowing that he will be observed and commented upon next reduces the trainee's temptation to be judgmental or compete for "favorite child" status with the supervisor. Through her comments and questions, the supervisor models for the trainee how to look at clinical material, how to avoid premature conclusions, and how to refrain from negative judgments about parents (or clinicians). The associate supervisor participates in helping the trainee to hone his observational skills, but she is also free to watch the senior supervisor's techniques.

After each child is seen, a debriefing takes place in the senior supervisor's office. The debriefing is immediately followed by coffee and then by another assessment/debriefing sequence. This is the time for the trainee who has done the evaluation to talk about her experience of the child and how she felt, and for everyone in the co-supervision group to share and check impressions. The "watch one, do one" sequence ensures that each trainee learns how different a child can feel to the clinician "in the room" from the way the child looks "through the glass." The supervisor's respect for the trainee's experience of the child in interaction, his interest in the technical problems of assessment, and his skill in helping the young clinician "keep questions open" rather than diagnose prematurely all contribute to the learning of the trainee who did the assessment under discussion.

The contributions and learning of the non-active trainee and the associate supervisor are equally important. The trainee who observed his fellow student's evaluation is encouraged to contribute his collegial, yet quasi-supervisory observations and questions; he may ask, for example, why the student did x instead of y at a certain point. Both the supervisor's modeling and the awareness that his own performance will be scrutinized shortly encourage the trainee to refrain from being unduly critical or competitive.

For the associate supervisor, learning is likely to be about how to discuss her observations with the trainee in the most helpful way possible. Having observed a trainee become exasperated with a difficult toddler and stop facilitating the child's efforts in the testing situation, for example, the associate supervisor may wonder how to help the trainee understand that a child has made him angry, without making him feel bad or useless, helpless or guilty. Her novice attempts usually meet with some defensiveness: "I'm feeling pretty criticized by you. You don't like the way I'm playing with children." Next time (or after observing the senior supervisor in a debriefing) she may be able to phrase her comment more skillfully: "Johnny must have made you feel you had your back to the wall—he refused everything. What did that feel like?"

## Using a relationship to teach a relationship

The relationships among members of the co-supervision group, like any good set of relationships, should be as open, reciprocal, honest, and trusting as possible. The group process needs to withstand negative and positive feelings about each other and the families and children seen. Confronting issues honestly and dealing straightforwardly with conflict are important clinical skills. Moreover, these are crucial supervisory skills, and they don't come easily. The co-supervision process encourages all involved to respect the other's experience, and offers ample lessons in humility. For example, an associate supervisor who had been an extraordinarily competent trainee found that she needed help from the senior supervisor in assisting a student who was struggling, as she hadn't had that experience herself.

One of the central responsibilities of the supervisor is to encourage, guard, and protect the clinician's empathic connection with the child. The supervisor has to be aware of what the child is feeling and what the clinician is feeling. Acknowledging the trainee's unique experience of the child supports the empathic connection with the child, and often results in more empathic connection between the clinician and the parents as well. As the supervisor, associate supervisor, or fellow trainee offers a sensitive comment or question, the atmosphere is "supportive but expectant."

Traditional individual supervision helps people to become better clinicians. However clinicians may demonstrate the result of good supervision in their competent daily practice without ever being aware of the process of supervision itself. Co-supervision allows each participant to witness the process, gaining a conscious understanding of supervision that will be helpful throughout professional development.

## Training supervisors

Supervisors in our center are no longer simply former supervisees willing to take on an often undervalued role. The co-supervision process produces supervisors who feel competent and an institution that appreciates that competence. After participating in a co-supervision group for two years as a trainee and then serving as an associate supervisor for a third year, a clinician has learned supervision as a distinct craft. Our supervisors define themselves less defensively and tentatively than formerly. They are better than they used to be at what they do. Furthermore, they seem to last longer, with less burn-out.

The lessons we have learned from the co-supervision process may be useful for a range of training and service settings. A one-way mirror is by no means an essential ingredient of the recipe. Videotape offers many opportunities for multiple observers of an interaction. A clinician's verbal presentation of a treatment session provides his perception of the process. What matters in co-supervision is that the supervisors and trainees confront the same material, so that all can observe how the supervisor deals with the training issues raised.

## Maintaining skilled supervisors

We have learned that the sharing of experience that occurs between senior and

> **The co-supervision process encourages all involved to respect the other's experience.**

**Regular meetings of supervisors are very important, because they help us monitor the quality of our work and affirm the values and standards of the institution as a whole.**

associate supervisors in the co-supervision process must be extended to all supervisors in our institution, although less formally. All supervisory staff meet four times a year to discuss how supervisees are doing and search for solutions to the problems that inevitably arise in this complex, innervating clinical work. Food is usually involved; the nurturing of supervisors is not only psychological.

To some extent these gatherings are venting sessions, where supervisors are free to air opinions about their trainees' professional and personal traits in terms less appropriate to supervisory debriefings. But supervisors also compare notes about experiences with particular trainees, describe trainees who are doing well, and organize support for those who are not. In sum, supervisors talk about what they are doing, why, and how they feel about it.

Once every three or four years, as a result of these meetings, a trainee is counseled out of clinical work and encouraged in another direction. No supervisor would do this without checking his perceptions with others first. Yet if the issue of counseling a trainee out of direct clinical work never comes up, the training institution is probably not doing enough quality control as a group.

Regular meetings of supervisors are very important, because they help us monitor the quality of our work and affirm the values and standards of the institution as a whole. Our anecdotes remind us of what we believe in. If supervisors do not meet and talk about how their students are doing and how they themselves understand and practice supervision, the students can leave the training institution with enormously varied experiences. This is unacceptable in an institution that sees itself as adhering to the highest level of interventive skill and as the transmitter of a clinical expertise that exists almost exclusively in the heads of its faculty.

# Supervision and Mentorship of Infant/Family Practitioners

The "professional use of self" may be the infant/family practitioner's most valuable tool in working with very young children and their families. The chapters presented here illustrate how reflective supervision and mentorship can support and guide practitioners as they learn to use their skills effectively in challenging, constantly evolving service settings.

# 10

# *The Professionalization of Early Motherhood*

## William M. Schafer

The preparation for this paper began almost four and a half years ago when I had the privilege of attending a clinical retreat for infant mental health professionals, hosted by the Training and Education Committee of the Michigan Association for Infant Mental Health. The participants had come from all across the state, from urban centers and rural areas. They represented many different professions, working in hospitals, schools, community mental health centers, and private clinics. All had experience making home visits. All, with the exception of myself, were women.

On the day in question we discussed cases. We spent over an hour talking about a 16-year-old girl who successfully "hid" her pregnancy from her own mother, delivered her baby with her boyfriend's help in the back seat of a car, then left the baby girl on a crowded avenue in the hope someone would find her and care for her. The authorities were called in, and the baby spent five weeks in foster care. Then, largely at the grandmother's urging, the baby was returned to the teen-age mother. Now the authorities had called in the infant mental health specialist "to make sure everything would be okay."

We spent much time trying to enter into the emotional state of that 16-year-old girl in order to find words which might, just possibly, respond accurately enough to her inner experience to engage her in serious work on behalf of her baby. Then, perhaps even harder, we tried to do the same for the grandmother who had engineered the fateful reunion.

It was during this prolonged exercise of entering into the young girl's consciousness that I became aware of a profound shift occurring within the group. The conversation turned from clients to clinicians, and to the toll this work levies on their own inner life. Someone spoke of feeling drained of maternal energies. Another spoke of the lingering resentment she felt from her spouse. A third told of the complaints her children voiced at her work. People described their outlets and releases: music, aerobics, horseback riding, running, drawing (I recall a vivid description of drawings of doors without handles and walls with bars), and endless telephone calls to set up workable support groups. As I listened I was struck by the difficulty of juggling professional with domestic roles. Then I realized something which to me was new: these women were not talking about a conflict *between* job and motherhood, but of the conflict *within* a job that turned motherhood into a profession. Their careers demanded that they enter daily into realms of feeling ordinarily reserved for special and time-limited periods surrounding the birth of one's own children. The draining of maternal energies resulted from the professionalization of early motherhood demanded of the infant mental health specialist.

As I look back on that day I do not think it coincidental that such an awareness should

*William M. Schafer*, Ann Arbor, Michigan

> **Early motherhood is the delicate emotional space between one's own childhood and that of one's child. It is within this space that the infant mental health worker spends much of her time.**

dawn during a discussion of the feelings which exist between an adolescent mother and her own mother. The exercise of entering simultaneously into both of those emotional worlds was precisely, I believe, what turned the discussion from clients to clinicians. In an existential sense, early motherhood is the delicate emotional space hovering like a dimensionless point between one's own childhood and that of one's child. Since it is within this space that the infant mental health worker spends so much of her time, it is not surprising that she should frequently experience an ongoing preoccupation with her own personal existence as a woman.

It is to that space, and to its development over time, that we now turn. For expository convenience I had originally intended to invent a hypothetical infant mental health specialist, and to follow her as she struggled with casework over the course of her career. But to do that I would have to invent a person, that is to say, I would have to endow her with a history. She would need to have this particular mother, this particular husband, this particular job, these children, and so on. In the end, her individuality would overshadow the more general developmental issues I wish to highlight today. I take some time and trouble to point this out, because I want to underscore my belief that in the long run our individual histories and the way they have shaped each of us are far more important to our eventual experience and conduct as clinicians than anything else. Although what we are talking about today is quite important, it remains secondary.

My thesis is that the professionalization of motherhood is an issue which one can think about as a normal developmental crisis occurring in four basic stages. I propose that the first of these could be called a crisis of one's acceptability as an attachment figure. It usually occurs as one enters the field, before one has had children of one's own. The second is a crisis of one's competence to be a maternal figure, and usually occurs

during those years when the specialist is beginning her own family while simultaneously establishing herself as a member of her profession. The third is a crisis of commitment to remain a maternal figure, and spans the professional's maturing years, often ending in a series of crises commonly known as burnout. The fourth is a crisis of confidence in the outcome of one's maternal activity. It typically occurs after one's own children have grown, during those more mature years when one has begun to take on some responsibility for administering, supervising, teaching others who will one day take one's place in the field.

## I. The crisis of acceptability

The young woman who enters the field of infant mental health directly from graduate school brings with her a wealth of information, expertise and knowledge about infancy and motherhood. If, however, she is herself unmarried or does not yet have children of her own, she may be able only to imagine what it must feel like to prepare for, deliver and tend to one's own baby. Her client has had a profoundly moving life experience which she herself has not yet had. The client has produced the baby for which part of the worker secretly yearns. Perhaps the worker had been able to graduate from her master's level program only because she had postponed marriage and/or childbearing. Such a choice is never made easily or unambivalently, but the full force of that ambivalence may suddenly descend upon her shoulders when faced with a client who has made the opposite choice, who actually has produced the longed-for baby, and who now says she doesn't love it.

Added to this is the fact that the entry level worker is new to clinical work. She has not yet had her first success. She has not even had her first client leave her. She carries with her many principles and tactics, but they are for the most part unpracticed and untried. She has been told over and over that the human relationship is the central element in any process of development, but she has not yet had the opportunity to experience such a relationship in a professional context. The closest she has been to an ongoing therapeutic process may be her own personal therapy. This can be a marvelous opportunity to learn what therapy feels like, and the new worker who is in therapy has a tremendous advantage over the one who is not, but it can have its disadvantages as well. For the young person who is just beginning to work with mothers and babies may also be a young person who has just come from her own therapy session where she was confronted by the full force of her angry disillusionments about her own mother. Now she is suddenly being asked to respond empathically to the needs of a woman who is openly neglectful or rejecting of a helpless child. The abrupt shift may be more than the worker can easily manage, with the result that she will be impelled into an unhealthy overidentification with the baby against the mother.

These issues of late adolescence and early adulthood, issues of separation from one's own parents, are ultimately the source of the crisis of acceptability. This is a time of life when a young woman is called upon to give up her adolescent fantasies about herself and her mother. The process involves two apparently contradictory yet dynamically related movements. On the one hand she must learn to revise her idealized constructions of her own mother and of herself. She has to give up the fantasy: "I had a perfect mother, and I was her perfect child." At the same time she must get in touch with the defensive wishes (and the pain they conceal) behind her lingering hostilities toward her mother. She has to give up the fantasy: "I did not have the perfect mother I deserved, which is the reason I never became a perfect child."

It is this struggle which the new infant mental health specialist brings to her clinical cases. As she offers herself as an attachment figure to each new client, part of her is hoping that she will be the client's perfect mother and the client will be her perfect baby. This wish is quickly frustrated by the client, who is brimming over with confusion and ambivalence about her baby, as well as about her worker. Then the specialist is tempted to retreat into a defensive stance in which part of her wants to tell her client that the client would have indeed found her a perfect mother, if only the client had been a better child.

It might be well for us to pause for a moment's reflection here. We are proposing that the crisis of acceptability as an attachment figure is rooted in the young worker's struggle to give up past illusions about her own mother. So far, that is nothing really very new. Is this not precisely the problem which is faced by any young social worker, nurse, or teacher, no matter which client population she serves? What is so special about the problem faced by the infant mental health worker? What makes this problem different?

It is the presence of the infant in the midst of the work. The baby is the concrete embodiment of the human race's illusion of perfectibility. Each baby is the world's new hope for healing. Each birth is a new dawning of innocence which is still beyond damage or evil. This is a natural, a normal phenomenon. It is good that we at times yield to this illusion. It gives us the faith we need as we attempt to renew ourselves through the birth of a new life. But it is an illusion that is meant to exist for a time only, within that delicate space between two childhoods which we call early motherhood. The difficult challenge of the infant mental health specialist is to learn to utilize the positive impetus of this illusion without being totally captivated by it. The special problem of her formative years is learning to harness the power this illusion holds over her client while she is simultaneously struggling to be liberated from its power over herself.

The resolution of the crisis of acceptability hinges upon the infant mental health specialist's acquisition of basic competency in her role. This competency in turn is com-

> **The illusion that each birth is a new dawning of innocence gives us the faith we need as we attempt to renew ourselves through the birth of a new life. But it is an illusion that is meant to exist for a time only.**

> **The young worker's doubts about her worthiness will be resolved to the extent she is carefully supported through her initial humiliations.**

prised of two elements: her acquisition of basic intervention skills, and her growing confidence in her ability to enter empathically into the world of a mother-infant pair with positive results. The first is accomplished through continued training, supervision and support. The second would seem more difficult to acquire.

As it turns out however, the crisis of acceptability carries within itself the very terms of its own solution. If we look more closely, we can see that the beginning infant mental health specialist is offering herself to a client-mother as an attachment figure without any prior experiential validation of her own worthiness to be such a figure. She has no history of successful outcomes, no memories of initially resistant parents who eventually found her invaluable, no mental pictures of competent babies who owe their competency in large part to her intervention. She can literally taste the cloud of doubt which surrounds her. And here she is, presenting herself to another young woman who is also offering herself as an attachment figure to her infant with little or no experiential validation of her worthiness to be such a figure. Both client and clinician are for the moment joined by their common experience of self-doubt and by their need to resolve lingering conflicts over a common set of fantasies about themselves and their own mothers. And here lies the groundwork for a solution. If the new worker can be given the guidance and emotional safety to explore and to understand this troubling situation within herself, she can be led to a deeper and richer understanding of the client-mother's emotional world. No longer will she stand at the periphery of the mother-infant relationship, a stranger to its bittersweet intimacies; instead she will be a partner to its pulsing dance. And even if at first she fails to catch on, and her first few cases seem to fail, she will still be in possession of an experience which can potentially link her to many of the mothers she serves, mothers who are also taunted by their own secret lists of prior failures. In an odd sort of way,

her doubts about her worthiness will be resolved to the extent she is carefully supported through her initial humiliations.

## II. The crisis of competence

The growing competency of the infant mental health specialist ushers in a new phase of work, and with it a new problem. As the specialist becomes a more experienced clinician, she is also likely to be moving ahead in her own personal life. One of the most powerful events shaping her life now is likely to be her own entrance into motherhood. With motherhood comes direct experience of that delicate space between two childhoods. This creates a new ability to empathically share another mother's experience. It also introduces a new set of tensions.

The new infant—the specialist's child—is a strong competitor for her affection and energies. She may temporarily leave her job to be with her baby. This may bring a loss of money, of friendships, of self-esteem. Or she may continue to work. This may bring feelings of guilt or resentment as she drops her child off at day care in order to begin her visits to other children's homes. She cannot help but draw comparisons between her own and her clients' children, between herself and her client-mothers. She may feel a small surge of pride and relief at the thought that she and her own children seem to be so much happier, followed by a stab of shame that she should allow herself this secret pleasure. If the competitive impulse is not held in check, she may find herself offering herself more and more as an attachment figure to the client-infant, to the subtle exclusion of the client-mother. Or, and perhaps more commonly, she may begin to feel growing resentment toward those "other" professionals who serve children and families (but wihout the infant mental health background)—which, of course, makes them virtually useless!

These kinds of tension are signs that the specialist has embarked upon another segment of the long, complicated road from one's own childhood to one's children's. The earlier conflict over one's acceptability has been transformed into a conflict about one's own competence. The earlier fantasies about having or not-having a perfect mother have shifted slightly and become: "I *am* a better (worse) mother than my own, for I have produced a better (worse) baby."

These issues of early parenthood—the lingering competition with one's own parents, the illusion that one might still become the perfect parent they failed to be—can complicate the clinical work of the younger specialist. But as in the case of the earlier crisis of acceptability, this current crisis also contains the elements of its own solution. Having a baby of one's own tends to normalize the whole range of feelings associated with early parenthood. One is able to experience for oneself the sense of being burdened and overwhelmed, the powerful wish for temporary escape, the welling up of resentments and anger. All of this serves to remedy one's earlier and somewhat naive visions of motherhood.

Actually, one's own baby can be a major force in helping to resolve this crisis. First of all, as one's baby passes through infancy into middle childhood, the basis for comparison with one's client-children tends to shrink. Secondly, it becomes obvious that one's own child, although competent and sturdy, is not *always* healthy, happy, and content. Consequently, it slowly becomes obvious that perfection is not necessary, either for the child or the parent. And most importantly, one becomes more fully aware that the child also has something of her own to say about how development shall proceed. All of this conspires to teach us that normal development has a somewhat broader range than we previously thought, and also that we cannot accept either total credit or total blame for everything that happens to our children.

A second major force in the resolution of the crisis can be found in one's professional life. One way to look at the crisis of competence is to understand it as a search for new bases of self-esteem, narcissistic supplies, and competitive victories. These can be obtained through setting up comparisons with one's clients, but that is not the only possibility. One can also search for these necessities in the arena of professional growth. As the infant mental health specialist gathers more experience she usually discovers that she now has something useful to say during staff meetings, case conferences and group discussions. She ceases to be the newest member of the team. She may be asked to write up one of her cases and present it at a meeting. She may take on new responsibilities, earn higher wages, learn that she is recognized and valued by her fellow professionals. Thus, she discovers that she can sublimate many of her narcissistic and competitive impulses into her professional life, rather than simply repeat them with her clients.

## III. The crisis of commitment

As times goes on, the infant mental health specialist may begin to feel that children fill her life from one end of the day to the other. There are all these client-children; then there are her own. They surround her until her life begins to seem like an endless preoccupation with infancy. She may learn to go through many facets of her day on a kind of automatic pilot. The initial poignancy of her first one or two really tragic cases diffuses somewhat, and she may experience her own inner reaction to new tragedies as less sharply focused but more broadly encompassing. It's the difference between a thunderstorm and an endlessly cloudy day.

It is at this point that she may begin to hear some rumblings of discontent. The first rumblings may actually come from her spouse, who complains about her seeming tired and preoccupied; or from her children, who complain about her being away from the house. When she talks with her colleagues about her work she tends to focus less upon specifics of case dynamics and intervention techniques, and more upon all the sadness and loss that is out there in the world. The rumblings of discontent now

> **Having a baby of one's own tends to normalize the whole range of feelings associated with early parenthood.**

seem to be coming from somewhere within herself. She is beginning to ask why she has chosen to surround herself with babies and with the feelings they awaken. Somewhat paradoxically she may also be mulling over whether or not to have one last child of her own. At times she explicitly wonders whether she should look for a different kind of work.

We usually talk about this process under the heading of burnout. That is unfortunate, because the term burnout connotes running out of fuel. It implies some insufficiency within the individual. Admittedly, burnout is a very complicated question, involving all sorts of personal, psychological, maturational and social factors. But very often the feelings we describe as burnout are simply signals that the person stands at a developmental crossroad. Far from having run out of gas, the person is poised to cross a new threshold. Often what is needed is not a new job, but a new integration of career into one's personal life. For the infant mental health specialist, this entails a yet deeper understanding of how to work within the illusions of early motherhood without succumbing to their power.

We may recall that early motherhood is a time of pliability and openness. It is a time when psychological boundaries are allowed to relax. It is a period of continual giving to an other who needs to be nurtured. At so many different levels, it is an experience of profound self-less-ness. However it is not meant to last, and we will cause ourselves endless trouble if we confuse this vision of early motherhood with motherhood in general, or worse yet, if we confuse early motherhood with being an infant mental health specialist.

People in our field are prone to a general belief, never quite stated as such, but there nonetheless, that we are the professionals who truly care about our clients. We pride ourselves on our openness to even the most painful emotional experiences, on our capacity to provide ongoing nurturance, care and support, and on our ability to intervene without confrontation or blame. We are, in a phrase, professional early mothers.

I believe that this is totally wrong. We are not professional early mothers; we are rather professionals who understand the implications of early motherhood. Learning the difference between these two visions of the profession is, I submit, the crucial task of gaining maturity as an infant mental health specialist.

Let me give an example of that difference. The professional early mother makes repeated appointments with a client who is rarely at home, and then when they finally do meet says very little about the missed appointments. The professional who understands early motherhood also makes repeated appointments, but when the opportunity to meet does present itself she spends a great deal of energy trying to understand why the client has found it so difficult to meet with her. The first worker believes that she will build a relationship of trust by not troubling her client too much. The second trusts that she can build something positive only by talking about what troubles the relationship. We could alter the example, of course. We could examine how each behaves when a client displays heated anger or hostility toward her child, or what each does when shown the telltale signs of substance abuse. The specialist who is confused about her role will find herself placating anger rather than pursuing its cause, she will offer transportation rather than the truth, she will set up appointments that are inconvenient to her rather than set limits which will be helpful to her client. Somehow, the confusion will confound the clinical work. The specialist who believes she must be an early mother invariably ends up behaving more like an uncertain stepmother who tries to win her new child's love by giving in to his every whim—while in fact she is being unresponsive to his most important feelings of unhappiness and mistrust.

That same confusion may also show up in the specialist's personal life. She may feel

> **We are not professional early mothers. We are rather professionals who understand the implications of early motherhood.**

somehow used and valueless, as though she has no right to her own happiness. She may find it hard to leave the tragedies at the office, and go about the business of enjoying her own life. Slowly, she may become a bit of a burden, first to her colleagues, then to her family, finally to herself.

Now there are many reasons why something like this should happen to a worker during her career. Many of them are rooted in the individual's own history. Sometimes, however I think it has to do with the development of the particular set of fantasies about early motherhood we have been describing. We have seen how they began as a set of fantasies about *having* a perfect mother, then became a set of fantasies about *being* a perfect mother. In the crisis of commitment they take on a slightly different form, and might be worded thus: "Only if I remain the perfect *early* mother can I find perfect happiness." It is a fantasy based upon an inner belief that the only good mother is the infinitely giving, patient and selfless early mother. The *later* mother, however, who sets limits, promotes independence and maintains a life of her own is seen as a bad mother. This is a fantasy which seems particularly prevalent among those whose own mothers took very good care of them as infants, but didn't always know how to care for their emotional needs as they grew older, leaving them with a strong inner need to recapture some personal lost paradise, (perhaps through infant mental health work).

This fantasy of finding happiness only by remaining an early mother can also be accentuated by the events of middle life. As is often stated, mid-life is a time of being confronted by life's disappointments. One didn't get the house one always wanted, or the position or degree—or perhaps the spouse. Furthermore, the disappointments of mid-life are framed differently from those of earlier days because one's sense of time has changed. When one is young, tragedy is no less awful, but one instinctively suspects that things will somehow change.

When one is at mid-life, tragedy is more likely to be experienced as permanent. A divorce, the loss of one's health, of one's child, or of one's hope of someday having children—all of these crises make it hard to imagine a future which is different, changing and developing. One feels compelled instead to imagine the future as more and more of the same. This tends in turn to reinforce old fantasies of finding perfection and happiness by remaining an early mother.

The resolution of this crisis comes only with time and effort. There are, however, a number of strategies one can employ to help the process along. On the professional level, one has to keep growing. For those of us who are in direct service, particularly for those of us who make home visits, this means finding ways to counteract the isolation which such work tends to create. It means finding other people with whom we can share our work in a context which offers, not just emotional support, but also the opportunity to learn new and better ways to do what we do. The cure for the "professional early mother" syndrome is to become more *professional*, and that almost always entails becoming more intimately connected with other professionals.

On the personal level, resolution means coming to terms with one's inner beliefs about motherhood and perfection. The early mother is not the perfect mother; she is simply the appropriate mother for a certain period of development. Resolution also involves the process of capturing and appropriating the positive memories of one's own childhood and of one's own later mother. This should gradually result in a clearer awareness of how one's mother and oneself, while far from perfect, nevertheless possessed many strengths together, for how else could one have survived and thrived as well as one has? Furthermore, resolution involves incorporating a new vision of the future as extending into an unknown in which change and development are still possible. Finally, it involves listening to one's family and friends who are so frequently

**On the professional level, one has to keep growing.**

**Some infant mental health specialists who are experiencing a crisis of confidence may seem grief-stricken and angry, overwhelmed by today's social problems. Others may speak unrealistically of infant mental health as a panacea for most human ills.**

reminding one that there is more to life than motherhood, that children after all grow up to have their own lives, and sometimes the best way to show them how to do that is to make sure one has a life of one's own.

## IV. The crisis of confidence

The maturing infant mental health specialist one day arrives at that point in life when her gray hairs outnumber all the others and her colleagues begin to look up to her as though she were somehow wise. Having arrived at this prestigious plateau, she may find that her parenting tasks have shifted somewhat. Her children may be grown, away at school, or starting families of their own. Her career has developed to the point where she now administers a program, supervises other clinicians, teaches students, or serves on various policy-making bodies. She is beginning to parent "at one remove."

This can be a very rewarding time, for it allows her the luxury of some distance from the daily fray, and gives her a vantage from which she can survey the field with a broader perspective. All of this helps her to find a better sense of balance about her work. Her years of experience, both with her cases and with her own family, help her to normalize the various situations she encounters. That is, she is more able to perceive the positive along with the pathological aspects of real life situations. She can more easily see her families and their infants not just as vessels of human loss and misery, but as the marvelous testaments to human adaptability that they often are.

This is not to say there are no problems. Some of these may show up in the older infant mental health specialist's remaining clinical work. By this time, she is probably quite skillful in the conduct of her casework. She is calmly self-assured about her own maternal capacities, she is gently supportive of the young client-mother's dignity, yet she is unafraid to speak plainly when necessary. She would seem the nearly perfect clinician. It is somewhat surprising therefore that such a superb clinician should sometimes carry a caseload comprised almost entirely of families whom she has known for a very long time. Many times these are families whose babies are now preschoolers who play in another room while she visits with the mothers. The intervention offered is often quite spectacular, but it is no longer infant mental health work.

This raises the sometimes difficult questions of how to distinguish between cases continued because further work is necessary, and cases continued because the specialist is having some inner difficulty terminating the case. It would seem that the answer often hinges upon a realistic assessment of the developmental status of the children. Sometimes it happens that the children seem to be doing well, yet their good development does not quite manage to assuage the specialist's worries about the families' ability to "maintain" the gains of treatment. Sometimes the specialist seems much more aware of her clients' liabilities than she is of their competencies. Whenever this is the case, one may fairly wonder whether the hesitation to end the work is the specialist's more so than the client's.

The crisis of confidence can also manifest itself in her administrative and educational work. Here it usually assumes of of two forms. In the first, a sense of global discouragement creeps into the specialist's manner. She may talk a lot about today's overwhelming social problems—drugs, poverty, teen-age pregnancy—as though there were no possible hope of solution. She may carry about a heavy burden of grief that rarely seems to lift. She may appear chronically angry at the institutions and professions which share responsibility for children and mothers.

On the other hand, one sometimes encounters the mature specialist who, once she leaves the direct clinical work, becomes an unrealistic visionary. She may begin to speak of infant mental health as though it were a panacea, able to cure most human ills—cheaply. At the same time, she may seem inordinately suspicious about new ideas and approaches. When she writes up her program or one of her cases, everything may become so simple and so successful that her students (and often colleagues) begin to shudder at the prospect of living up to her claims.

Both of these apparently antithethical sets of behaviors imply a certain crisis of confidence in the outcome of one's maternal efforts. The first worker seems to feel that none of her clients or programs or methods are strong enough to survive on their own. Her sense of being indispensible really seems a cover for her uncertainties about her professional offspring. The second worker seems to share this sense of insecurity, but attempts to mask it behind her denials. Returning once more to the series of fantasies about motherhood and perfection which I have been pursuing throughout this paper, it is as though these specialists are saying: "All my children must be perfect, because only by producing perfect children can I avoid utter failure as a mother."

By now it should be obvious that the series of fantasies I have been describing throughout this paper are all variations on a common theme. In one way or another, they all have to do with the search for perfection. The developmental crises we have been describing are related to this search, to the illusion that it can be successful, and to motherhood as one major arena in which this illusion must be surrendered. It seems likely that all individuals are called upon to wrestle with this problem. Everyone must in some way learn to give up the belief in one's own perfection, whether it is couched in a belief about one's perfect parents, one's perfect self, or one's perfect offspring. The problem for the infant mental health specialist is that she is called upon to do this in the midst of the continual celebration of life's renewal that defines infancy.

The infant literally begs us to believe that everything is possible. The magic of giving birth, of holding that tiny being to our cheek and *feeling* its breath, motion and warmth, is a momentary epiphany of something greater than ourselves breaking through the veil of everyday existence. Watch next time you attend a funeral. Watch what people do as they return to the family home. Especially watch what the old people do. They turn to the babies, for the babies are the guarantors of our belief that death shall not prevail over life.

This magic is necessary, helpful and good. Infant mental health work in particular is the beneficiary of this biological gesture of kindness, and those of us who do this work know just how dependent we are on that magical surge of hopefulness within the heart of even the most hardened client-mother. But it is dangerous to live continuously under its spell. And it is positively disastrous to allow oneself the illusion that one is its permanent dispenser.

Spending one's professional life within this delicate and magical space is not an easy task. It calls for humility, selflessness, professionalism, and a willingness to surrender to the inevitability of life. The reward, however, can be the realization that as one has struggled through each of these crises one has also grown personally, that one's professional work has left one calmer, warmer, more honest and wise.

**Everyone must in some way learn to give up the belief in one's own perfection, whether it is couched in a belief about one's perfect parents, one's perfect self, or one's perfect offspring.**

# 11

# Supervision as a Catalyst in the Evolution of an Integrated Infant Mental Health/Developmental Intervention Program

**Barbara Ivins and Nancy Sweet**

*Barbara Ivins, and Nancy Sweet*, Child Development Center, Children's Hospital, Oakland, California

The Parent-Infant Program at Children's Hospital in Oakland, California is a parent participation program that serves an exceptionally diverse group of families with developmentally disabled and at-risk infants in Oakland and the urban eastern Bay Area of northern California. Our commitment to providing and developing new services for this population has been longstanding. We emphasize both direct service to individual babies and families and involvement in the development of local, regional and state early intervention policies.

We have become passionate proponents of a service model that fully integrates mental health and developmental interventions for infants and families. The evolution of this approach has been gradual, but unswerving in its direction, as our program has grown from a staff of three serving 16 families in 1977 to a staff of 15 working with 100 families in 1991. Clinical supervision has proved to be extremely important in the development of our program. Looking back over almost 15 years, we realize that the status of supervision at any point in our program's history says a good deal about our program's overall development at that time. We can also see that clinical supervision has served as an important catalyst for change in the ongoing development of our program.

In the pages that follow, we offer a natural history of our program and approach. We will pay special attention to the role that clinical supervision has played, and continues to play, in helping our program to offer more effective support to infants and families.

## Stage I: Parent education and support

The first early intervention program in the Child Development Center (CDC) of Children's Hospital, Oakland, began in 1977 with a model demonstration grant from the U.S. Department of Education. Since one of the senior CDC staff who developed the proposal had studied with attachment theorist John Bowlby, the Parent-Infant Program focused from its very beginning on supporting early family relationships as well as ameliorating the impact of the baby's developmental problems.

In the home-based Parent-Infant Program, the interventionist was a developmental and behavioral consultant for the family. Through weekly home visiting, this primary intervenor developed a strong relationship with each family. Our home-based model promoted a transdisciplinary approach. The program's first generic "infant development specialists" had backgrounds in special education and early childhood education; later, people with backgrounds in developmental psychology, occupational therapy, speech therapy, and nursing joined the staff. Center-based programs for groups of parents and infants were added to complement home-based services.

The program was small, and the supervisory model was intentionally one of collegial support. Staff members acted as a supportive "family" for one another; this enhanced their ability to be supportive, in turn, to the families with whom they worked, often in the (professional) isolation of the family home. Staff cohesion stayed strong in the face of unstable funding, limited facilities, and the emotional demands involved in supporting families who were confronting the newly diagnosed disabilities of their babies.

Our conception of "work with families" changed with experience. A service model that called for parent participation in every aspect of the program resulted in opportunities to work with caring, articulate, committed parents, whose diversity and capacity for coping we learned to respect enormously. The notion of "educating" parents about the needs of their babies changed very quickly to a model of *supporting* parents, as they went through the process of adjustment to a vulnerable baby or a baby with disabilities.

From the beginning of the Parent-Infant Program, our experienced social worker provided marital and crisis counseling for families and support for the intervention staff. We also began parent support groups. Still, there were families with whom we felt our interventions failed. Acute and chronic mental illness, child abuse and neglect, family violence, and the combined impact of multiple problems challenged our staff's skills. If we referred these families to more child-centered early intervention programs, we felt uncomfortable: We knew that respite might be beneficial for the parents, but we also knew that significant family relationship problems would not be addressed. We looked for a new approach.

## Stage II: Specialized mental health intervention program

In 1983, a second model demonstration grant enabled us to develop a special program for "double jeopardy" infants—babies who were both biologically and pychosocially at risk. When we recognized attachment problems or other parental risk factors in families of developmentally disabled or delayed infants who came to the Parent-Infant Program, we assigned a clinical psychologist as the primary intervenor with the family. She provided intensive mental health interventions, working with an infant development specialist and the staff clinical social worker as a supportive team. This was our first opportunity to blend infant mental health and developmental intervention approaches.

Grant support also enabled us to begin a training program for all early intervention staff in infant mental health concepts, attachment theory, family systems theory, and interaction observation techniques (Bowlby, 1969; Bromwich, 1981; Greenspan, 1981; Provence, 1983). We expanded our common thinking about how to work with parents and infants and blended ideas from our diverse professional backgrounds. The clinical psychologist led multidisciplinary clinical supervision with staff, but these opportunities could only be used in relation to infants included in the "double jeopardy" demonstration project. Meanwhile, the developmental staff began to meet weekly in the early morning before the Center opened, to continue to provide collegial support and discuss developmental concerns about infants and families who were not in the project.

This demonstration program achieved very positive outcomes for infants and families, but proved to be a stressful model for staff. At this stage in our program's development, we were struggling to address both the psychological needs of parents and the developmental needs of infants by integrating the perspectives and intervention approaches of infant mental health, child development, and social work. Sometimes, however, we seemed to be offering three parallel interventions, with mental health intervention the new and dominant intervention for most families. To the extent that staff struggled for control over the intervention with a family, we lost the potential power of a truly transdisciplinary effort.

## Stage III: Growing pains and a growth spurt—toward integrated services and supervision

In 1986, foundation funding allowed us to hire a full-time clinical psychologist to provide infant mental health services and staff support. While the psychologist who had worked with us previously worked only part-time in our program, the new clinical psychologist became a fully integrated member of our staff.

The clinical psychologist's first task was to understand the scope of the Parent-Infant Program and the ways in which she could use her skills to support staff and families most effectively. She had expected initially that colleagues would want to refer multiple-problem families to her for direct clinical intervention. This was not always the case. Instead, the psychologist found that other staff members came to her when they found it hard to be the only professional working with a family. Sometimes parents were depressed or actively grieving; sometimes questions of infant-parent attachment were troubling; sometimes multiple and complex needs seemed to be overwhelming both families and staff. Staff tended to feel that they should be always available to families and somehow "responsible for everything." Not surprisingly, they often experienced an acute sense of failure.

Much of the pressure on staff could be traced to changes in the external milieu surrounding our program in the mid-1980s. Family needs were becoming more acute, but societal resources were shrinking. The crack cocaine epidemic began in earnest. More and more families referred to the program had multiple problems. More of their babies had been born prematurely; more were medically fragile; more lived in single-parent families, or in households whose members spoke no English. More families needed help with housing, respite, and basic communication with other therapists and medical staff.

At the same time, the steady pressure toward program growth had resulted in a larger, more diverse early intervention staff. Challenged to serve such complex children and families, we felt increasing confusion and discomfort about professional roles, appropriate interventions, and the limits to our services. Many developmental specialists felt that their own training and experience were not being used, while they were being expected to take on unfamiliar roles as social worker, case manager, or provider of emotional support to families. Staff discussions began to focus on the discrepancies between what we thought we were providing to children and families and what we actually were providing. We were going through our own growing pains.

We had no regular staff supervision at this time. All staff members spent most of their time in one form or another of direct service to families, who participated in varying combinations of center-based group activities, a parent support group, in-home developmental intervention, counseling, or infant-parent psychotherapy. Three or more staff members might have weekly contact with a family, but contact with each other would be limited to brief conversations. Only one hour a week was available when the whole staff could meet together to discuss "problem cases" in a program that now served up to 70 families at any one time.

## Taking care of ourselves: Implementing supervision

There were many reasons why we "couldn't possibly" establish an organized, regular system of clinical discussions among staff. Once demonstration projects that had included opportunities for communication, training, and supervision as core elements of a good program were completed, we faced the harsh realities of state and local reimbursement for direct client contact only. To survive financially, we carried higher than optimal caseloads. We could not get reimbursed for time spent making chart notes, formulating developmental plans, writing reports, consulting, or discussing cases. Case discussion disappeared, and in this context the idea of an organized case review felt more like an extra burden than like help. Staff were frustrated and ambivalent—we wanted to talk about cases, but felt that there was no time.

Another barrier to regularizing supervision may have been our unwillingness to acknowledge the implications of our own growth. Key staff kept their sense of the program as it had been when everyone on staff knew all the families in the program, and when collegial interaction and support were part of our daily working lives. Our desire to remain the small, intimate program we had been was at odds with the reality of the larger and more diverse program we had become.

Fortunately, we were able to take three steps toward positive change:

• **We produced a one-page philosophy statement.** After what seemed to be agonizing months of weekly discussion, we found a way to describe in four sentences what we were trying to do with families and what our version of early intervention meant. We said,

*We believe that the family is the most important influence in the development of an infant and therefore seek the active participation of family members in our program. We are committed to promoting healthy parent child relationships that balance the needs of parents with those of children and the whole family. The Parent Infant Program (PIP) recognizes the wide range of needs and complex feelings experienced by families with infants who have special needs and offers support in facing stress, uncertainty and often difficult decisions. In helping families to understand and accept the strengths, limitations and developmental potential of their child, and in providing a safe place to share concerns with others, we hope that parents will become better advocates for their child and feel more satisfied, confident and competent.*

We could give this statement to families at intake to help clarify for them what our program stood for. We could use this statement, which crossed disciplinary boundaries, to define our own role with families in a new way. Now we felt freer to provide a more flexible intervention to families, based on assessment and need rather than dictated by requirements of funding sources or shaped by the training paradigm of a single professional discipline. Now it felt legitimate to consider a more integrated approach to developmental, educational, emotionally supportive, and relationship-promoting interventions. When we followed the principles of our philosophy statement, we felt that we were "doing the job"—the job that we had defined together, that we had given ourselves permission to do.

• **Simultaneously, we established a weekly supervisory hour for each home visiting infant specialist.** Because of our continuing concern about possible fragmentation of the various home- and center-based services that families used in our program, we designed a model for supervision specifically to reflect our model of service delivery. Each infant specialist began to meet weekly in a group that included the clinical psychologist (who had now been designated as Director of Clinical Services for the program), the program's clinical social worker (who saw all families at intake and also facilitated parent support groups), and the center program coordinator (who was the one staff member who saw all of the children and families in the center-based portion of our intervention program.) Since the discussion in each such meeting flows from the infant specialist's caseload, this format allows us to focus our attention on individual families, to remain more aware of the impact of multiple services and multiple relationships on families, and to coordinate the home- and center-based portions of our program more effectively. In these weekly hours, the clinical psychologist encourages staff members to explore different ways of thinking about parents' and children's experiences and to reflect on their assessments and interventions. She may meet alone with the infant specialist for part or all of the weekly hour if this seems appropriate and may also schedule extra individual sessions for new staff members.

• **We reserved an hour of our weekly meeting of the entire direct service staff for free group discussion of problems, ideas, program changes, and interventions.** Thus we institutionalized the infant specialists' informal early morning meetings.

## Stage IV: Increased infant mental health staffing, including a parent/professional

A mental health perspective had become an integral part of our program's direct services to families, consultation to early intervention staff, and supervisory process. In 1989, we gained a richer parent perspective as well. This came from a new staff member who is a professionally trained infant mental health specialist with personal experience as the parent of a child with developmental disabilities who was served in an early intervention program.

Many families in our program have found the opportunity to share feelings and experiences through support groups and individual parent-to-parent contact uniquely valuable. The addition to our staff of a peer parent who is also professionally trained in infant mental health intervention has offered a new dimension of support to these parents, who often feel cut off from families of typically developing babies. Group and individual counseling may be particularly effective for some families when these services are provided by a parent who has shared some of their experiences in caring for a baby with disabilities.

## The current supervision experience

Reflecting on supervision in the Parent Infant Program in its current stage of development, we realize that each infant specialist in our program uses her hour differently. Most of the time, the home visitor and center program coordinator spend part of each hour "checking in" and coordinating home-based and center-based approaches. But there is no set format for a supervisory hour, and each infant specialist uses the time according to her own style, interests, and concerns about particular families.

The supervisory hour is a time when the four people in the group (infant specialist, clinical psychologist, center program coordinator, and social worker) can raise questions together about relationship concerns, family dynamics, intervention strategies, or the developmental potential of a child. It is a time when we can consider whether our program is working for a particular family and whether alternative resources are available in the community. We do not expect that an infant specialist will review all her cases or treatment plans each week.

Some vignettes from supervisory hours offer illustrations of issues raised and the way we handle them:

• Supervision helped a new staff member who was unfailingly optimistic about the developmental outcome for even the most severely disabled baby to deal with her feelings when a family found it hard to match her cheery enthusiasm. We were able to discuss the kind of "fix-it" fantasies and expectations frequently generated in working directly with children with disabilities (this staff member had been a children's speech therapist for many years) and to look at the impact of her own hopeful attitude on this particular family. We thought hard together about what the intervention should be, how the work with the child might feel to the parent, and how the infant specialist could begin to support the parents in their own current experience with the baby, without feeling a failure herself.

• Supervision helped an infant specialist think about how to present to a single parent assessment results that suggested moderate to severe retardation in her infant. We were able to explore the staff member's own ideas about the likely impact of such news on this mother, and her concerns about being one of the professionals discussing this information. Together we identified a style of communication that we thought would be comfortable for the infant specialist and meaningful to the mother.

- Supervision helped a staff member think about a parent's ongoing drug use and the impact it was having on her intervention with the child and family. We were able to discuss the infant specialist's frustration over the failure of previous attempts to discuss this issue with the mother and to devise new strategies for bringing up her concerns. We also talked about options inside and outside the program for additional treatment and the infant specialist's growing concerns about the child's development.

- Supervision helped a staff member explore the complex relationships involved in a child protective services case. An infant who had been in long-term placement with a supportive foster mother, who was an active participant in our program, was suddenly returned to her biological father, who was clearly ambivalent about our services and unclear about our program's connection to his reunification plan. In this situation, we were able regularly to discuss the complexities of establishing a good working alliance with the father so that, among other things, he could help his child cope with the loss of the foster mother, her primary attachment figure. We spent considerable time discussing the feelings that the child's removal from a long-term and loving home aroused in all the staff members who knew this infant.

In general, weekly supervisory meetings with the early intervention staff provide guidance, consultation, and joint problem-solving concerning the relationships between infant specialists and the families with whom they work. Our model of supervision affirms the early intervention staff's expertise in developmental intervention and helps them to address mental health needs of infants and families—and their own feelings in relation to families. Infant specialists do not see themselves as psychotherapists (when appropriate, families can be referred to one of the program's mental health staff for consultation or therapy), but they are comfortable and effective in a role that **includes** an infant mental health perspective.

## Benefits of and constraints on supervision

Our current model of supervision has been in place for two and one-half years. Establishing and using clinical supervision in our early intervention program has required an enduring commitment to the process, a commitment made easier by our dedication to the goal of integrating developmental and mental health services for the population of babies with developmental disabilities and at-risk factors that we serve.

The benefits of this commitment have been considerable.

By recognizing themes that recur in individual supervision hours, we have been able to identify areas where the whole staff can benefit from training and discussion. For example, staff have learned to accept and recognize grief and the different ways parents in our program may express grief as nonpathological (Moses, 1983). Similarly, recognition of differences in the training paradigms of our multidisciplinary staff has enabled us to discuss fruitfully such issues as confidentiality, didactic vs. non didactic intervention, the elements that constitute emotional support to families, and the difference between direct "hands-on" work with infants and working through the parents. Staff as a whole can discuss these conceptual and theoretical issues. In supervision, we can explore the application of concepts and theories to work with individual families.

Supervision has helped us address the feelings staff experience as they work with infants who are disabled, medically fragile, and/or drug-exposed, and with large numbers of multiple problem families. Infants who are not progressing or who are hospitalized repeatedly are now common in our program; it is essential for staff to have a place to explore feelings and potential interventions. Supervision helps staff to become more able to look at their personal effectiveness and styles with families and clearer about the limits to our help and responsibility. We can recognize how important our personal involvement is to families. We can acknowledge how hard our work is. As a result, we see less general anxiety about cases, and a somewhat diminished feeling of burnout.

When staff know that they can receive guidance, feedback, and support each week in supervision, they are more likely to pursue new intervention styles with families. For example, staff members who had been most comfortable working directly with the baby have developed more interest and confidence in working with relationship problems or issues of parental self-esteem. As individual staff members become more flexible, our entire program grows closer to the integrated approach we seek.

Finally, our supervisory model allows early intervention staff and the clinical director to make difficult administrative decisions together. Staff feel a dual loyalty—to the individual families with whom they work and to the program as a whole. When there is a conflict between family needs and what the program, given ever-present fiscal constraints, can provide, discussion in the supervisory hour about how to proceed can alleviate pressure from the staff. The clinical director takes final responsiblity for administrative decisions.

Although supervision has helped staff and the program as a whole, maintaining our model has not been free of problems. Since four staff members are involved in each hourly supervisory meeting and many staff members work part-time, committing this much time to supervision is not easy, and scheduling itself is extremely difficult. Since we are not a training program, we must continually search for funds to cover the costs of supervision. Finally, the creation of the position of Director of Clinical Services has made a hierarchical structure explicit in a program that had seen itself originally as a "supportive family." The Director of Clinical Services is responsible for both clinical supervision and the yearly staff performance evaluations required by the hospital; she and staff continue to discuss ways of achieving a comfortable, fair evaluation process.

## Guidelines for implementing clinical supervision in an early intervention context

Since we began the Parent-Infant Program in 1977, we have experienced a variety of supervisory models, beginning with peer support and most recently featuring individual and small group consultation with a Director of Clinical Services, trained as a clinical psychologist. Supervision has worked as a catalyst to providing more flexible intervention to infants and families, intervention that integrates mental health and developmental perspectives. Although we continue to refine our intervention program and expand our thinking about supervision, we believe that the following guidelines will continue to serve us well:

• **A multidisciplinary program must respect disciplinary differences while integrating perspectives and practice.** In our program, staff members function as general infant development specialists when they work as primary intervenors with families. However, staff members also use their more specific training and expertise in joint consultations or joint home visits with colleagues. In this way we try to learn from each other, expand our understanding of individual children, and recognize the particular contribution of each of our staff members to the program at large.

- **Our current supervisory model recognizes the individuality of staff members and tries to accommodate their individual interests, strengths, and limits.** We encourage staff to work in ways that promote their own sense of success and expand their repertoire of skills and perspectives. Our supervisory model gives staff members time to know each other as individuals and permits regular discussions with infant specialists about the kinds of interventions that they feel most comfortable with, the kinds of situations that are more difficult, and the circumstances in which it would help to involve another staff member for additional intervention with a family. We accept an infant specialist's decision about whether she wants to work with a certain kind of child and family. Demonstrating respect for the individual differences of our staff members helps them to maintain a similar respect for the individual differences of infants and their parents.

- **It has helped to have the supervisory role grow with the program.** Our supervisory model was created, and has changed, in response to the needs of a staff that has grown and changed, in response to the needs of a population of families that is changing continually. We have been fortunate to have had a committed, stable staff since the inception of our program. Our deepening understanding of these individuals, as well as of program needs and goals, has helped us to create a model that is right for us.

## Replicating the integration of infant mental health and developmental perspectives

The successful evolution of an integrated model in our program for infants with developmental disabilities has encouraged its application in other early intervention programs within the Child Development Center. Infant mental health specialists have joined the staff of the hospital's Neonatal Follow-up Program for NICU graduates, the NICU Developmental Intervention Program, and an intervention program for drug-exposed, medically high-risk infants. The model of integrated mental health and developmental interventions, with ongoing clinical supervision, is proving its value in the evolution of each of these intervention contexts.

## References

Bowlby, J. 1969. *Attachment.* New York: Basic Books, Inc.

Bromwich, R. 1981. *Working with Parents and Infants: An Interactional Approach.* Baltimore: University Park Press.

Greenspan, S. 1981. *Psychopathology and Adaptation in Infancy and Early Childhood.* Clinical Infant Reports Series of the National Center for Clinical Infant Programs, #1. New York: International Universities Press.

Moses, KL. 1983. The impact of initial diagnosis: Mobilizing family resources. In Mulick, JA & Pueschel, S (Eds.). *Parent-Professional Partnership in Developmental Disability.* Cambridge: Academic Guild Publishers.

Provence, S. 1983. *Infants and Parents: Clinical Case Reports.* Clinical Infant Reports Series of the National Center for Clinical Infant Programs, #2. New York: International Universities Press.

# 12

# The Professional Use of Self in Prevention

## Judith Bertacchi and Julie Coplon

*Judith Bertacchi and Julie Coplon, The Virginia Frank Child Development Center of the Jewish Family and Community Service, Chicago, Illinois*

*"There are as many pathways to health and adaptation as there are to illness and maladaptive outcomes."* (Emde, 1988)

### Prevention/intervention: An unnecessary dichotomy

In the fifteen years that we have had established prevention programs for families with young children, our ideas about whom we serve, how we provide that service and how that service helps have changed. This article is about the therapeutic gains families make in prevention programs and the role of the professionals in developing meaningful relationships within the context of a prevention program.

Prevention programs were often designed with dual purposes. Families experiencing normal stress associated with a life stage were expected to use prevention programs for education, support and/or socialization opportunities. The hope was that these programs would mitigate against the likelihood of symptom formation and prevent the need for clinical services. The helpful aspects of the programs were thought to be increased cognitive awareness and reduced isolation. For families who were already exhibiting significant symptom formation, prevention programs were viewed as a vehicle for referral to more intensive clinical services.

This view of prevention programs as distinct from clinical services did not adequately reflect the subjective experience of families.

Some families consider as normal and age appropriate child behavior and development that professionals would worry about. Some parents, for example, feel children must be trained by age one, and other parents are comfortable with their four-year-old's use of diapers. Early childhood professionals are likely to be uncomfortable with both of these extremes. But if a pediatrician or day care provider refers a family that is comfortable with their child's development to a clinical service, the family often feels confused, misunderstood or harshly judged. The family is more likely to end its relationship with the referral source than to act on the referral.

In prevention/family support programs designed for parents with infants or toddlers, the common experiences are more compelling than the differences between who has "symptoms" and who doesn't. The mother of a two-year-old who is anxious about effective strategies for toilet training may make a comfortable and helpful connection with the mother of the one-year-old and the mother of the four-year-old also dealing with toilet training. At a drop-in morning or informal discussion group, families raise the issues that are uniquely triggered for them by the external stimulus of their child's development. (Professionals may understand the issues that are evoked and reexperienced in terms of attachment, dependency and autonomy or in terms of separation-individuation.)

Even for families without "symptoms" who are experiencing the normal stress associated with the transition to parenthood and the caretaking of an infant or toddler, the subjective experience of a prevention group is likely to be quite different from the description in the program design. Many groups for new parents, for example, are billed as "parent education." Yet a major psychological impact of the first stage of parenthood involves the reawakening of unconscious, preverbal issues stemming from a parent's own experience of infancy and toddlerhood. Precisely because this early experience is preverbal and not readily available to consciousness, "education" about such emotionally charged issues as dependency, helplessness, separation and autonomy is likely to fall on deaf ears. but the *relationship* to the professional leading the group, however limited, often serves as a powerful vehicle for the expression of these preverbal issues. In a professionally led prevention program, preverbal issues are communicated through the nature of the relationship formed with the professional staff. Talk serves as the vehicle for forming these relationships, but content is seldom meaningful in and of itself. The issues that unfold and are enacted in the relationship with staff usually parallel the issues experienced between parent and child. How the staff members understand and respond to these issues becomes the core of the work that takes place, making the dichotomy between prevention and clinical intervention unnecessary.

For some clients, prevention programs are in fact the "clinical" service of choice. Significant work can take place in these programs, even though, or perhaps because, the work is not taking place within a diagnostic framework. The client is not required to identify him or herself as needing help: she or he is not required to listen to a formulation as to what is wrong; and she or he is not required to enter into an agreement to work toward change. Many clients, and particularly many families at risk, are not able to see their way through one or all of those requirements, which are typically prerequisites for entering any treatment relationship.

### Case vignette: Jane and Erika

Jane was an isolated mother whose beautiful two-year-old, Erika, could do no right. At the twice-weekly drop-in mornings, Jane sat by herself, though she would respond if approached by a staff member. Her answers to our inquiries were always the same—complaints about how difficult Erika was. Erika had particular likes and dislikes, wanted to do things her own way, didn't want to cooperate with Jane, etc. When we responded that Erika was working on just the issues two-year-olds work on, Jane ignored us. But despite her negativism, Jane was open to being approached by staff and seemed to enjoy complaining to us. Slowly a parallel process began to emerge. The staff accepted Jane's negativism with interest and respect, and didn't try to change her attitude toward Erika. Over time, Jane's complaints about Erika didn't change, but the feeling she conveyed by her complaints did. Jane could speak of her own exasperation without focusing on Erika as a bad child. She began to describe Erika's difficult behavior, with some humor and, we suspected, even some pride.

As we accepted Jane's negativism and Jane began to accept Erika's negativism, Jane started to become more open to positive feedback about Erika. She also became more responsive to staff's attempts to engage her in conversation with other mothers. A year later, it was not unusual for Jane to arrive at the drop-in with stories of how adorable Erika had been. (It is important to note that a year later Erika was three and not two).

### Assessment and planning: Jane and Erika

When Jane and Erika first came to the drop-in they were isolated from other families. Jane's constant complaining about Erika didn't fit with the cute, developmentally-on-target two-year-old that staff saw. The first

> **In a professionally led prevention program the issues that unfold and are enacted in the relationship with staff usually parallel the issues experienced between parent and child.**

professional response of the team members was to generalize about the age-appropriateness of Erika's behavior in hope that the information would change the meaning of the behavior to Jane. Jane reacted to their "educative approach" by alternately ignoring the content of what they said and actively rejecting it. However, at no time did staff feel that Jane did not want to be approached. She simply responded to everything they said with a "no!". Staff's felt impulse was to be critical of Jane. Professionalism tempered this impulse, but was often ineffective in curbing the tendency to ignore Jane. In a room with thirty-five mothers and children, the tendency to ignore a particular mother-child dyad can be easily overlooked as a meaningful action.

The first part of assessment and planning is based on staff's observations of a mother-child dyad. Staff noted that Erika was a bright, curious, well-developed child. She had good verbal skills for her age and was able to explore the environment. Her attention span was age-appropriate. While she didn't particularly interact with other children, she was able to participate in the one organized activity (Roll the Ball). She was physically well-cared-for, well-groomed and dressed, and she was a very pretty child. Staff didn't see much of the negativism that Jane described, but they began to see in Erika a depressed affect that mirrored Jane's. Mother and child avoided each other during the course of the morning, each of them seeming alone and isolated. While Jane's negativism colored all of her interaction with Erika, she was very concerned about her daughter and could describe her with great accuracy. Jane continued to care for Erika and didn't try to avoid her by putting her in a program by herself. Instead, Jane chose to bring Erika to a mother/child drop-in run by a child development center and led by professional staff.

The second part of assessment and planning is based on the nature of the relationships mother and child form with professional staff and the feelings evoked in staff by the relationship. Staff was unanimously critical of Jane. This was noteworthy, as clients sometimes share different parts of themselves with different staff members and the feelings staff have about a parent can be quite diverse. Staff members also have different personal reactions to and toleration of various parenting difficulties and this too accounts for staff having different reactions to clients. But with Jane, each staff member felt annoyed, critical and ineffectual. Jane rejected all of their kind, helpful, educative and supportive input.

The third part of the assessment and planning, is based on how theoretical understandings are applied to a particular mother-child dyad. Based on how well developed Erika was, staff speculated that the relationship between Jane and Erika had been basically positive until Erika's budding autonomy had been expressed through negativism. Staff speculated that Erika's negativism had rekindled in Jane her own early issues that had not been worked through. As these issues were basically pre-verbal, Jane was not able to tell staff about her experiences as a two-year-old, but was re-enacting them with staff. Staff decided that their task was to accept Jane's negativism and in this way help her accept Erika's negativism. While the supportive and comfortable atmosphere of the drop-in may have been enough to help Jane weather Erika's "terrible twos," it was the therapeutic relationship with staff that allowed Jane to grow from the experience of this phase, not just to survive it.

## Case vignette: Sallie and her three little girls

Sallie and her three little girls were brought to the drop-in by a friend. Sallie's double buggy only accommodated two of her three children, but her friend had a double buggy with a vacant seat. When the team tried to comment casually on her children's play she responded in sentences that trailed off and left staff hanging. Though there were concerns about Sallie and her children, staff members backed off. Sallie was always greeted warmly. Attempts were made to make her comfortable with the group and to facilitate her children's participation.

Betsy, aged two and a half, seemed depressed and withdrawn. At times she played and at times she fought with her younger sister Ann, aged eighteen months. Ann was an outgoing, spunky child who had the greatest ability to engage Sallie. Rita, the baby, was just a few months old and was left in the buggy for most of the morning or was nursed. Sallie, who looked to be about twenty-five years old, seemed passive and depressed. She usually sat with other mothers. At times Sallie was aware of her children and available to them; at other times she did not seem to hear or see them. Her children were relatively well-behaved, but had a forlorn quality about them.

After a number of weeks, Sallie came to drop-in and came right up to Helen, the team leader. Her friend told her to do this. She launched into a long, wordy narrative about Betsy. She felt that Betsy was too rough with her younger sisters and nothing Sallie did helped the situation. As Sallie talked, Betsy approached and began to pat the baby, who was on Sallie's lap, and continued to pat her more and more roughly. Sallie seemed not to notice. The rough pats continued and finally Sallie said, "See what I mean?" Eventually, in a tired and defeated voice, Sallie told Betsy not to hit her sister. After Helen had discussed various ways Sallie could handle the situation, Sallie said that her friend had assured her, "Rebecca can help you with this!" Helen then gently explained that she was Helen, not Rebecca, but she was still very glad that they had spoken.

Sallie continued to talk to Helen over the next several weeks. Her basic complaints of helplessness and hopelessness remained unchanged, but two themes began to emerge. Betsy, aged two and a half, was a bad and immature girl because she fought with her sisters, and Sallie would be criticized by her family because her children weren't well-behaved. A pattern began to develop between Helen and Sallie. Sallie eagerly sought Helen's advice about this issue, but none of her advice helped. Helen felt ineffectual, helpless and hopeless. Sallie continued avidly to seek advice on this same issue. This is as far as the relationship progressed.

## Assessment as a dynamic process: Sallie and her three little girls

At this point, the staff member does not know enough about Sallie to explain or understand the nature of the relationship developing between them. What the staff member does know at this point is that: 1) she will not insist on focusing on a technique for handling the sibling rivalry; 2) she will not suggest that Sallie talk to other staff members who might have better ideas about handling sibling rivaly; and 3) she will not discourage Sallie from reiterating the same complaints again and again.

Instead, the staff member will listen to Sallie and try to be aware of her own impulse to turn a deaf ear to her, i.e., passively to let Sallie complain while disengaging from any meaningful attention to her. The staff member will watch Sallie do this to her children, who are basically well-behaved, well-endowed children. The staff member will think about Sallie's expectations that Betsy be grown up at age two and a half because the baby carriage only has two seats. And she will think about Sallie's inability to be helped by her; after all, her suggestions were good ones. The staff member will sit with Sallie and listen to her. She will talk to her about Betsy's strengths and how young she really is. Mostly she will talk to her about how hard it is to be the mother of three children under the age of three.

The staff member will not expect Sallie to respond to her observations or even listen to them. But if Sallie and the staff member sit together and the staff member listens to Sallie and, most important, does not expect anything of Sallie (for example, that

> In order to be successful, staff must maintain an openness to examining their reactions and their feelings, both positive and negative, toward the families who come.

she should be more grown up and competent than she is and that she should do what the staff member tells her to do) then this relationship has the potential to help Sallie. It also has the potential to improve Sallie's parenting even though she will never follow any of the suggestions that she will continually require the staff member to make. The task for the staff member in prevention, like the task for a therapist in a conventional treatment setting, is to use an ongoing assessment of the nature of the transference as a basis for further assessment and planning.

## Supervision

The same principles that guide our clinical parent-child work are fully operative in prevention programs. Staff members working in prevention programs need supervision that includes support and attention paid to the parallel process issues being enacted within them. Just as parents re-experience the issues and affects of their children, so do caretakers and professionals working intimately with these very same issues. The issues may be readily observed and felt in the young children but only experienced in an affective mode through interactions with the parents. In order to be successful, staff must maintain an openness to examining their reactions and their feelings, both positive and negative, toward the families who come.

Staff members also grow in their ability to assess functioning and form hypotheses in the here and now; that is, within the situational moment and in any environment where the family is met by the staff. This could be in a corridor, a bathroom, a busy group, the lobby or a hospital room. Frequently, professional staff members working in prevention function as a team. Supervision must enable them to share with each other, to raise differences of opinion, differences of perception, and to tolerate conflict and tension. With time, they gain in their ability to understand these tensions as not solely personal issues but further refinements of communications from parents and their young children.

There are specific tasks and strains for staff working in prevention: An overriding task for staff is to become comfortable with utilizing their clinical acumen, but implementing it in very different ways from a clinical interview. For example, the skill of assessment is used for planning interventions that are within the scope of the boundaries of the program (See Jane/Sallie.) The contract existing between a staff member and a family is a subtle one and time-limited, i.e., "I am coming to your professionally led preventive service for today, based on what I read in a flyer or heard from my friend or neighbor." Supervision addresses this task by exploring the contract that is operating between staff and families within any preventive experience. The limits and boundaries of intervention need to be frequently clarified.

Staff does not always receive feedback on how a family is doing or how a particular discussion or comment was understood by the parent. This leads to concern and worry about certain families, especially those considered vulnerable or at risk, and who have not, for example, "dropped-in" lately. The supervisory task is to listen and participate in the concerns, thus sharing and at times containing the anxiety. Frequently, the supervisor's task is to review the fact, easily lost, that the family knows we are here; again, holding to the contract.

Staff members struggle continuously to make themselves desirable attachment figures. Within this process they accept the complex communications resulting from these attachments. The non-verbal dynamics of the group process and the expressed, ongoing normal maternal dependency needs of mothers in this life stage can continue to create in staff a phenomenon of wanting to do more and more for parents. Momentarily they can feel just like the mother, being prone to similar regressions and defensive strategies. The supervisor's task is to work toward helping staff accept those very same maternal feelings of neediness and occasional entitlement. That shared experience, if understood, can deepen the empathy team members gain for the parental tasks of this life stage.

This task often comes forward when families begin to request changes in the limits and boundaries set within a program structure. By virtue of being "outside the process" the supervisor becomes aware of staff regressions paralleling the parents and of guilt beginning to drive decision-making. To understand and empathize with a parent's neediness and sense of entitlement is quite different from being caught up in this neediness. To hold limits in an empathic, respectful manner is to accept the parent but interfere with their potential to destroy the very "holding environment" for them as parents that they crave. The supervisor works to help staff regain perspective; then staff can provide without burning out or beginning to hate those who ask so much of them. Again, the supervisor points out the close parallel to a primary parental task.

Staff members in prevention programs learn to advise more freely than is usual in some of their clinical work. They gain in their ability to understand that their advice will not always be taken and may be serving another purpose within the transferences that develop between parents and staff. They learn to participate in small talk while using their clinical skills in understanding metaphor and transference.

The team and staff are uniquely strained by those families who, in their vulnerability as parents, present staff with multiple examples of "bad parenting". The supervisor must continually hold out "hope" to staff working with these high-risk families. This is particularly true at those times when team members begin to feel the despair and exhaustion shared with them by the families. This sharing may occur when quietly sitting with a mother who looks depleted, depressed and/or is not available to her child while she is with us. This intervention is a poignant non-verbal communication occurring within a preventive transference relationship. Further, the supervisor can also point out the value of this mother being less isolated, being "held" while observing other parents who are functioning. We have learned that a mother in distress does not necessarily spoil the experience for other mothers (an early apprehension of ours). Being with a parent who is struggling can provide relief for other parents. They observe and realize that they might not be the only one who ever faltered in their parental tasks.

In parallel fashion, the supervisor sits with staff and listens. By sharing observations of slight change in the family or reviewing the unresearched value of caring for the mother and providing respite, the supervision goes beyond listening and provides ongoing training. The supervisory support lies essentially in the theories that help us better understand both adult and child personality development within the context of a caring, informed relationship.

Supervision helps staff deepen their understanding of parental ambivalence as they explore their own complicated reactions to certain parents and children. Our teams are frequently made up of social workers and child development specialists. Thus the staff teams often represent the continuum of identifications from baby to mother. Their positions and belief systems slowly undergo change with all ideally moving to a more middle-of-the-road, dyadic stance. Those who always move first to the children will need to recognize with Winnicott that, "There is no such thing as a baby" ... only a mother/father and a baby. Those who enter the work from the other end of the continuum, focused on the mother, will learn to appreciate the expanding parental identity struggles that always include the child. The learning task will become, to paraphrase, "There is no such thing as a mother, there is always a mother and a child." The internal changes necessary for dyadic work do not diminish the unique insights and talents that individual team members need to share and utilize. It only means that interventions need

> **The supervisor works to help staff regain perspective; then staff can provide without burning out or beginning to hate those who ask so much of them.**

The Professional Use of Self in Prevention 89

to be dyadic and directed toward the parent-child relationship. The supervisor's task here focuses on the talents of the team members. This is a crucial task for the team, to learn to focus, discuss and plan interventions for dyads, rather than individual parents or children.

## Summary

The professional use of self in prevention is the process by which a staff member lends him/herself to enter the arena of preverbal issues. Staff make themselves available to receive these communications through the relationships they form, through the role they have been assigned by a client and the feelings that role evokes in them. Staff members use these experiences to form speculations as to the issues a client might be struggling with. This process usually involves use of supervision, as it is not solely the clients' preverbal issues that are evoked in an arena such as this. Staff member and supervisor form a working assessment of the family's issues and use this assessment to guide staff actions.

While transference reactions occur and have meaning in any therapeutic arena, in "zero to three" programs they are a special vehicle for communication. Families with infants and toddlers are living in the realm of preverbal issues—their children's and their own. These issues are usually unconscious, can seldom be communicated in words, but are an important dynamic of parenting during the preschool years. When prevention programs are designed to include parents and children together, preverbal issues are always part of the relationship between parents and child and often reproduce themselves in the relationship between parent and staff member. It is careful attention to the parent-professional relationship within prevention programs that allows them to serve as vehicles for change, not just as vehicles for repetition.

## Bibliography

**Books**
Anthony, E and Benedek, T (Eds.) 1970. *Parenthood: Its Psychology and Psychopathology;* New York: Little Brown.

Fraiberg, S (Ed.) 1980. *Clinical Studies in Infant Mental Health, The First Year of Life,* New York: Basic Books Inc.

Provence, S (Ed.) 1983. *Infants and Parents, Clinical Case Reports,* New York: International Universities Press.

Winnicott, DW. 1975. *Through Paediatrics to Psychoanalysis.* New York: Basic Books.

Winnicott, DW. 1965. *The Maturational Processes and the Facilitating Environment.* New York: International Universities Press.

**Articles**
Benedek, T. 1959. Parenthood as a Developmental Phase: A Contribution to the Libido Theory, *Journal of the American Psychoanalytic Association,* Vol. 7, pp 389-417.

Schames, G. 1981. Boundary Issues in Countertransference: A Developmental Perspective, *Clinical Social Work Journal,* Vol. 9, No. 4.

**Journal**
Emde, R. 1988. *Infant Mental Health Journal,* 9, 2.

# Lay Home Visiting Programs: Strengths, Tensions, and Challenges

## Mary Larner and Robert Halpern

The efforts described in this paper were generously supported by the Ford Foundation under its Child Survival/Fair Start Initiative. The authors thank their colleagues in the CS/FS home visiting programs for sharing their experiences. In particular, Minnie Bommer, Barbara Clinton, Lupe Manujano-Garcia, Wanda Newell, and Emily Vargas Adams contributed quotes and many insights used in this paper.

Visiting poor families in their homes to provide guidance, information and, more recently, social support has long played a modest role in efforts to ameliorate the consequences of poverty. In the latter decades of the 19th century, well-to-do volunteers known as "friendly visitors" dispensed "moral guidance" to poor families (Davoren, 1982). In the early part of the current century, home visiting was part of the repertoire of social workers and public health nurses, many affiliated with the settlement house movement (Melosh, 1982). But it is only in the past 25 years, starting with the community action programs of the federal War on Poverty, that talented but nonprofessional members of the target community itself have been called on to serve as home visitors (Hewett, 1978; Travers, Nauta, and Irwin, 1982).

In the 1980s, lay home visiting programs are again proliferating, amid high hopes that these labor-intensive, personal program strategies can successfully link low-income families to formal services and can support them in their efforts to cope with poverty and the host of stresses it creates for parenting (Cochran and Woolever, 1983; Dawson, Robinson, and Johnson, 1982; Lyons-Ruth, Botein, and Grunebaum, 1984; Zigler, Weiss, and Kagan, 1983). Lay home visiting programs have both unique strengths and inherent tensions. For example, the programs provide a way of maximizing the the acceptability and cultural consonance of supportive services, while holding down the cost of making individual visits to families. The strategy forms an uneasy union between characteristics of professional intervention (circumscribed, disciplined, goal-oriented, and knowledge-based) and features of informal social support (relatively unbounded, reciprocal, multi-faceted, and based on exchanges of personal experience). Along with its appeal, then, that amalgamation brings difficulties that too often take program administrators by surprise.

In this paper, we focus both on the strengths of the home visiting strategy that uses lay community workers and on the tensions and implementation challenges that make it difficult to achieve the potential embodied in this approach to service delivery. Before addressing those implementation challenges, however, we will review the general reasons why home visiting has been so persistently popular as a way of serving poor and high-risk families. Then we will examine how reliance on lay workers multiplies many of the strengths of the home visiting approach, and will also consider the unique management challenges that accom-

---

*Mary Larner*, National Center for Children in Poverty, New York City

*Robert Halpern*, Erikson Institute, Chicago, Illinois

pany that strategy. Finally, we will look at some of the persistent tensions that lay visitors confront in their work with families.

The insights in this paper are drawn from the accumulating experiences of a set of home visiting demonstration programs supported by the Ford Foundation in its Child Survival/Fair Start Initiative. In these community-based programs, home visitors work to improve pregnancy outcomes, infant health, and family conditions that influence child development among a heterogeneous group of at-risk populations: migrant Mexican-American farmworkers, young black mothers in rural Alabama and Tennessee, isolated Appalachian families, Haitian immigrants and refugees in South Florida, and Mexican-American residents of urban Texas barrios. In some programs the visitors are "natural helpers," neighbors and peers of the families they serve; in others they are individuals with more education and experience who nevertheless come from a similar cultural background.

The authors have worked alongside program staff, assisting with evaluation and helping clarify emerging general lessons (Bond and Halpern, 1987; Halpern and Larner (a), in press). The reflections in this paper are drawn from a study of program development and implementation involving extensive interviewing of program staff at each of the local sites. The Child Survival/Fair Start programs differ considerably, however, and the generalizations in this paper cannot do justice to the variations in their programs and experience.

## The nature of home visiting practice

Home visits in parent support and education programs typically combine a number of core activities—information-sharing, modeling, demonstration, emotional support, joint problem-solving, and service brokerage and assistance in meeting pressing needs—in creating an approach that will foster growth and support parenting in the families served (Chamberlin, 1980; Halpern, 1986). Individual home visits usually incorporate a mix of these activities interwoven in the fabric of the developing relationship between visitor and family. The balance struck among the elements differs from visitor to visitor; the same visitor may emphasize different elements in her work with various families; and the priority given to each element changes over time as needs and interests evolve.

When she (home visitors, whether lay or professional, are overwhelmingly females) enters the home, the visitor typically catches up with the new mother on significant events and appointments since her last visit, discusses relevant health or child development topics, and demonstrates and asks the mother to try out infant care and stimulation activities. She may remind the mother of coming medical appointments, and together they plan the topics that will be covered on the next visit. Often the task-oriented "educational" portion of the visit is preceded or followed by a more relaxed time of sharing about social activities, feelings, concerns, and personal problems. The visitor both empathizes with the mother and helps her to come up with ways of dealing with difficulties.

Home visits represent a reaching out to a young family and do not, on the surface, require the family to actively seek help and support. They place the helping interaction in a relatively less threatening environment than that found in most agencies, although it cannot always be assumed that the home is a comfortable setting for private conversation. Home visits also give the family worker a fuller appreciation of factors in the physical and social context that influence childrearing, and they lend realism and relevance to the home visitor's demonstration and modelling of parent-child interaction and caregiving. Most important, they provide the sustained contact that allows a mutual relationship to develop. Because the program is embodied in the one-to-one relationship between the visitor and mother it can respond flexibly to the interests and needs of each family.

## Home visits by lay community members

The decision of a program to rely on lay workers as home visitors amplifies many of the strengths of the generic home visiting strategy. For example, programs that emphasize the case-finding aspect of outreach often find that lay workers are well-suited to learn of and seek out eligible families, using their networks of personal contacts and knowledge of local "hang-outs" and activity patterns. Once initial recruitment is accomplished, a home visiting program continues to bring its services to the family's door; thus it can often maintain contact even with difficult or passive clients. Lay visitors tend to be accepted by families and their neighbors more quickly than professionals often are, and their persistent efforts to locate mothers provoke less suspicion than similar pursuit by many types of professional visitors.

At her best, a local visitor slips easily into the rhythm of conversation in the home. Her cultural familiarity enables her to read behavioral cues, frame her messages in understandable terms, and anticipate responses to her suggestions. She knows when she is bucking traditions, and is often skilled in the local art of persuasion. While any home visit affords an opportunity for staff to observe and learn about the family's surroundings, a worker from the community joins the program with substantial prior knowledge of the physical and social conditions in which families live. She can draw from personal experience to understand the issues confronting families. She has coped with poverty, and knows intimately its daily toll; she has heard how neighbors talk about "spoiled" infants, and listened as her own grandmother taught her about childbirth, remedies for fever, and signs of good health in babies. She is not surprised by the problem of the beliefs of the families she visits, and her empathy and understanding often make her suggestions more welcome.

The relationships developed in lay home visiting programs resemble the informal helping relationships that exist within natural social networks (Gottlieb, 19833). Peer helping is usually reciprocal, and while lay visitors do not request assistance from the mothers they visit, they do exchange ideas and often share personal experiences to illustrate a point and to build empathy. "Formal" lay helping, like informal helping, is often multidimensional, integrating emotional support, cognitive problem solving, and concrete assistance in an ongoing relationship that offers continuity and stability, creating a context of confidence and trust. When a relaxed, trusting alliance develops between visitor and mother it is a mechanism of considerable power, if it can be harnessed.

## Challenges of program management

As we suggested earlier, the very strengths of lay home visiting as a strategy give rise to tensions in implementation that can undermine program effectiveness. These tensions are often most pressing during the early months of implementation, but they suffuse the full range of program development tasks. Implementation challenges that are directly related to the use of lay home visitors include: (1) articulation of a realistically delimited role for the lay workers; (2) discovery of the skills and personal qualities demanded of home visitors; (3) establishment of a training system that builds on strengths and allows for the introduction of specialized knowledge; and (4) provision for a supervisor who will nurture and monitor the continued development of the lay workers.

### Articulating a role for lay visitors

The first and most difficult challenge for those responsible for planning lay home visiting programs is to spell out and at the same time critically evaluate the expectations that are being laid on the visitors' shoulders. This delimitation process should be grounded in sober thought about what kinds of support tasks local community members (with several weeks as opposed to years of training, a basic curriculum, and some supervision) can realistically accomplish, and it should lead to plans for providing back-up personnel, resources, and referrals to ensure that the visitors will not have reason to overstep the limits of their expertise. In the course of their visits, lay workers come face to face with a wide range of family problems, and they often feel an internal pressure to respond. If the program provides mechanisms for linking families to professional services, the home visitors can make appropriate referrals and focus on what they do best—offering education guidance, support, and assistance in such a way that the mother's self-esteem and autonomy are maintained.

Even when the home visitor's general role and purposes have been established, the task of supporting and educating families through home visits often (though not always) remains relatively unstructured. That open-endedness can lead to considerable insecurity for fledgling home visitors. Both the mechanics of conducting home visits and the criteria for evaluating them are often not clearly described, leaving the visitor to wonder: "Was that what a home visit is supposed to be? Did I spend too long listening to her talk about her husband's family? She looked bored when I explained the benefits of breastfeeding; should I have dropped the topic? Did I push too hard? Was she agreeing with me only to get me to leave?" It takes time before any new worker can develop the skills to manage home visits, but the process is greatly helped if expectations are clear and there are early opportunities to observe experienced home visitors in action.

### Discovering appropriate recruitment criteria

Far more than in professionally oriented services, the nature of the treatment received by each family in most lay home visiting programs is shaped by the personal characteristics of the worker. As a result, knowing what qualities to search for in recruitment is virtually as important a program development task as is the creation of a relevant and potent training program to build on those strengths. Criteria for selecting potential home visitors tend to emerge out of a trial and error process that often weighs credentials (education, prior experience, status in the community) against personal characteristics (social ease, sensitivity, maturity, and self-awareness). Different Child Survival/Fair Start programs have tipped that balance to correspond to the specific demands they make of lay visitors. For example, in two urban programs, the home visitors had frequent contact with professionals in other agencies and played a public role as advocates. These programs placed more stake than the others in educational achievement, since the visitors had to gain the respect of professionals and community leaders. The visitors in other programs focus more exclusively on interpersonal work with families; they are recruited primarily on the basis of personal qualities such as empathy, warmth, and openness. Finally, programs using lay workers as culture-brokers to link families to the mainstream service system have needed to find individuals who combine a comfortable awareness of their cultural roots with cognitive flexibility and an interest in new ideas.

### Establishing an effective training system

Preservice training offers a modest opportunity to cultivate the skills that lay workers may lack, and it provides a chance for the program to discover the beliefs and values that trainees hold about matters like childrearing, human services, or family needs. All too often, however, training becomes a one-way process in which the knowledge and attitudes of the home visitors are ignored, as trainers hurry to teach them the information they are to convey to families. An overly didactic preservice program can undermine the experiential sense of mastery and successful coping that made these women a natural source of information and support to other community members. As one supervisor said:

*"We've got caring people as natural helpers and we need to use that fact. We need to give them the resources to work with—not overload... Let's not try to make them overnight professionals. They can lose their effectiveness."*

If the training leaves lay workers feeling insecure about their limited mastery of the material, they may retreat to a rigid recital of the curriculum on their visits, and the key strengths of the lay visiting model will have been forfeited.

On a more mundane level, time management and documentation may pose difficulties for lay home visitors. Their role is an unusually autonomous one—in many programs they have no fixed schedule (work hours are spent in the homes of program participants, driving to and fro, on preparation and follow-up) and little objective documentation of their own. Learning to manage that autonomy is a challenge, since the prior work experience of those lay workers who have held jobs has often been in closely supervised settings like factories or restaurants. One of the program directors puts it well:

*"When the home visitor is in the field working with a family, she is alone, without anyone to hold onto, no one to guide or to supervise her. If you have someone who is still trying to find out what a working day is like, as well as learning what home visiting is, and how to become a person of respect to the family you are going out to visit—that's a lot of pressure on a young person with little organizational experience."*

Demands for visit planning and record-keeping weight heavily on lay workers who are not accustomed to writing. Effective documentation often requires that visitors be able to interpret family needs, plan interactions and assess progress, tasks that rely on subtle skills of observation and self-scrutiny that develop only gradually in any family worker.

## Providing supportive supervision

The challenge of monitoring and sustaining home visitor performance over the long term typically falls to a professionally trained supervisor who works primarily or solely with the team of lay workers. The supervisor, who has often guided the recruitment and preservice training programs, becomes as well the pivotal individual shaping the development of the home visiting program and of the lay workers. As trainees take on their new roles as home visitors, most begin by emphasizing the tasks they find personally most fulfilling—teaching, helping out in a crisis, or playing big sister to a troubled teen. But their emerging sense of their role is also influenced by their supervisor's professional background and personal style, since they often come to identify with her.

Supervising a lay home visiting program is primarily an educational process, not an administrative one. The success of the supervisor often lies in her ability to motivate, teach, nurture, evaluate and reward the lay home visitors. Through one-to-one supervision and team meetings, supervisors help lay workers: to understand the limits of their role and responsibility, to use concrete observations of family life and parent-infant interaction in planning, to learn to make nondisruptive transitions between educational and supportive interactions, to deal with hard-to-like clients, to make suggestions without passing judgment, to manage the demands of needy clients without encouraging dependence, and to recognize how their own feelings and past experiences may influence their work with families. One supervisor pointed out that she works to create a growth-enhancing relationship with her home visitors that resembles the relationships the lay workers cultivate with program participants.

## Tensions confronting the lay worker

In addition to the managerial challenges that the lay home visiting strategy poses to program implementors, this approach confronts the lay workers themselves with persistent, unsettling tensions. These fall primarily in four areas: (1) defining a new social role that is half-friend and half-intervenor; (2) juggling the conflicting interpersonal purposes and styles demanded by the role; (3) moving back and forth between two cultures; and (4) finding a way to build on experiences acquired through the home visiting work, in order to achieve personal goals in the wider society. Understanding the dynamics associated with each of these tensions can sensitize us to the rewarding but difficult role that lay home visitors have accepted.

## Defining a new social role

As we have pointed out, lay home visiting programs incorporate elements of both professional intervention and natural social support. For all their informality, home visits are not "natural" social interactions. Cultural rules guide the behavior between guest and hostess, and these do not typically give the guest the authority to pick topics of conversation, ask personal questions, or tell the hostess how she should go about doing things. Early visits often have a tentative quality because the visitor and the mother are uncertain what to expect of each other. Though the lay worker stands much closer to the mother than any professional service provider, she and mother are not "equals." As one supervisor put it:

*"Once a community woman has been selected as a home visitor, the community tends to view her differently. No longer is she thought of as a relative of someone who lives down the street, but rather as a contributing, upwardly mobile person."* (Newell, 1987, p. 118).

That subtle difference in status can make interactions awkward. If, however, the lay worker can be both relaxed and respectful, her visits can be comfortable for both parties while remaining "special events."

## Striking a balance interpersonally

Home visitors balance precariously on a series of tightropes as they try to create a useful, acceptable role with each family they visit. The lay workers must be assertive enough to approach strangers in order to recruit them into the program and confident enough to direct the attention of the mothers they visit to the program's agenda. Yet if assertiveness becomes didactic, domineering, or judgmental, the mothers will quickly lose interest in participating in the visits.

Even when rapport is established, each home visit can be marked by a tension between support and education, as the visitor balances her responsiveness to family interests and needs with a goal-oriented awareness of the agenda she wants to cover. Unless monitored, some visitors spend very little time on the curriculum, focusing instead on family needs or the personal concerns of the mothers. In the words of a supervisor: "It's very easy to be seduced into talking about all the mother's problems and never really give her anything back in terms of new information about child development." Yet single-minded emphasis on educational goals can invite problems of a different sort if the visitor does not embed her advice in the supportive give-and-take of a trusting relationship. One home visitor put it this way: "In order to help people, you've got to be listened to, and if I turn you off, you haven't heard a word I've said anyway. We're just going through the motions."

The lay visitor's willingness to share her own personal experiences can be a powerful aid to forming a trusting personal relationship. But it is difficult to share at this level and still maintain the perspective required to see the most effective way to help. The over-identification between visitors and families caused problems in one case:

*"Often the home visitors' own personal problems were not dissimilar from the problems they were trying to solve for the families—and that was extremely difficult to handle... We want people to be compassionate and understanding, but not to the point that they become part of the problem."*

Because home visiting work with families is not based on standard scripts but draws heavily on interpersonal exchange, the demand for sensitivity and self-awareness is unending.

## Straddling two cultures

In many situations, the lay home visitor functions partly as a culture-broker, and that aspect of the work is fraught with ambiguity and tension. It is expected that lay workers will be respectful of the families served by the program, sensitive to cultural issues, and able to translate program messages into culturally accepted terms. Their very closeness to that culture means, however, that many beliefs and practices are too deeply ingrained in their own life experiences to change easily. While the lay workers may respect the expertise that undergirds the program's recommendations, they only gradually become comfortable discussing ideas that fly in the face of traditions, and incorporating them in behavior is more difficult yet. As a result, individual lay workers often maintain "domains of silence," individual topics they avoid or address only tentatively, well beyond the period of preservice training (Halpern and Larner (b), in press).

Training inevitably alters the "layness" of lay workers, and some observers have warned that paraprofessionals can be "co-opted" by the professionals who surround them, coming to adopt a stereotypic agency-based view of family needs and problems rather than helping reshape the program to fit community values and concerns (Gartner, 1979; Powell, 1982). Some programs have fought this tendency by deliberately involving home visitors in ongoing adaptations of the program's curriculum, materials, and approach. Nevertheless, it can be difficult to train lay workers to convey the program's agenda without sacrificing some of their identification with the families they are serving.

## Struggling to achieve personal goals

A final tension may arise between the lay worker's perspective on the future and that of the program that employs her. Put briefly: the home visitor hopes to advance, and the program hopes to keep her. A near-universal characteristic of low-income communities served by these programs is the absence of employment opportunities, and even talented, resourceful women like those chosen to be lay workers are often handicapped in the local job market by a lack of education and work experience.

The lay home visiting program can help local women enter the white-collar world of human service agencies, because it values the skills they already have and it offers a supportive way to build new ones. In the nurturing context provided by the supervisor and a team of peers, the personal growth of many lay workers is startling: one completes her high school equivalency exam; another learns to drive and buys a car; a third leaves an abusive husband and enrolls in the local community college. Advances tend to come in three broad and important areas: in education, in job-related skills and in confidence and self-esteem.

Unfortunately, many home visiting jobs are not linked to further opportunities within the agency or in the wider community. During the 1960s, the creation of paraprofessional positions served two purposes: their presence was intended to alter the culture of the agency, making it more sensitive to the needs and values of the people being served; and the positions themselves were depicted as "new careers" that created ladders of employment by which community members could climb out of poverty (Austin, 1978; Pearl and Riessman, 1965). Some of the current generation of lay helper programs seem to have lost sight of those former ambitions: many administrators do not solicit the views of lay workers about agency policies, and they seldom plan opportunities for advancement within the agency. To continue their personal growth (and earn a more acceptable living), lay workers often seek other jobs, leaving the program, their supervisor, and the families in their caseload behind.

Staff turnover is stressful, both for the program that must train new workers, for the lay worker confronted by the new demands of a different job, and for the families who are asked to form a relationship with a new home visitor. Even this unplanned and wasteful process can benefit the larger community, however. The lay home visiting program's efforts to identify, nurture, and develop the skills of talented local women often launches them toward careers in human service or community leadership (Clinton and Larner, in press), enabling them to contribute in new ways to the well-being of their community.

## The challenge ahead

It sometimes appears to these authors that we put too much on the shoulders of lay home visitors. It is crucial that we continue to clarify appropriate roles, expectations, and tasks for lay home visitors, taking into account their characteristics as helpers, as well as the nature of the problems facing the families they serve.

Yet there is a further danger—that too much may be expected of parent support and education generally as a vehicle for altering the likely futures of poor children and parents. No single support strategy, whether interpersonal or financial, can address adequately the range of obstacles to healthy development that poor children and adults face. A variety of complementary strategies are needed. In that light, lay home visiting is an attractive element of a broader package of family support strategies we should all be promoting.

## References

Austin, M. 1978. *Professionals and Paraprofessionals*. New York: Human Sciences Press.

Bond, JT and Halpern, R. 1987. The role of cross-project evaluation in the Child Survival/Fair Start Initiative. In H Weiss and F Jacobs (Eds.), *Evaluating Family Programs*, Norwood, NJ: Ablex.

Chamberlin, R. Conference exploring the use of home visits to improve the delivery of preventive services to mothers with young children. Evanston, IL: American Academy of Pediatrics, June 1980.

Clinton, B and Larner, M. Rural community women as leaders in health outreach. *Journal of Primary Prevention*, forthcoming.

Cochran, M and Woolever, F. 1983. Beyond the deficit model: The empowerment of parents with information and informal supports. In I Sigel and L Laosa, *Changing Families*. New York: Plenum Press.

Davoren, E. 1982. The profession of social work and the protection of children. In E Newberger (Ed.), *Child Abuse*. Boston, MA: Little, Brown and Co.

Dawson, P, Robinson, J, and Johnson, C. 1982. Informal social support as an intervention, *Zero to Three*, 3(2), 1-5.

Gartner, A. 1979. The effectiveness of paraprofessionals in service delivery. In S Alley, J Blanton, and R Feldman (Eds.), *Paraprofessionals in Mental Health*. New York: Human Sciences Press.

Greenspan, S and Wieder, S. 1984. Dimensions and levels of the therapeutic process. *Psychotherapy*, 21(1), 5-23.

Gottlieb, B. 1983. *Social support strategies: Guidelines for mental health practice*. Beverly Hills, CA: Sage Publications.

Halpern, R. 1986. Home-based early intervention. Dimensions of current practice. *Child Welfare*, 63(4), 387-398.

Halpern, R and Larner, M. In press. The design of family support programs in high-risk communities: Lessons from the Child Survival/Fair Start Initiative. In D Powell (Ed), *Parent support and education: Consequences for children and families*. Norwood, NJ: Ablex.

Halpern, R and Larner, M. In press. Lay family support during pregnancy and infancy: the Child Survival/Fair Start Initiatives. *Infant Mental Health Journal*.

Hewett, K. 1978. *Partners with parents: The Home Start experience with preschoolers and their families*. Office of Human Development Services. DHEW Publication No. 78-31106. Washington, D.C.: U.S. Department of Health and Welfare.

Lyons-Ruth, K, Botein, S, and Grunebaum, H. 1984. Reaching the hard-to-reach: Serving isolated and depressed mothers with infants in the community. In B Cohler and J Musick (Eds.), *Intervention with psychiatrically disturbed parents and their young children*. San Francisco, CA: Jossey-Bass, Inc.

Melosh, B. 1982. *The physician's hand: Work culture and conflict in American nursing*. Philadelphia, PA: Temple University Press.

Newell, W. 1987. *Supervisor's guide to home visitation programs*. West Alabama Health Services, Eutaw, AL.

Pearll, A, and Riessman, F. 1965. *New careers for the poor*. New York; Free Press.

Powell, D. 1982. From child to parent: Changing conceptions of early childhood intervention. *Annals of the American Academy of Political and Social Science, 416,* 135-144.

Travers, J, Nauta, MJ, and Irwin, N. 1982. The effects of a social program: Final report of the Child and Family Resource Program's infant and toddler component. Cambridge, MA: Abt Associates, Inc.

Zigler, E, Weiss, H, and Kagan, S. 1983. *Programs to strengthen families.* New Haven, CT: Bush Center in Child Development and Social Policy.

# 14

# *A Developmental/Relationship In-Service Training Model for Public Health Nurses Serving Multirisk Infants and Families*

## Serena Wieder, Robert Drachman and Tippie DeLeo

Many thanks to Ann Kelley, B.S.N., R.N., and Esther Herman, M.S.W., of Protective Services; the planning committee; and the nurses and social workers whose participation in this training program allowed us all to learn.

In Prince George's County, Maryland, just beyond the borders of the District of Columbia, Community Health Nurses in the Bureau of Child Health Services dedicate 60 percent of their time to home visiting and case management. Their practice involves reaching out to high risk families with young infants who have not been using the health care system or who miss appointments at the county's seven clinics. These Public Health Nurses are seeing families with more complex needs and difficulties than was formerly the case. Fifteen percent of the infants born in the county were probably exposed to illicit drugs in utero. Almost 11 percent (1290) of the county's births each year are to teen parents; more than a third are to single mothers.

Young children and families whose problems include maternal drug abuse, infant drug exposure, low birthweight, failure to thrive, potential child abuse or neglect, non-compliance with medication regimens, and cognitive impairments create new demands and anxieties for Community Health Nurses as they do for other human services professionals. Work with such families also calls into question traditional Public Health Nursing approaches and rewards. Nurses who have been trained to provide preventive care and information for parents to use in caring for their children find that this model of practice often does not meet family needs. Multiply stressed families fail to keep appointments; may not remember child care information; nod in response to suggestions but do not follow through; seldom if ever express appreciation for the nurse's help; and may even be hostile and angry when pursued. These families, with overwhelming, multiple, complex problems place their infants at great health and developmental risk; to intervene effectively, providers need new skills and insights.

This set of circumstances, in which practitioners are challenged to redefine themselves and the meaning of their work, would be described by adult learning theorists as a state of "cognitive disequilibrium." Stressful as it may be, disequilibrium is seen as necessary to bring about the kind of change in perspective that can, in turn, change the way individuals experience, interpret, and understand their world (Mezirow, 1979).

In Prince George's County, in 1987, Community Health Nurses responded to the markedly changed demands on their professional capabilities by requesting a training program that would assist them in providing more effective services to multirisk infants

*Serena Wieder*, Silver Spring, Maryland

*Robert Drachman*, Prince George's Hospital Center, Cheverly, Maryland

*Tippie DeLeo*, Child Health Services, Prince George's County Health Department

and families. The Program Director sought out and requested the assistance of a clinical infant psychologist with extensive experience in dealing with low-income, multiproblem families and infants with developmental difficulties. This article will describe the process she initiated of conceptualizing and implementing a training model for Public Health Nurses and Protective Service Workers. The "Developmental/Relationship Training Model" builds on the conviction that it is the quality of the relationship between professional and parent that determines the likelihood of parental changes in behavior to benefit the care and development of the infant. Training must stress the importance of the worker/parent relationship in accomplishing infant care and parenting goals and must sensitize and instruct workers in the insights and techniques required to establish such a supportive relationship.

## Defining the work, defining the training needs

A planning committee of nurses, supervisors and administrators met to explore the concerns raised by working with increasing numbers of infants and young children with multiproblem homes in high risk communities, and to define what they wanted to learn. They spoke for nurses all over the county; common concerns seemed to be independent of age and experience. Interestingly, discussion did not focus on specific knowledge or information that nurses could learn and impart to families; rather nurses wanted to know how to motivate and help families use existing information and services, use the nurses' help in supporting the attachment and development of their infants, and identify health and developmental problems as early as possible. Some specific questions were raised.

- **Suppose I only have one chance to engage a family and guess wrong about a baby's safety?** When called upon by Protective Services Workers to evaluate a home or when dealing with a crisis, particularly in areas where their personal safety was a real concern, nurses, like other human services professionals, frequently found problems so overwhelming that it was difficult to know what they were dealing with, let alone whether they were doing their job well. They worried that they might get only one chance to engage a family who did not want them in the home, and that they might misjudge an infant's safety.

- **How do I decide whom to see and whom not to see?** Nurses found that increasing caseloads and increasing complexity caused a constant redefinition of administrative priorities. Finding a balance between easier and more difficult families was unlikely. The comments, "You have seen her long enough" or "She is too dependent on you" would be heard. Nurses wondered whether families were being discharged for the wrong reasons—increased staff anxiety, rather than improved function. But they also wondered whether they might be persisting with families for the wrong reasons—a need to "make" something work to protect one's professional self-image.

- **How, day by day, do I work with difficult families?** Nurses wondered how to promote attachment when they saw so many babies failing to bond with their mothers, how to help highly stressed, drug-using mothers care for drug-exposed infants so fussy and irritable that even the best mother would be at a loss. They wondered what to do when parents did not show up for their appointments or said they would do something and didn't. They asked how to compete with the television for a mother's attention and how to respond to a grandmother who asked that Protective Services be called to investigate her daughter.

A major concern was how to set **realistic** goals for families that accurately reflected their capabilities.

Most professional in-service training efforts attempt to impart information, enhance competencies and provide a forum in which nurses can share experiences and

**Training must stress the importance of the worker/parent relationship in accomplishing infant care and parenting goals and must sensitize and instruct workers in the insights and techniques required to establish such a supportive relationship.**

> We needed to help staff become able to identify and respond empathetically to difficult, frequently ambiguous situations and emotions in more self-confident and realistic ways.

meet with colleagues. However, the relevance and utility of the knowledge and ideas imparted are often uncertain, and the impact on families ambiguous. Now, given the opportunity to define what they wanted to learn to support daily nursing practice, the Community Health Nurses sought a more differentiated view of the work and their professional role. In order to engage and motivate families more effectively, they wanted to better understand both their families and themselves. Above all, they wanted to know how they could know that they were doing their work well and how practically to measure success or failure.

What proved to be essential for the trainer was expertise on how people learn, change, and use relationships to develop. By staying focused on this process, the trainer could integrate the specific "topical" knowledge nurses wanted on development, interaction, play, the impact of drug exposure, etc. into the ongoing training program. While it might have been possible to have a number of specialized experts present at large meetings, the training model would still have required someone to "personalize" the knowledge presented, tying it to participants' thoughts and feelings in both small and large sessions. The continuity provided by a single trainer also meant that the consistency and persuasiveness of the basic "message" concerning the importance of relationships could be delivered in many different ways, as the nurses discussed and examined their ideas and feelings. By seeing the participants each month, the trainer got to know their strengths, special talents, knowledge base, concerns, resistances and anxieties, and could address these issues.

## A conceptual framework for training

Researchers in education describe developmental levels of conceptual functioning and relate these levels to specific behaviors among practitioners (Harvey, 1966; Murphy and Brown, 1970). For example in stage one, practitioners value authority and believe that any question has a single right answer. Stage two is characterized by uncertainty, but behavior does not alter. In stage three, practitioners tend to use group consensus rather than established rules to guide behavior. In stage four, individuals regard knowledge as tentative rather than absolute and are able to consider situations from different points of view. Researchers describe this stage of development as characterized by increased flexibility, differentiation, tolerance of conflict and ambiguity, and comfort with conceptual complexity, characteristics that enhance both interpersonal functioning and effectiveness at work (Hunt, Kohlberg and Loevinger, reviewed by Glassberg and Oja, 1981).

Can an in-service training program promote such development? That was the challenge the planning committee faced. We needed to make training an opportunity to understand the work being done, to support it, and to learn from it. Nurses had described very substantial challenges to their practice; the training program would have to present a conceptual framework that would be relevant to their work. We sought to create a training model that would enhance the functional practice level of Child Health Nurses in the program. We needed to help staff go beyond trying to use familiar terms to interpret new experiences and challenges; we needed to help them become able to identify and respond empathetically to difficult, frequently ambiguous situations and emotions in more self-confident and realistic ways.

Development during the earliest years of life, when parent-infant relationships and feelings provide a foundation for learning, offered a conceptual framework highly relevant to Community Nursing practice with young children and families. The parent's caregiving and attention to health issues in the child present a process that is parallel to the nurse's efforts to engage challenging families. Therefore, in our training program, we wanted to make sure that not only the content, but the structure and process of training as well, would embody a developmental perspective.

## Goals, structure and content of the training program

This training was designed to build upon the strengths of the Community Health Nurses. Some staff had already intuited ways to use their own strengths and support from colleagues to deal effectively with difficult families. We sought to create an environment in which all nurses could build upon their own and one another's expertise. The nurses met to define for themselves what they wanted to learn, developed the curriculum to address areas of greater needs, evaluated the training midway, and revised the curriculum and approaches accordingly.

We set both affective/relationship and behavioral objectives for training. Affective objectives included the development by nurses of a more complex, differentiated, and integrated understanding of themselves and the families with whom they were working. Behavioral objectives included an increase in knowledge about child and parent development; the enhancement of skill in promoting interaction and positive relationships between infants and parents; and the development of strategies that would allow a nurse to assume a variety of roles with families, depending upon the circumstances.

The developing relationship between the trainer and the nurses proved central to meeting the affective objectives of the training. We realized that this relationship would need to include the same elements we wanted to see in relationships between nurses and families and, more important, between parents and infants. Toward this end, the trainer met with the entire "family," from the Chief of Child Health Services, to the Assistant Chief and Professional Development Specialists, to District Supervisors, to Nurses. This process produced a sense of total commitment within the Bureau of Child Health Services to common goals. Approximately 50 Protective Services Workers and Nurses attended the large group lectures and later divided into three smaller District case conference sessions with 15-20 staff. Furthermore, the trainer made home visits with nurses to families identified as particularly difficult to work with; this practice allowed the trainer to join the nurse's efforts as well as to better understand the reality of the nurse's work. Finally, the trainer was responsive to the personal as well as the professional concerns that the nurse expressed.

The structure of the training program, like its goals, was arrived at through discussion. Like development, the training program was designed to be an unfolding process. Conducting training over a ten-month period permitted practice, application, and integration of content. Different approaches were designed to accommodate the different ways people learn. Large group lectures and discussions, role playing, small group case conferences, readings, and accompanied home visits complemented each other and offered nurses different ways to learn and participate. Role playing offered an opportunity to practice active listening and empathic responding. Home visiting, where so much of the nurse's work actually is done, offered an opportunity for applying new learning.

The range of experiences and opportunities offered within the overall training program were designed to relate to each other and to validate the important work that the nurses were doing. By experiencing together meetings or home visits that had some emotional intensity or significance, the learners and the trainer developed a sense of "shared meaning" about what had occurred. Over time, it was no longer necessary to spell out everything in words—a look or a "shorthand" phrase could convey what was important about an experience, or how it felt. Shared meanings, achieved through a variety of shared experiences, were also the essence of what would need to be developed between nurses and mothers, and mothers and infants, for learning and development to proceed.

## Implementing the training program

Between 50 and 60 people participated in the training program, including **all** the Child

> By experiencing together meetings or home visits that had some emotional intensity or significance, the learners and the trainer developed a sense of "shared meaning" about what had occurred.

Health staff and about ten Protective Services Workers, including three supervisors, who had been invited to join the training program so that they and the nurses could better understand each other's work.

During the ten-month course of the training initiative, five bimonthly large group lecture and discussion sessions were held. These day-long events were used to present a variety of interrelated material regarding infant development, parent-infant interaction, nurse-parent relationships, and the specific challenges involved in working with adolescent or drug-abusing parents and their babies. Theoretical and conceptual frameworks such as Greenspan's developmental-structuralist model (1981) and Klein and Feuerstein's mediated learning experience (1985) provided the structure to undergird new perspectives. The close connection between training topics and the professional concerns that the nurses had identified led to active participation in discussions, role playing and responses to provocative videotapes. The focus always remained on the work to be done—intervention strategies and specific techniques to engage and promote interaction—and on the nurse's experience in doing this work. (See p. 107 for approaches to mediating successful parenting, as presented by Wieder during the course).

Case conferences, conducted at three District Centers, allowed for more interaction within groups of no more than twenty staff. The cases selected through discussion between supervisor and staff were often those that presented exceedingly difficult problems and left nurses feeling "stuck," uncertain about how or whether to proceed. These cases were also selected because they confronted the nurses with their own strong feelings, ranging from protectiveness to anger, fear, and the bitterness accompanying failed expectations.

The case conference format provided an excellent opportunity to examine the complexity of each situation and the nurses' need for increased flexibility, tolerance of ambiguity and acceptance of their own limitations. Their understanding of themselves and the families became more differentiated as they could sort out positive and negative feelings, what they identified with in families and what they rejected.

Case conferences also served to validate the significance of the nurses' developing relationships with parents. Conventionally, nurses' productivity and the outcomes of their efforts were typically measured by numbers—of families seen, immunizations completed, referrals made, or records updated. Professional realtionships with parents were assumed. The case conferences, however, focused on the process of the nurse's work and the importance of her interaction with parents. Developing relationships with parents were emphasized as important goals to be accomplished since relationships were the vehicle for promoting parents' abilities to support the physical health and development of their children.

In the course of the case conferences, certain responses to work with infants in multiproblem families emerged as typical. The examination of these responses, within the case presentations, provided the substantive content of training.

**1. Nurses often underestimated the importance of the relationships that they had managed to establish, often through persistent outreach.**

**2. Nurses tended to see strong feelings about families—either positive or negative—as evidence that they were getting "too involved." Some did not consider their reactions in relation either to the specific effect parents had on them or to their own expectations or attitudes.**

**3. Nurses were often so consumed during case conferences by efforts to decipher the overwhelming, anxiety-producing family "dramas" they encountered that sometimes the infant in the family was lost to their attention.**

**4. Because very little interaction or "play" occurred between either parents and infants**

or nurses and infants during their contacts, opportunities for pleasure and reciprocity were missed that could have helped to strengthen all the relationships involved.

5. On occasion, giving information and instructions could serve as a defense against getting closer to a frightening family or environment.

6. When family problems seemed overwhelming, family strengths were often overlooked. Similarly, nurses tended to lose sight of their own strengths and successes.

7. Focusing on psychopathology created a safe distance and was used to alleviate insecurity about being able to help certain parents.

8. Nurses often felt pressured to find solutions to insoluble problems; when they could not, they would tend to withdraw before giving themselves a chance to review what was going on and learn from the experience.

9. The nurses had a unique opportunity to facilitate "successful" parenting, which would provide an important source of self-esteem to parents facing future challenges.

Each case presented was discussed by the trainer in terms of the developmental and therapeutic relationship issues (Greenspan and Wieder, 1984) raised. Each case provided an opportunity to recognize strengths and challenges and to support the nurses' efforts. While the child and family's "story" was certainly important, the conference also focused on **how** to think about the family. The trainer tried to help participants conceptualize each situation with regard to the process of engagement, the differences between the perceptions of the family and those of the nurses, the feelings triggered in the nurses as indicators of the family's experience, the expectations of nurses and families, and how they affected each other. As we shared what different ideas and behaviors of each family might mean and the experience of working with them, the nurses could shift perspective. They could return to the case with renewed energy and redefined goals. After the case conferences, they could more readily apply the knowledge of infant development and skills to promote interaction and positive relationships that they had learned in the larger sessions.

Home visits where the trainer accompanied the nurses provided the most individualized learning opportunity for nurse and trainer to work together to address concerns about a family. These visits were used to evaluate further the developmental levels of infants and parents, their interaction, and the approach being used to engage the family. By bringing toys and books, the trainer could also model specific techniques for the nurses, such as inviting both parent and children to "play"; encouraging the parenting identity in talking with the parent, and leaving a special notebook with pictures and ideas; singing songs; and noticing the strengths of the infant. These visits became the opportunity to introduce new ideas and to help parents experience a sense of success and pleasure through interaction with the child. Following the visit, trainer and nurse could discuss the dynamics of the intervention, the stage-specific issues, the next steps in development, and the methods needed to engage families' attention, facilitate reciprocity, and, most importantly, to play and have fun together. Only by taking the time together to play and mediate pleasure and success would parents come to believe that this was important.

These home visits were also discussed in small group meetings whenever possible. The willingness of the trainer actually to go on home visits with the nurses, sharing their concerns and dangers, provided credibility and support for this special aspect of their work.

Any service system should include learning opportunities for every level of staff. As part of our training program we planned a special session for nursing and protective service supervisors, to address the specific stresses and challenges present in their work. Here, too, the developmental/relationship perspective was helpful; supervisors were able to consider alternatives to unrealistic expectations that they held for themselves—that they had to have all the answers, absorb all of their staff's anxieties, or be the sole source of protection and support for staff in the system.

### Evaluating the training program

Evaluating a training program is probably no less complex than evaluating a service program. In evaluating the Child Health Nursing training effort, it would have been ideal to address changes in the nurses' professional developmental level, observable changes in actual practice, changes in nurses' professional self-image and perceptions of their own work, and the impact of the training program on parents and infants. Unfortunately, limited resources did not permit a systematic study of these complex issues. However, informal observations and feedback from the nurses indicated that the more receptive nurses were to looking at themselves and to new learning, the more confident and competent they felt, the more they enjoyed their work, and the less likely they were to leave the unit.

The trainer and planning committee learned a great deal from the nurses' own evaluations of the training, which occurred in the middle and at the end of the ten-month program. Using a five point scale from exceptional to unsatisfactory, the nurses rated the overall quality of the course, the various training formats, and the usefulness of content. That ratings became more positive from the middle to the end of the program may reflect the developing relationship between nurses and trainer. All the participants found the overall program interesting, with large majorities also finding it relevant to their work (89%) and being able to apply course content (86%). Small group case conferences and home visits were rated highest among training formats, followed by large group lecture/discussions and nurse presentations. The readings seemed to be the least useful way for participants to learn. A follow-up study will examine what aspects of the training nurses continue to find useful and how nurses may have changed their perspectives and perceptions of their work.

### Conclusions

Our training program, planned in three months and implemented over a ten-month period, attempted to integrate adult learning and developmental/relationship models in order to address the training needs identified by Health Department Child Health Nurses and Protective Services Workers in Prince George's County, Maryland. The training model seems particularly appropriate for in-service staff development programs in which a group that faces common work issues can meet together over time.

The features of our model included:

- a conceptual framework for the goals of the training, with affective and behavioral objectives to guide the training and efforts to increase participants' developmental level;

- definition by the participants of what they wanted to learn and the personal and professional challenges presented by their work;

- a variety of training approaches that addressed individual learning styles and provided opportunities to practice and integrate the concepts being presented;

- active participation by the trainees in the learning process, through discussions, case presentations, role playing, and presenting; validation, through these activities, of trainees' strengths and abilities to organize their own learning;

- joint learning by staff of several agencies, with the goal of developing mutual understanding of each other's work in order to reduce professional and interagency tensions and facilitate collaboration;

- an emphasis on direct interaction and play with mothers and babies as the means to promote relationships which support health and development;

• an extended training period, which permitted relationships, as well as new perspectives to develop over time.

Finally, learning is an ongoing process. It supports and rewards the practitioner's daily work. The new initiatives undertaken in their practice and interest in further learning that we have observed among participants in our training program suggest that our model opened doors to individual learners. We could not ask for a more satisfying outcome.

## References

Glassberg, S, & Oja, SN. 1981. A developmental model for enhancing teachers' personal growth. *J. Research & Development in Education, 14* 59-70.

Greenspan, S with Greenspan, N. 1989. *The Essential Partnership.* NY: Viking.

Greenspan, S, & Lourie, RS. 1981. Developmental structuralist approach to the classification of adaptive and pathologic personality organization: application to infancy and early childhood. *Am. J. Psychiatry,* 138:6.

Greenspan, S & Wieder, S. 1984. Dimensions and levels of the therapeutic process. *Psychotherapy,* 21, No. 1.

Harvey, OJ (Ed.) 1966. *Experiences, Structure and Adaptibility.* NY: Springer Publishing Co., Inc.

Klein, P & Feuerstein, R. 1985. Environmental Variables and cognitive development. In Harel, S & Anastasiow, N (Eds). *The At-Risk Infant: Psycho/Socio/Medical Aspects.* Baltimore: Paul H. Brookes, Inc.

Klein, P; Wieder S; and Greenspan, S. 1987. Prediction from mother-infant interaction patterns to preschool performance based on observations of mediated learning experience. *Infant Mental Health Journal,* 8, 2, 110-129.

Mezirow, J. 1979. Perspective transformation. *Adult Education,* 28 (2), 10-110.

Murphy, P & Brown, M. 1970. Conceptual systems and teaching styles. *American Educational Research J.,* 7, 529-540.

Rogers, ME. 1989. Creating a climate for the implementation of a nursing conceptual framework. *J. Continuing Education in Nursing, 20,* (3), 112-116.

# *Mediating Successful Parenting: Guidelines for Practitioners*

## Serena Wieder

Parents learn to be parents in many ways. Some read books, pamphlets or magazines available at every check-out counter. Others watch T.V. talk shows, talk to their friends or neighbors, call their mothers, or remember their own childhoods. Still others take courses and join other new parents.

*Serena Wieder,* Training Consultant, Silver Spring, Maryland

Hopefully, all learn from their infants as they care for them, enjoy them, and grow together.

At risk parents are often unable to use these resources to learn. They may be distressed by overwhelming realities, overwhelming pasts, and previous failures and fears which continue to interfere with their functioning in general, and as parents in particular. Too often they do not have the chance to enjoy what other parents enjoy with their children, singing songs, dressing up, taking pictures, or playing.

Whatever the structure or goals of an intervention program, working with these parents and infants involves interacting and relating in many ways. Specific techniques are described below to mediate more successful parenting. They are derived from therapeutic and mediated learning experience models which can be integrated into common interactions and play during time spent together.

***Give the concept of being a mother or father positive meaning and identity—build consciousness and awareness of being a parent.*** It is important not to assume that having a child means feeling like a parent. Even if someone begins to feel like a parent, nurture this new identity with as much support as possible. This is done by admiring the parents, giving them credit for what they do, having fun together with the infant, and reassuring them the child is doing well. To do this, indirect comments are useful. For example, when seeing a baby who is dressed nicely or attractive, one might say to the baby being held by the mother, "Mommy dressed you so beautifully today, she knows exactly what looks good on you!" Or, "You're so big, Mommy knows exactly what/how to feed you to make you grow!" Or, "Mommy knows how to dress you beautifully, Suzy, you're a lucky girl!" Or, "What an athlete Daddy is making out of you." Such comments help a parent feel proud, focus on the process of what they have to do to feel competent; and lessen the risk of parental jealousy of the infant. One does not assume the parents appreciate or take pleasure in having their child admired when they are not directly credited or referred to.

***Make the mother and father feel unique.*** To support the special attachment and investment parents need to make in their infants, reinforce the uniqueness of the parent to the child. This too can be done through a variety of comments to the parent, such as, "Mommy gets the best smiles from you; I know who is in love with you!" as the baby smiles at the parent. Similarly, when noting the baby looking at a new or strange face, say, "You sure know your mommy best of all because I can see you staring at me and you don't know me at all!" In the course of following an infant, many opportunities arise which can highlight the parents' unique function. For example, when a baby fusses the intervenor might say, "Mommy will know how to comfort you best of all," as you guide or support the parents' response to calm the infant. Here too is an opportunity to give the parents credit for anything they do, for the purpose of enhancing their special relationship with the child and supporting their self-esteem.

***Focus on the infant's or parent's experience rather than right or wrong.*** It is possible to communicate to the parent that infants have feelings and experience things in different ways through straightforward comments, or "talking through the baby." For example, one might say, "Hold me tight, I like to be all wrapped up tightly too." Or, "Don't turn me so fast; it's scary and I'm afraid I'll fall." Noticing how the infant might be feeling is especially important for the parent who does not empathize readily, or does not think in terms of the infant's feelings, or may not be handling the baby very well and does not notice the effect she or he is having. Such comments support the parent's efforts without the practitioner's taking over or necessarily knowing what is going to work best. This approach encourages exploring different attempts to calm the baby by reading signals with the parent and relating to these signals as expressions of feelings.

***Focus on issues relevant to the infant"s specific stage of development.*** For example, when helping parents learn to read the baby's cues and signals as they begin to communicate in purposeful ways, highlight the meaning of these behaviors. For example, "You want to tell mommy something, don't you?" Or, "Figuring out what you want isn't easy at all; tell/show mommy what you want again." "Oh, look how he turns around to look at you just after he crawled away; he wants to make sure you're still there!" "Boy, you need your daddy's help, don't you, it's hard!" Such comments accomplish multiple things. They focus on what is important for the parent to respond to at specific ages. They preempt misinterpretations of the meaning of behavior which can lead some parents to withdraw or reject or retaliate against their children if they disapprove. It is also easier for parents to learn an infant's language if they feel it is directed towards them. These comments support the attachment, identity and uniqueness of the parent.

*Focus on the impact of current behavior on the future.* With parents who do not relate current development to later achievement or success, or parents who have little sense or hope for the future because of being overwhelmed in the present, it is useful to create a sense of future success for the infant and the role parents can play. For example, when encouraging reading baby books, you might say, "When you grow up, you will be so smart because mommy is getting you ready already!" Or, when observing a child play with blocks, "I wonder if you will be an engineer or an architect, you build those blocks so well!" Or, "Daddy is so good with tools and you are following his footsteps already." Encouraging the ability to transcend the present is important so that parents identify infant learning with future success in school or work. But it is important to focus on the *process* of learning and not the product, i.e., discovering, exploring, trying new things, using toys or objects in novel ways, rather than being able to name letters, numbers and other concrete skills.

*Build parental self-esteem by selecting and admiring success.* Whenever a child is doing something well, it is worthwhile pointing that out and building an image of the child as a successful learner and the parent as a successful parent who can be effective and help the child learn. General admiration or clapping such as, "That's great!" or "You're so good!" is not as useful as specifying what made the act successful or what difference it makes. For example, if a toddler is stacking rings, then he might be admired for, "you figured out which one should come first and second and third; that's good thinking!" Even if the child cannot yet understand these words, commenting guides the parent to think in terms of thinking and problem solving rather than just the end product which may or may not be well done. Focusing on the process of how or why something succeeds encourages the parent to pay attention to what to do, rather than what they will get or other concrete results. For example, admire the parent's success in getting the child to attend, "You really got him to listen when you got him to look at you before telling him what to do." When these behaviors are noticed in the course of natural interaction they convey the idea learning is going on all the time. They also put the parent in charge and reinforce effective behaviors rather than only focusing on problems and parents' inadequacies.

# Issues for Supervisors and Program Directors

Reflective supervision becomes an important part of a service program's shared culture only when it is valued and protected by management. The chapters that follow illustrate the "tenacity of commitment" required to establish and maintain regular, collaborative, reflective supervision for all infant/family practitioners.

# Supervision and the Management of Programs Serving Infants, Toddlers, and Their Families

## Linda Gilkerson and Carol Lou Young-Holt

*Building and sustaining the settings in which individuals can grow and unfold, not 'kept in their place' but empowered to become all they can be, is not only the task of parents and teachers, but the basis of management and political leadership—and simple friendship.* (Bateson, 1989, p. 56).

Supervision may be a relationship **for** learning, but it is also a relationship that occurs **within** an organization. Without management support, supervision gets lost in the daily demands of direct service. But when reflective supervision is valued and protected by management, it becomes an important part of a program's shared culture.

It is the responsibility of the program director to make sure that reflective supervision for individual staff members is **fully** incorporated into the program. First, there must be an organizational commitment, philosophically, to provide supervision for **all** staff members. Second, dollars need to be allocated and time must be set aside on a regular, scheduled basis for supervision activities. This means that supervision is built into job descriptions, that there is an articulated performance system for the organization which is tied to each person's job description, and that time for supervision is expected and allocated as each person's job responsibilities are assigned. Just as an audit is an expected accountability element of the fiscal system of an organization, supervision must be an equally expected accountability element of direct services to infants and families. It is the director's responsibility to ensure that the staff as a whole has regular, predictable opportunities for "slowing down the process" of daily work and reflecting on issues that affect the entire program. Finally, it is the program director's responsibility to establish and maintain a reliable system of support and consultation for herself.

We have been led to the observations that follow in part by our experiences as directors of child care and early intervention programs, as consultants to program directors, and as teachers of students preparing for a variety of professional infant/family roles. Our ideas have also been shaped by our reading in the professional literatures of organizational management, child care, and human development. Just as this *Sourcebook* as a whole is designed to stimulate further inquiry among its readers, so we hope that this essay will lead readers to consult the books and articles listed in the bibliography.

## Metaphors for management of infant/family programs

Programs that serve infants, toddlers and their families are organizations. They are systems, comprised of interrelated and interacting components, that exist within an external environment. The literature on

*Linda Gilkerson*, Erikson Institute, Chicago, Illinois and *Carol Lou Young-Holt* Far West Laboratory, Sausalito, California

organizational structure and development and on systems theory has much to teach the infant/family field. However, infant/family programs are special kinds of systems and organizations; some of their uniqueness may be captured through the metaphors of "community" and "program family."

## Community

Everyone in the entire management system must work in concert to achieve program excellence and to meet the needs of children and families. When this happens, the program becomes a viable, healthy **community.** The community offers a vision or philosophy of what the program intends to accomplish. It includes and nurtures everyone involved—children, parents, staff, directors, administrators, board members, and the larger community.

John Gardner writes compellingly about community. For those of us working with children and families, his definition offers a powerful metaphor to illustrate the leadership, guidance, and involvement that must form the foundation of our daily and long term work.

*It is in community that the attributes that distinguish humans as social creatures are nourished. Families and communities are the ground-level generators and preservers of values and ethical systems. No society can remain vital or even survive without a reasonable base of shared values—and such values are not established by edict from lofty levels of the society. They are generated chiefly in ... intimate settings in which people deal with one another face to face....*

*We know that where community exists it confers upon its members identity, a sense of belonging and a measure of security. Individuals acquire a sense of self not only from observation of their own bodies and knowledge of their own thoughts but from their continuous relationships to others, especially close familial or community relations, and from the culture of their native place, the things, the customs, the honored deeds of their elders ... Humans need community—and a sense of community.* (Gardner, 1991, pp. 1-2).

It may well be that much of the impact of infant/family programs may come from the fact that they are (or have the potential to become) "intimate settings in which people deal with one another face to face." Within large, impersonal medical centers and office complexes, adults and children in NICUs and in on-site child care facilities form communities. Store-front family resource centers and the homes on the early interventionist's route are "intimate settings" where, one hopes, "continuous relationships to others" are being nurtured.

Gardner identifies nine elements of healthy communities, all of which seem relevant to infant/family programs. These elements are:

- Wholeness incorporating diversity
- A reasonable base of shared values
- Caring, trust, and teamwork
- Effective internal communication
- Participation
- Affirmation
- Links beyond the community
- A forward view
- Institutional arrangements for community maintenance.

The sidebar on page 115-116 suggests a list of questions, adapted from Gardner's essay, for directors, staff, board, and participants to ask themselves and each other as they consider the "community" they are creating in their infant/family programs.

## The program family

A second metaphor for management is that of the "program family." By this we mean people who work together regularly—the team, the work group, the staff. For adults in contemporary America, the work group is a source of primary relationships. It can be an ongoing source of support for personal as well as professional growth. In infant programs, we need to pay attention to both the participating family and the program family. In order for participating families to be well served, a program's group process and supervisory model must address the emotional themes and issues of the program family.

Self-knowledge should be valued as a legitimate professional competency. No one needs this quality more than the program director, for his or her strengths and weaknesses will be mirrored in the staff's relationships and performance. One of the many essential roles that a program director plays is to think about the program family, its individual members, and its collective process.

## The importance of program structure

Like families and communities, infant/family programs require clear administrative structures for role definition, planning, emotional support, education, conflict resolution and performance appraisal. Well-meaning, even highly committed staff and an "open door" management style are not sufficient to sustain a program as it grows, or as it experiences stress.

A clear administrative structure almost always involves some hierarchical organization. Yet the notion of a "healthy hierarchy" in administration is an uncongenial one to many early childhood professionals. Many infant/family programs, particularly smaller ones, were built by team effort. Everyone pitched in to develop the program, decisions were made by consensus, role boundaries were fluid, and the organizational chart was flat. But although these characteristics may represent strength in the development phase of a service program, they may become stresses as programs move into a maintenance phase of service delivery. A hierarchical organizational structure does not imply a power-oriented management model. On the contrary, teams and committees representing all levels of staff and program participants may be charged with major management responsibilities. What is important is a clear, explicit administrative structure for the program.

## Ensuring supervision for individual staff members

It is the responsibility of the director of an

## Questions to ask ourselves:

- Does our program support *diversity of the whole community?*

  ★ How are individual and cultural differences considered for each child and family?

- What are the *shared values* in our infant/family program?

  ★ How are these values shared and expressed?

  ★ What is the philosophy of our program?

  ★ How do we articulate this philosophy to one another on staff? With our program participants? In the broader community?

  ★ Does the allocation of resources (time and money) reflect these values and beliefs?

  ★ What are the visions for the program community?

- Everyone who works with young children needs to be supported and nurtured. How does our community *care* for its members?

  ★ What are the everyday and long-term actions that demonstrate caring?

  ★ How is the program director providing leadership for caring in the community?

  ★ How is the community nurturing the director?

- What is the level of *trust and teamwork?*

  ★ Is there respect among all community members for one another?

  ★ How do people demonstrate this respect with one another?

  ★ Do staff members understand and appreciate each person's role and responsibility as it relates to the whole program?

- Is there effective communication?

  ★ Is communication regular, predictable, written as well as verbal?

  ★ Does everyone discuss with one another a range of topics related to the program, such as accomplishments, issues, and concerns?

  ★ Is there a commitment to inform?

  ★ Is communication direct and open, or is it closed and/or indirect?

  ★ Is communication interactive or one-way?

  ★ Is there a predictable, agreed-upon process for conflict resolution?

- How are members of the community encouraged to participate fully?

★ Who defines the terms of participation?

★ In what ways is participation invited?

★ Is there group consensus, or do a few individuals control the community, with others restricted in their involvement?

- How are community members affirmed?

★ Are people affirmed and appreciated for being who they are? Are their unique contributions integrated into the whole community?

★ Are "shared beliefs" clear, explicit, and related to the goals of providing the best care for infants and families? Or is affirmation tied to other issues, not directly related to supporting children and families?

- How is our program linked to other communities?

★ Do we work with colleagues and other service settings, or is our program isolated and/or territorial?

- Is there a forward view for our community?

★ What are the visions of our program, and how are these visions being translated into accomplishments by each person?

- How is the program nurtured and maintained?

★ Does the program's board provide leadership and guidance to management? Does the board define and expect competent management?

★ Are areas needing improvement looked at honestly and openly?

★ Are solutions developed for problems, and remedies supported by everyone involved?

---

infant/family program to ensure that a clinically rich model for staff supervision is in place. This means allocating time in the program for supervision to occur, and incorporating supervision into the job descriptions of appropriately skilled people. This means embedding and protecting funds in the budget to pay for the staff time involved in supervision—even when the time is not reimbursable.

Especially when programs are small or resources are scarce, program directors may assume that they themselves should provide clinical supervision. This may be a mistake. Directors are personally responsible, first and foremost, for accountability in the system. There is no way that a single program director can supervise individually a staff that has grown to 40 people. The director's personal priority must be assuring acceptable service to program participants; responsibility for the professional growth of staff can be delegated.

In addition to ensuring supervision for her staff, the program director must identify and establish support for herself. Directors of infant/family programs commonly experience the loneliness and lack of appreciation that are part of being at the head of any organization. Because of the multidisciplinary character of the infant/family field, program directors may feel the lack of specific skills or information that was not a part of their own training or work experience. Although directors may feel "out there by themselves," usually they can establish a circle of helpful connections if they are willing to take the initiative. Within a program, a "director's committee," composed of staff from different levels can provide information and counsel. Organized outside contact, such as a consortium of program directors or a time-limited series of seminars for directors (see Bertacchi & Stott, this volume) can be helpful. Budgeting for outside consultation for the director may be as important as budgeting for supervision for front-line staff.

## Opportunities for reflection by the whole staff: "Slowing down the process"

Just as individual professional competence grows within a supervisory or mentoring relationship, so the competence of a whole program can be enhanced by regular opportunities for reflection. These opportunities develop, affirm and transmit shared values. They are the predictable rituals of the healthy "program family," the honored traditions of the program "community."

For many programs serving young children and families, the school calendar offers natural occasions for periodic reflection. Staff can talk about the comings and goings of children, marking progress but also acknowledging the losses that staff feel as children and families move on. In other settings, staff may reflect on the program's own annual cycle: Was it a year full of accomplishment? A hard year? A transition year? Based on where we have been, where are we headed? What were the significant markers and the more subtle, but nonetheless important signals that we have seen? Quarterly program reviews can be used to look at client evaluations of service and to set quality improvement goals for the quarter to come.

Articulating a program's services to participating families and then asking them about their experiences yields valuable insights. Articulation in itself is a means to accomplishing program goals: It explains services, access, and availability. It can also become a vehicle for dialogue with participants.

If obvious beginnings, middles, and ends do not exist in the program, regularly recurring opportunities for reflection need to be created.

A program's regular staff meeting structures may offer opportunities for "slowing down the process." Most organizations must deal with three orders of business: 1) logistics and immediate planning; 2) the substantive content of the work; and 3) long-term planning. Unless firmly circumscribed, administrative issues tend to take over any meeting. Some infant/family programs find it useful to alternate the agenda of regularly scheduled staff meetings: One week's meeting will be devoted to administrative issues, the next to an in-depth discussion of work with a specific child and family. Other programs have two types of meetings, clinical and administrative. Each type is likely to require a different leader and a different format. Program directors can help by posting or circulating agendas and inviting participation. An outside consultant can give a staff a fresh look at themselves by bringing an outside perspective on staff "group issues."

Long-term planning need not occur frequently, as long as staff do have predictable opportunities they can count on to look at their own group process and to think ahead. These may include agency off-site retreats and quarterly planning sessions along with regular content-based staff meetings.

A staff handbook can be an excellent vehicle for reflection. Preliminary drafting can be assigned to a committee rather than the director. Each staff member can review her own job description and suggest changes. Of course the director's input is critical. In one program, a director who felt that her staff constantly criticized and devalued each other added "professional support and collegiality" to practitioners' job descriptions.

## Linking the "program family" to the broader infancy community

By seeking out ways to connect her program to other infant/family programs and human services initiatives, the program director can achieve opportunities for collaboration, refueling, recognition, and reflection for herself and her staff. Vehicles for connection include infant/family publications; local, state, and national conferences; and multi-site research, demonstration, and training initiatives. Each vehicle presents opportunities for connection at several levels.

Infant/family publications range from informal newsletters to scholarly journals. Delegating responsibility for choosing the publications to which a program will subscribe to a committee of staff who represent a range of interests and expertise may stimulate reflection on training needs in the program in general. The committee might also think about the ways publications are used in the program: It may be appropriate to acknowledge and reward staff members' intellectual curiosity by investing in subscriptions to key publications for each staff member, perhaps with the expectation that there will be group discussion of particularly relevant articles. Writing for publication about some aspect of the program or preparing a case study for publication can be a useful group exercise in reflection, as well as an opportunity for public recognition of the program's achievement. (Nancy Sweet and Barbara Ivins, for example, used the draft of their chapter about the evolution of supervision in their infant/family program [this volume] as the background paper for a staff retreat.)

Participation in conferences is typically seen as a chance for individual refueling and networking, especially for program directors. However, if several staff members attend a single conference, they can use the occasion as a mini-retreat. They can set aside time during the conference and at home to discuss the implications of conference sessions for their own program's practice. Preparing an abstract for presentation at a conference, like writing an article, can be an opportunity for group reflection on program philosophy, approach, and achievements. At the presentation itself, audience responses are likely to stimulate even more staff analysis of program issues and approaches. Conference attendance and participation can help to build an agency's professional team; avoid duplication of services, by helping programs define their niches in the service system; and give managers an opportunity for collegial support from their peers.

Multi-site research, demonstration, or collaborative training initiatives are generally designed to increase knowledge and understanding in the field as a whole. Reflection, in the form of process evaluation, is typically part of such an initiative. However, staff of individual programs may see requirements for documentation as an unwelcome burden unless they are allowed sufficient time for this responsibility and given regular feedback as data are collected. Participation in a multi-site initiative may bring new resources to a program, in the form of outside technical assistance or consultation. This outside perspective may be particularly valuable since it is likely to draw on broad experience with programs facing similar challenges. In one collaborative research and demonstration initiative, semi-annual site visits included "reflective process interviews" with each staff member and half-day feedback sessions for the entire staff. These sessions provided an opportunity for consultants to give feedback on common themes and issues raised in individual interviews; description of the organizational dynamics of the site; reflection on where the program was compared to its status six months ago; goal setting for the next time period; and team building and support (Als, 1989).

## Conclusion

Staff supervision is a key element in an overall value-driven management system. A supervision process that emphasizes reflection and that is characterized by collaboration and regularity reinforces these values throughout the program. At the same time, supervision must be supported by management—in word and in budget—in order to become and remain a meaningful program element. The kinds of learning and support that occur in reflective supervisory relationships can be encouraged in a variety of program activities, ranging from preparation of staff manuals to participation in multi-site research and demonstration initiatives. It is the program director's responsibility to establish and protect regular supervision for her staff, and to encourage reflection throughout the program. To do this, the director herself needs ongoing support and consultation.

## References

Als, H. 1989. National Collaborative Research Institute for Early Childhood Intervention (NCRI-ECI): Family-focussed developmental care and intervention for the very low birth-weight preterm infant at high risk for severe medical complications and developmental disabilities. US Department of Education, Office of Special Education Grant # H024S9003.

Bateson, MC. 1989. *Composing a Life*. New York: Plume.

Gardner, J. 1990. *Community*. Stanford, CA: Graduate School of Business, Stanford University.

# Bibliography

*Child Care Information Exchange* is a publication that includes articles on supervision and related topics on a regular basis.

Bloom, PJ, Sheerer, M and Britz, J. 1991. *Blueprint for Action: Achieving Center-Based Change through Staff Development.* Lake Forest, IL: New Horizons Educational Consultants and Learning Resources.

Jones, Elizabeth. 1986. *Teaching Adults: An Active Learning Approach.* Washington, D.C.: NAEYC Publications.

The Program for Infant/Toddler Caregivers. 1988. *Visions for Infant/Toddler Care: Guidelines for Professional Caregiving.* Sacramento, CA: California State Department of Education.

# 16

# Management in the South Carolina Resource Mothers' Program: The Importance of Supervision

## Madie A. Robinson

*Madie A. Robinson, Healthy Start, Florence, South Carolina*

In South Carolina's Resource Mothers program, women selected for their personal warmth, successful parenting experience, knowledge of community resources, demonstrated ability to accept responsibility, and evidence of natural leadership work with adolescent mothers from their own community during pregnancy and the infant's first year of life. Resource Mothers are expected to assume the roles of Teacher, Role Model, Reinforcer, Facilitator, and Friend. They fulfill these roles by finding potential participants, negotiating a participation agreement with each adolescent, making closely structured home visits, and establishing relationships with the participant, family, school, and community agencies—all with the goal of reducing infant mortality and supporting the development of maternal and infant health competence.

Within the carefully designed relationship between Resource Mother and pregnant adolescent, warmth and closeness flourish. Resource Mothers often accompany girls to the hospital when they go into labor, even in the middle of the night, and stay with them throughout delivery. Young women typically describe their Resource Mothers as being "always someone to care."

We have found that continuing supervision of Resource Mothers by a masters' level social worker is essential to maintain program standards, provide guidance, and enable Resource Mothers to maximize their "natural helping skills." But as the Resource Mothers Program has moved from demonstration grant status (supported originally by a grant to the Medical University of South Carolina by the Robert Wood Johnson Foundation, to implement the Rural Infant Care Project) to become an established component of South Carolina's Division of Maternal Health, it has not been easy to protect an adequate level of supervision. This article will discuss the blend of selection, training and supervision that we have found necessary to help dedicated Resource Mothers fulfill their complex roles.

## Selection and training of Resource Mothers

The goal of the Resource Mothers Program is to support the development of maternal and infant health competence, through the use of paraprofessionals. To be eligible for employment as a Resource Mother, a woman must demonstrate personal warmth, successful parenting experience, knowledge of community resources, ability to accept responsibility, and evidence of natural leadership. She must also live in the community where she will work, be willing to be contacted at odd hours, have a car available during work hours, and be a high school graduate.

When Resource Mothers began as a pilot project in 1980, we recruited throughout the three-county target area and invested three months in the selection process. We realized that special efforts to get the best qualified people for the positions were important, because the paraprofessionals' success would be based on their ability to relate effectively to a wide range of individuals, on written and spoken language competence, and on other subtle interpersonal skills.

More than 100 people applied for the six Resource Mothers positions available in the pilot project. Applicants provided basic information in writing about their feelings about children, their work, and community experiences. The social worker and pediatric nurse practitioner interviewed applicants initially; promising candidates were then interviewed by the developmental psychologist and certified nurse midwife. Using rating sheets and group discussion, the team as a whole selected the six Resource Mothers.

An intensive six-week training program for the first group of Resource Mothers was designed to teach, reinforce, and enable them to be positive role models as they worked with pregnant adolescents. The curriculum included material on pregnancy, labor and delivery, family planning, nutrition, communication skills, infant stimulation, home visiting techniques, well-child development, community resources, referral skills, and work with extended family. Training emphasized inherent strengths, within both the adolescent and her environment, that could be used to enhance decision-making and the development of life skills.

Currently, training is done on the state level in two two-day sessions each year, to develop skills and allow time for the Resource Mothers, now numbering 16 women in 12 counties, to share expertise. Other training opportunities are available through the Division of Maternal Health and inservice programs of other agencies. When a new Resource Mother is hired, the District Coordinator is responsible for her general orientation and instruction in specific content areas. The statewide training sessions offer an opportunity for a new Resource Mother to form relationships with her colleagues from other counties.

## Supervision of Resource Mothers

As the demonstration phase of the Resource Mothers Program evolved, a masters level social worker, using a "social support" model of supervision, assumed responsibility for weekly supervision of each Resource Mother. The supervisor helped the Resource Mother to understand the principles underlying her work with adolescent mothers, their families, and the health care system, rather than telling the Resource Mother what to do in any given situation. In addition, because the use of paraprofessionals was new in the region's health care system, the supervisor took on the role of liaison between Resource Mothers and professional service providers. The supervisor identified and clarified the Resource Mothers' role within the health care system. She assured professionals and administrators that the goal of the project was to enhance, not to undermine their work, and that Resource Mothers would help pregnant adolescents become better users of established health care services. To make this possible, the supervisor assisted Resource Mothers in identifying barriers to care and in working with and through systems, as well as in supporting and reinforcing adolescents in appropriate behavior.

Now that the Resource Mothers Program is part of the Department of Health and Environmental Control, a State Program Director is responsible for overall supervision and coordination of the program. Four District Coordinator/Supervisors, under the supervision of District Social Work Directors, are responsible for the hiring, training, and day-to-day supervision of Resource Mothers. District Coordinator/Supervisors are also responsible for working with nurses, social workers, nutritionists, health educators, physicians, and other health profession-

> **The supervisor helped the Resource Mother to understand the principles underlying her work, rather than telling the Resource Mother what to do in any given situation.**

> Faced with diminished guidance and support, some Resource Mothers have coped by persuading themselves, consciously or unconsciously, that they can handle difficult situations without supervision.

als to get referrals for Resource Mothers, and to negotiate potential systems barriers. Finally, the District Coordinator/Supervisor may intervene directly in cases that need intensive follow up; she has, in effect, a caseload of her own.

Supervision of Resource Mothers includes monthly group conferences to review patient caseloads, solve problems, and provide continuing education in specific subject areas. The District Coordinator/Supervisor makes one supervisory home visit monthly with each Resource Mother. In individual conferences, held at least monthly, the Coordinator/Supervisor reviews the Resource Mother's entire caseload and helps her to work with selected cases, acquire insights into human behavior and relationships, use resources, and modify systems barriers to the services adolescent mothers need. Conferences focus particularly on identifying patient and family strengths, helping teens understand the need for good maternal and infant health, and resolving specific problems.

The following vignette illustrates the issues that may arise in supervision.

**Kecia delivered her first child, a 5 lb., 8 oz. boy, when she was 16 years old. Kecia lives with her widowed father and three younger siblings; she is expected to handle all household duties as well as care for Johnny. The baby's father is not involved, and this is a problem for Kecia. By almost three months after his birth, Johnny had gained less than a pound and did not seem alert to his surroundings. The nutrition staff at the clinic gave Kecia advice on feeding, but the baby did not gain weight. Mrs. A., the Resource Mother working with Kecia, explained to her the consequences for Johnny of continued failure to thrive. Mrs. A. did not understand why Kecia was not following the nutritionist's directions, even though Mrs. A. repeated them to Kecia during each home visit.**

Here the Supervisor needed to address relationships on several levels. Resource Mothers generally feel so close to program participants that they refer to them as "my girl" and "my baby" when discussing cases with each other. But Mrs. A. and Kecia had not begun to work together until late in Kecia's pregnancy and had not developed, before delivery, a high level of trust. Another issue of trust involved Mrs. A. and the clinic nutritionist. When the Resource Mothers Program became part of the health department, we learned that some professionals were uncomfortable with the idea of paraprofessionals functioning so independently. Paraprofessional Nursing Assistants or Community Health Aides were visible in the clinics, but the Resource Mothers' activities, taking place in homes and in the community, are less visible and may be undervalued.

The Supervisor worked with Mrs. A. to help her consider Kecia's experience as a new mother who had recently lost her own mother, could not count on her baby's father (whom she had previously trusted), and had no real support system for herself. The Supervisor emphasized the need to develop a relationship with Kecia before any other progress was possible. At the same time, the Supervisor emphasized Mrs. A.'s value as a member of the health team concerned about Johnny and Kecia—both to Mrs. A. herself, and to professional team members.

Unfortunately, this model of supervision has been compromised since the Resource Mothers Program became part of the state public health system. District Coordinator/Supervisors have been assigned to provide direct service as social workers in public health clinics. The demands of clinic work reduce supervisors' ability to review regularly and consistently the 60-65 cases carried by each Resource Mother. The time that supervisors have available, especially for individual conferences with Resource Mothers, has decreased, as has their day-to-day accessibility to the Resource Mothers.

Faced with diminished guidance and support, some Resource Mothers have coped by persuading themselves, consciously or unconsciously, that they can handle difficult situations without supervision. The danger, where these energetic, dedicated women are concerned, is not that they will slacken their efforts without supervision, but rather that they will try to do too much.

**Resource Mother B.** was working with Pam, a 16-year-old who was seven months pregnant, anemic, and having multiple family problems, especially with her mother. One night, after an argument and some physical confrontation with another sibling in the home, Pam's mother put her out, with no place to go. Pam called her Resource Mother, who took Pam to her own home for the rest of the night. Although Ms. B. had received training about what to do in situations of abuse and neglect, she did not contact her supervisor. The supervisor first found out what had happened the next day, when Pam's mother called the program, trying to locate her daughter. When the supervisor was finally able, after several tries, to reach the Resource Mother, she learned that Ms. B. and Pam had already gone to the Housing Authority to apply for housing for Pam.

Ms. B. had been doing her best to fill the role of "friend" to Pam. She sought to help the girl but failed to understand the danger in which she put herself during the middle-of-the-night "rescue" or to think the situation through clearly. She did not see the need, at the time, for consultation with her supervisor. It is only regular, individual conferences that give a skilled supervisor time to ask leading questions and carefully probe suspicious-sounding situations.

**Andrea was a 17-year-old experiencing her first pregnancy.** She had strong feelings for Joe, 19, the father of the baby, but was only seeing him off and on. He was seeing other girls. Andrea was so upset that she swallowed 11 prescription pain relief tablets. After she was taken to the emergency room, she called Mrs. C., her Resource Mother, to tell her what happened. There was no harm to the fetus or to Andrea, and she was sent home after some hours of observation. The Resource Mother decided not to inform her Supervisor about the incident immediately, but to wait until her scheduled supervisory conference, later in the week.

Mrs. C. first told her Supervisor about Andrea's gesture in a casual conversation several days after the incident. When the Supervisor asked Mrs. C. why she had not told her about the incident immediately, Mrs. C. replied, "I was going to tell you during our conference. I didn't want to call and bother you over at the clinic—I know you're so busy. Anyway, Andrea said she didn't mean to kill herself, just create a scare." Mrs. C. continued, "I talked to her, and I don't think she needs to go to Mental Health, but maybe get some family counseling."

One has to be very careful in helping paraprofessionals to understand their

> It is only regular, individual conferences that give a skilled supervisor time to ask leading questions and carefully probe suspicious-sounding situations.

## The origins of South Carolina's Resource Mothers Program

In 1981, South Carolina had the highest infant mortality rate in the nation. Six counties in the Pee Dee Region had an infant mortality rate one and one-half times that of the State rate, and 70 percent higher than the national infant mortality rate from 1976-1981. These circumstances were the basis for a four-year demonstration grant awarded in 1980 to the Medical University of South Carolina by the Robert Wood Johnson Foundation, to implement the Rural Infant Care Project. The goal was to lower the Pee Dee perinatal mortality rate to the State rate. The Rural Infant Care Project was jointly managed and implemented by the Medical University, McLeod Regional Medical Center, Pee Dee Area Health Education Center, and the Department of Health and Environmental Control—Pee Dee I Health District.

A component of the Rural Infant Care Project was the Resource Mothers Program. The Resource Mothers Program was piloted in Dillon, Florence, and Marion counties, all of which were poor, rural, and lacking in accessible health care and educational resources. These areas also constituted "high risk pockets" where health problems had been resistant to traditional interventions.

limitations. It is true in many instances that Resource Mothers have a closer working relationship than any professional with many program participants, and that they indeed know a great deal more about participants' everyday situations because they are constantly in and out of their homes. But while Resource Mothers receive some training in counseling patients in various situations, they do not understand all of the dynamics involved in crisis intervention. The Coordinator/Supervisor's responsibility is to help the Resource Mother understand how she fits into the entire service team. The Supervisor can and should acknowledge that the Resource Mother may be the most positive force in an adolescent's life, but the Supervisor must also, supportively but effectively, help the Resource Mother understand the limitations of her role.

Being "professional"—for professionals and paraprofessionals alike—involves calling for consultation and assistance in order to provide participants with the best quality services possible. In this instance, the Supervisor discussed with Mrs. C. what might have happened if Andrea had succeeded in committing suicide, reviewing not only the tragic consequences for Andrea and her family, but also the potential impact on the professional careers of the Resource Mother and Coordinator/Supervisor and on the entire Resource Mother Program.

The two incidents above, and other less dramatic examples, have taught us the dangers of failing to maintain adequate professional supervision in a service program. We are moving toward restoring the weekly individual supervisory conferences that were in place during the demonstration grant phase of our program and are reducing the clinic responsibilities of District Coordinator/Supervisors so that they can be more easily accessible to Resource Mothers.

## Some lessons from experience

South Carolina's Resource Mothers are extremely proud, dedicated, and serious about the work that they do. If they and other paraprofessionals are to be successful within a health care bureaucracy, they need support, flexibility, and supervision. A careful selection process, appropriate training, clearly defined tasks, and professional social work supervision are all factors that we believe have contributed to the successes of South Carolina's Resource Mothers Program. As others look to the Resource Mothers model as an effective, efficient response to a major national health problem, we urge that ongoing training and supervision be recognized as essential to the establishment and maintenance of high program standards and to the achievement of our ultimate goal—healthy and competent mothers and infants.

# 17

## Toward Tenacity of Commitment: Understanding and Modifying Institutional Practices and Individual Responses That Impede Work with Multi-problem Families

**Barbara Fields**

Intensive work with multi-problem families can be immensely satisfying, but it is also emotionally and physically depleting, and at times unrewarding. While the despair and frustration of members of such families have been amply reported, the feelings of clinicians who work with these high-risk infants and their parents have received scant attention. I believe that it is important to look at two sets of feelings that practitioners who work with this population may experience—first, those feelings associated with the administration and supervisory structure of the settings in which the work is done, and second, those feelings that are elicited by children and parents themselves. Many such emotional responses can cause even an experienced clinician a great deal of discomfort, and, if denied, can seriously interfere with treatment. If, on the other hand, we can understand our own feelings and those of our colleagues and supervisees, we may be better able to support each other in the difficult work we do and to serve deeply troubled families with greater compassion and skill.

Because multi-problem families present such an array of difficulties, workers from a variety of disciplines may find themselves in one way or another involved with them. Thus, clinicians who work primarily with children whose biogenetic endowment is compromised are seeing an increasing number of organically impaired infants born to multi-problem families. Not only must additional services be provided for these infants and parents, but professionals in such fields as special education, occupational therapy, physical therapy, nursing, and speech, language and hearing also need to expand their conceptual and clinical framework in order to address the problems these families face. At the same time, many of us in the mental health professions are realizing the need to deepen our conceptual and clinical understanding of multi-problem families, particularly since we now realize that traditional psychological and psychiatric interventions have failed at the most basic level, that of developing and sustaining meaningful contact with members of these families.

Unfortunately, the service providers who are faced with meeting the range of interrelated developmental and parental needs presented by multi-problem families seldom have training beyond that required by their specific discipline, and have little access to new advances in developmental and

*Barbara Fields*, New York, New York

clinical formulations. They have, in particular, little formal preservice training or on-the-job guidance in recognizing, understanding, and ultimately using the powerful feelings that inevitably accompany work with this population.

## Confronting an array of difficulties

As service providers working with children from birth to three, we are charged with the challenging task of developing and implementing programs in a range of primary care settings for infants and their families.

These infants and parents fall roughly into two categories, with a great deal of crossover between groups. In one group are babies whose biogenetic endowment renders them developmentally vulnerable. Parents of these children are faced with the critical task of promoting optimal growth in their handicapped infant while concurrently attempting to work through their own complex responses to feelings of defect and deficit in themselves and their child.

In the second group are infants who are considered developmentally at risk due to serious limitations in their caregiving environment. These infants usually are referred for preventive intervention or for alleviation of the symptoms of developmental stress, distortion and delay they already exhibit as babies and toddlers. (Fraiberg, 1980, Provence and Naylor, 1983, Greenspan, et al., 1987). Additionally, these children may be organically impaired. The children in this second group belong to what are commonly described as multi-problem families. These families, designated also as hard-to-reach or multi-risk, are characterized by an array of individual, parental and environmental problems which call for new and creative approaches to meet their multiple, interrelated psychological and concrete needs.

As I have suggested, feelings associated with our work are of two types, related to the administrative and supervisory structure of the setting in which we work, and to the children and families we serve in one form or another. These latter responses may have to do with the feelings, impulses and ideas that are elicited in the clinician by the case material or by behavior reflecting the child's or parent's inner life. I will describe some of my own responses to a particular parent that contributed to an unsuccessful outcome because I did not understand them well enough at the time. Before I do that, however, I want to discuss feelings related to administrative and supervisory practice which also elicit responses that can profoundly affect our work.

## Institutional practices

It is my contention that unquestioned institutional practices contribute all too frequently to feelings of futility and anger on the part of staff. Interestingly, clinicians' responses to the institutions in which they work are similar to feelings of hopelessness, helplessness, anger and despair expressed, usually behaviorally, by the families they treat. These responses are also similar to feelings of anger and futility we may have toward and about a particular child and parent at various points in the treatment process. (J. Fields, Yorburg and Turkel, 1970, Rigamer and J. Fields, 1971).

It is generally agreed that certain elements in any program have enormous influence on the overall attitudes and morale of staff. Provence and Naylor describe staff support as taking several forms including intellectual stimulation, an atmosphere of intellectual inquiry and curiosity, the ability to respond promptly to staff members' distress about problems with a parent or child, and provision of channels to address the inevitable strain that arises among people working together.

In most settings, however, inordinate and pressing demands upon administrators force them to subordinate their efforts to provide the climate of intellectual inquiry, training and empathy with staff concerns that Provence and Naylor suggest is vital to effective intervention. Beyond this, recent advances in the understanding of developmental processes have not yet been well integrated into the training components of many primary care settings. But with multi-problem families, the ability to conceptualize issues and treatment approaches is particularly essential for staff, adding a dimension that increases theoretical and clinical mastery. Without this dimension, staff feels at sea, puzzled by issues they cannot understand or grasp, and dependent upon traditional interventions that at best address a few aspects of a multi-faceted problem.

As early as 1970, J. Fields et al. drew attention to another administrative dilemma—that the time needed for staff to understand and assess each family in depth, and to provide meaningful intervention over time, is incompatible with the inordinately high caseloads and extensive paperwork many agencies require. Seventeen years later, there have been no apparent changes in agency practice, and the question Fields and his colleagues posed then is equally relevant today. Since most of the families we see require more, not less time to address their multiple needs, why is it almost a matter of unquestioned policy to assign more cases to staff members than they can possible manage?

As Fields, et al. suggest, one result of such practice is a staff that is often harried, overwhelmed, dissatisfied and unable to utilize their individual talents and knowledge. Administrators are forced to focus their energies on meeting the demands of funding sources and spend whatever time is left over meeting a variety of crises. Staff development and support necessarily falls lower and lower on their list of priorities. Supervisors are responsible for more cases than they can handle. In my experience, in all but a few demonstration settings, supervisory conferences of necessity consisted of highlighting the most critical aspects of eight or nine cases rather than an in-depth scrutiny of their theoretical and clinical issues. Case conferences as well tended to focus on management rather than on deepening conceptual and clinical understanding.

Additionally, the bureaucracy beyond the immediate work setting may negatively affect staff morale. For example, departments in many hospitals are run like small fiefdoms with little communication between disciplines. A physical therapy department without a social worker can refer a parent for mental health intervention—but then what? Unless the physical therapist and the mental health worker communicate informally or convene a special case conference, they often operate independently of each other, limiting effective intervention. Further, this fragmented treatment approach runs counter to new advances in developmental and clinical formulations that see development as involving multiple, interrelated pathways and needs that are most effectively addressed by a well integrated approach on the part of the individual practitioner and by the interdisciplinary team.

Caseloads that are too large, inadequate time for assessing and understanding each family in depth, insufficient intellectual stimulation, or training that does not encompass more recent formulations, and supervision that tends to be superficial, crisis oriented and limited in conceptual scope, along with a fragmented treatment approach, lead to the demoralization of both senior and junior staff. Feelings evoked are those of personal and professional inadequacy, incompetence, dissatisfaction, anger, helplessness, and despair.

Painful as these feelings are in themselves, the lack of their validation by administrators and supervisors can lower staff morale further. And it is often the case that overwhelmed administrators and supervisors, responsible for the overall program, feel criticized when negative feelings are voiced and therefore discourage their expression. Conflicts which arise among members of various disciplines as they attempt to work together can be another source of stress. These conflicts derive in part from honest disagreements about the best course to pursue in a given case, but just as often

**The time needed for staff to understand and assess each family in depth, and to provide meaningful intervention over time, is incompatible with the inordinately high caseloads and extensive paperwork many agencies require.**

involve territorial or competitive feelings which are difficult to sort out in the best of circumstances and almost impossible to resolve in the climate described.

## Psychological factors influencing effectiveness

The discussion so far has focused on those elements in administrative structure and practice which can contribute positively or negatively to staff feelings of competence and selfworth. I want to turn now to psychological factors that have equal impact in affecting the overall effectiveness of staff.

It is my impression, shared by others (Rigamer and Fields; Fraiberg; Provence and Naylor), that these more elusive factors stem from countertransference issues that staff encounters in work with high-risk families. The term "countertransference" is meant by the authors cited, and by this author, to include all emotional responses on the part of the clinician toward or about the individual he or she treats. Further, it is generally agreed that countertransference, in this broad interpretation, is a factor in all levels of intervention in work with young children and their families, from home visits geared to the transmission of parenting skills to psychotherapy. Countertransference critically affects outcome. As Rigamer and Fields specifically note, the clinician's emotional responses require continual self-monitoring and attempts at self awareness. Indeed the clinician can make good use of these responses in work with multi-problem families but only to the extent that he or she is aware of them.

For example, some years ago I was assigned as the social worker for an 18-year-old woman whose baby was enrolled in the program in which I worked. Nancy was an angry and defiant young woman, prone to aggressive and sexual acting out. She tended to view people as all good or all bad, and had marked mood swings, reflecting a relatively primitive inner life and level of functioning. Many early developmental tasks had been poorly negotiated or not achieved. These traits also were reflected in Nancy's behavior toward her infant son. While she was not especially physically abusive, Nancy was extremely neglectful and both rejecting and overstimulating, depending on her mood. She found it difficult to allow David even the autonomy to explore a toy in his own way—he was to explore it "the right way," i.e., her way or not at all. Further, although Nancy presented herself in crisis after crisis and seemed beset by inner and external stress, she frustrated all attempts to help her. She was unable, for instance, to keep appointments that would confer eligibility for public assistance, necessitating beginning the entire process again and again.

Soon after we met, Nancy began extolling my virtues to everyone in our center, to the extent that some of the other mothers began to express envious and competitive feelings. Needless to say, the tables soon turned and I became as despised as I had been admired, and Nancy did not hesitate to express these feelings about me either! What I had done, if anything, to incur such intense rage is still unclear. The important fact is that after my initial attempts to sort out Nancy's seemingly sudden change in feelings were met by continued hostility, I began to distance myself emotionally and even physically from her, avoiding going to the infant room, which I supervised, when I knew she would be there. First of all, I am embarrassed to admit, my pride was hurt. Although I had thought I had been well aware of the quixotic nature of Nancy's positive feelings for me, I realized a part of me had really warmed to her many compliments. More significantly, issues in my own history and inner life made me unrealistically afraid of Nancy. Her unpredictability, loose boundaries, highly charged emotions, and primitive level of functioning stirred up a complexity of uncomfortable feelings. My defense against these feelings was to distance myself and to view Nancy's situation and any possibility for change as hopeless. Not only did I view Nancy through this darkened lens, the entire staff began to complain about the futility of treating her and her child (an idea used by all of us to further justify minimum engagement). If I had been more aware, I might, at this point, have been an advocate for Nancy with day care staff, helping them to understand the roots of her behavior and planning with them some alternative, possibly more effective interventions with this young woman and her little boy.

It is important to mention that initially I was only half aware of my discomfort and only somewhat more aware of my wish to avoid Nancy. In addition, because of the urgency that surrounds our work, I had seven or eight other mothers who also needed my attention. I found myself thinking less and less about Nancy and increasingly about other, less nettlesome mothers and babies. More honestly stated, this shift in focus became a defense against scrutinizing my responses to Nancy. It took time to sort out the feelings described, and longer to understand how they might have interfered with treatment. The major point is that while it is uncertain whether or not Nancy could have formed a therapeutic relationship, my feelings may have contributed as much to the therapeutic stalemate as did Nancy's own characteristics.

## Awareness of feelings: A catalyst for growth

I have described my experience with Nancy for two reasons. First, and most important, although I was unable to establish the kind of relationship with her that might have led to even incremental change, I learned about aspects of myself that became a catalyst for personal and professional growth. I have since worked with a number of mothers whose problems were similar to Nancy's. My work with them has been more successful not simply because I have become more clinically sophisticated or have additional years of experience, but because I am more aware of the inner forces which shape my particular responses toward these young women. Without careful monitoring of our own responses, including an awareness of the kinds of defenses we are likely to use in warding off uncomfortable or painful feelings, it is difficult, if not impossible, to distinguish between families with whom a therapeutic relationship truly cannot be forged despite all our best efforts, and those whose treatment is impeded by countertransference issues that are not well understood or even within our conscious awareness.

It is equally important, however, to consider institutional practices as they contribute to, and in some instances actually support typical countertransference problems encountered in work with hard-to-reach families. As Rigamer and Fields point out, in settings where the pressure for service and the urgency of need is great, it becomes especially easy to withdraw from individuals who are trying, or whose problems are chronic and seemingly "refractory to treatment." Unable to grasp the real nature of their problems and/or unaware of our own responses, we begin to share the hopelessness of those we seek to treat, become frustrated or angry at what looks like their stubborn resistance to our intervention, and feel there is little we can do. We begin to feel relieved when family members fail to keep their appointments and view their "recalcitrance" as further proof that intervention is futile. This sense of futility is often supported by the supervisor whose sense of annoyance with the therapist is only once removed from the family itself (Rigamer and Fields). Both therapist and supervisor eventually relegate such families to the bottom of their list with the tacit agreement that they are "unworkable." If this state of affairs continues, the family will resist whatever level of intervention is offered or will remove their child from the program. This all-too-frequent scenario contributes to a loss of self-esteem (not being able to adequately do one's job), and a sense of hopelessness, helplessness and anger in practitioner, supervisor, and administrator,

> **In settings where the pressure for service and the urgency of need is great, it becomes especially easy to withdraw from individuals who are trying, or whose problems are chronic and seemingly "refractory to treatment."**

> It is important for trainees to hear about their supervisor's experience—blunders as well as success—and of the supervisor's struggle to make sense of the problems she or he faced in learning to work productively with troubled families.

who begin to blame each other and the family for the unsuccessful outcome. Since members of multi-problem families struggle with similar feelings, long before intervention is officially deemed a failure a pervasive sense of futility has most likely become an unacknowledged accompaniment to the therapeutic work, precluding the sense of competency and efficacy we want to feel about ourselves as clinicians and to impart to the families we treat.

## Is improvement possible in the "real" world?

Most of us do not work in demonstration projects. On the contrary, we try to serve multi-problem families in programs that themselves face multiple problems. Given the fact that meeting institutional, administrative and clinical demands takes up most available working time, how can administrators promote an atmosphere of intellectual inquiry and emotional support among staff? How can administrators prepare themselves and their trainees to be more aware of their responses to agency presures and to participating families? How can administrators help themselves and their trainees to cope with these feelings more successfully?

We do know that a climate of openness is conducive to promoting both intellectual curiosity and the expression of attitudes, feelings, and ideas. Creating such a climate presents a challenge to administrators, but I think it is a challenge that can be met, at least on some levels and to some extent. For example, I urge senior staff to think about how new advances in theoretical and clinical understanding can be conceptualized for staff in ways that apply to the problems they bring to supervisors or case conferences about a specific parent or child.

I also recommend that supervisors become more open in recounting to those they supervise, their own experiences with hard-to-reach families. The critical nature and special pressures inherent in our work often produce feelings of vulnerability in staff about their own knowledge and skills. In addition, as my experience with Nancy suggests, some of our responses to these families can cause a fair amount of discomfort. For both these reasons, it is important for trainees to hear about their supervisor's experience—blunders as well as success—and of the supervisor's struggle to make sense of the problems she or he faced in learning to work productively with these troubled families. In such a climate, less experienced staff might feel freer to ask questions and to express their own feelings, attitudes and ideas without fear of judgment. Just as traditional interventions with multi-problem families need to be modified or expanded in scope, traditional modes of supervision also may need modifying with the aim of facilitating the kind of dialogue between supervisor and supervisee that helps the latter to understand and feel comfortable about a range of responses. The degree to which this can be accomplished depends in large part upon the supervisor's ability to accept disturbing feelings in him or herself and others.

I want to end on a note of encouragement. Probably the most helpful analogy I can make to work with multi-problem families is that of raising children. This analogy rests not on the attributes of the individuals we are trying to help, but on the degree of commitment needed. Just as parents must be able to sustain their relationship with their growing children through difficult emotional times, so clinicians need to pursue their relationship with members of multi-problem families despite moments when a complex of negative or ambivalent feelings threatens the integrity of the therapeutic bond. This commitment is in itself rewarding. The tenacity of this commitment can often bring, in its wake, meaningful environmental and psychological change.

# References

Fields, JH, Yorburg, L, Turkel, M. 1970. The quest towards treating the untreatable. Presented at the Philadelphia Meeting of the American Association of Psychiatric Services for Children.

Fraiberg, S. (Ed.) 1980. *Clinical Studies in Infant Mental Health: The First Year of Life.* New York: Basic Books.

Greenspan, S, Wieder, S, Nover, R, Lieberman, A, Lourie, R, Robinson, M. 1987. *Infants in Multi-risk Families: Case Studies in Preventive Intervention.* Madison, Connecticut: International Universities Press.

Provence, S, and Naylor, A. 1983. *Working With Disadvantaged Parents and Their Children.* New Haven and London: Yale University Press.

Rigamer, E and Fields, JH. 1971. Hopelessness and the therapist. Presented at the American Academy of Child Psychiatry, Boston.

# 18

# A Seminar for Supervisors in Infant/Family Programs: Growing versus Paying More for Staying the Same

## Judith Bertacchi and Frances M. Stott

*Judith Bertacchi, The Virginia Frank Child Development Center of the Jewish Family and Community Service*

*Frances M. Stott, Erikson Institute, Chicago, Illinois*

*"There was that law of life so cruel and so just which demanded that one must grow, or pay more for remaining the same."*—Norman Mailer, *The Deer Park*

Leaders in the "helping professions"—especially women—struggle with experiencing anger and establishing and enforcing rules. Making judgments, setting limits, and dismissing staff members do not come easily, but they are part of a program director's obligation to ensure good service to program participants. Leaders in the helping professions commonly feel isolated, without peers to share their pain and difficulties. Few have had training in the process of intervention with staff or the relationships involved.

Recognizing these problems, Linda Gilkerson, Co-Director of Erikson Institute's Irving B. Harris Infant Studies Program, conceived the idea of a seminar for people in supervisory positions in programs serving infants, toddlers and their families. For the past three years, we have invited eight to ten administrators or program directors from early intervention, child care, family support, and hospital-based programs in the Chicago area to participate in a nine-session supervision seminar. The sessions are held every other week on Friday afternoons; the atmosphere is informal, and members bring refreshments.

The supervision seminar reflects Erikson Institute's conviction that good supervision is one of the keys to developing competence in students and to establishing and maintaining quality in service programs. The supervisory process is intensive and time-consuming. The supervisory relationship is a mechanism for teaching, solving problems, and helping supervisees make both "outer" changes in their skills and "inner" changes in their image and use of the professional self. In most programs serving young children and families, supervisors must also evaluate the job performance of supervisees and make judgments about the promotion, reassignment, or dismissal of staff members. As co-leaders of the seminar for supervisors, we have crafted a model based on psychodynamic theory, supervisory tenets drawn from the professional literature, and principles derived from clinical practice with families and young children. The seminar addresses leaders' isolation by providing a forum for exchange. It uses a process model to help directors broaden their professional identity to include new competencies.

As co-leaders we assist those responsible for supervising the daily practice of others to examine such issues as:

- understanding oneself and using oneself as a vehicle for good practice;
- learning how to establish and maintain a supervisory relationship, particularly in difficult circumstances; and
- learning how to ensure that professional goals of staff match program goals.

We designed the seminar on the assumption that once members have experienced the process, they will be better able to make supervisory and administrative decisions on their own, or know how to get consultation for themselves built into their program budgets. Our experience with the first seminar groups has confirmed this hypothesis.

The seminar does not teach the tenets of supervision directly. Although we provide readings and a bibliography on supervision, these are not required reading and are brought up during the seminar only if one of the group members chooses to do so. The focus of the group is on problem solving. We model leadership by dealing honestly and forthrightly with issues that arise inevitably in the work of supervising staff and, in some cases, administering a program.

Interestingly, the work problems that group members present typically have very little to do with the dynamics of families or children being served, but involve, rather, the struggles that supervisors and supervisees experience within agency or institutional systems. Of course, families are in our discussions—indirectly. The emotions that are connected to the struggles and pain of families with problems or compromised infants permeate our working atmosphere. And families' struggles are reflected in supervisors' struggles with staff. We see a series of parallel processes going on.

The following vignettes (with details changed to protect confidentiality) illustrate the process of the seminar for supervisors. Basic themes are raised in the vignettes—including the mutual sharing and clarification of expectations, the role of the supervisor as change agent, the handling of strong emotions and conflict, and distinctions between supervision and consultation.

## Eileen, Annie, and Helen

Eileen, a member of the seminar, supervises a large staff in a successful urban corporate day care center for employees whose children are 6 weeks to 5 years of age. In the first meeting of the seminar, she presented for discussion a problem involving a work violation by one of her staff members. She was pressed for time, she said, because the problem demanded an immediate intervention and possible sanctions.

Eileen told us that Annie, an experienced assistant teacher in the infant room, had begun to harass Helen, the newly hired young head teacher. The harassment, according to Helen, involved verbal slurs about Helen's competence, usually made within earshot of other staff members. Annie also made sarcastic comments directly to Helen, especially when Helen was picking up one of the babies that Annie thought should be left alone for awhile. These verbal attacks had begun to escalate to veiled threats to Helen both in and out of the day care setting. Annie also had begun first to avoid, and then to refuse to work with individual babies when Helen differed with a care plan initiated by Annie.

Helen had demanded of Eileen that Annie be disciplined, as she was fast becoming both afraid of Annie and enraged at her. Other experienced day care staff members had also approached Eileen and had given her their ideas of how this now impossible situation should be handled. Several had confided their suspicions that Annie might have an addiction problem (but never on the job!). Everyone knew that Annie had a young child with severe developmental disabilities, for whose care she was responsible when she was not working. Annie's old colleagues had begged Eileen to urge, if not force Annie to use the Employee Assistance Program that was available to her as a staff member.

Eileen said that after she gathered the facts from Helen privately, she called Annie into

> **The focus of the seminar for the supervisors is on problem solving. We model leadership by dealing honestly and forthrightly with issues that arise inevitably in the work of supervising staff and administering a program.**

> Valuing change intellectually is very different from being faced with personal issues that we are not aware of, that others are aware of, and that are impeding our work.

her office, reviewed the details with her, and suspended her for a few days. Annie left Eileen's office self-possessed and without saying a word. When Helen learned through the center grapevine about the disciplinary action, she asked to see Eileen and demanded a stronger sanction. She felt the suspension was "too little" for "too much."

At this point in Eileen's exposition of the problem in the seminar, one of the leaders interrupted and began to ask questions to gather more details. Eileen told us that Annie saw Helen as having an "attitude" problem and thought Helen saw her as "lowly." Using dynamic terms, we re-framed Annie's feelings for Helen as a powerful negative transference. We took this opportunity to teach the group about the broadest meaning of "transference"—that is, the projection of relationships from the past onto a person in the present, regardless of whether such a correspondence is logical, deserved, sensible, etc. We emphasized that this is an *unconscious* process at work, beyond a person's control.

We went on to explore Helen's position as a victim. Since Helen was clearly the target of unjustified and upsetting behavior, we wondered why Helen had not stood up to Annie directly, as well as (rightfully) reporting this conduct immediately to her supervisor. This work problem now clearly involved two players. Helen's passivity toward Annie may in fact have escalated the conflict. It became clear to us that whatever happened in the future, Helen and Annie should not be together in the present.

Before a solution to the problem could be developed, we needed to help Eileen explore and review her own alliances and allegiances. As Eileen shared more information with us, she became increasingly angry. From our point of view as outsiders, Eileen no longer seemed to be a neutral problem-solver. In a moment of great honesty, Eileen said that if there were no personnel or legal restraints to be considered, she would feel like firing Annie on the spot. She followed this revelation by increasingly judgmental statements, such as: "We're supposed to be adults here ... jobs are not being done ... children are not being well served ... I do not want Helen to quit; it is damned difficult to get trained people to commit to this work."

Fran intervened here (as we will discuss later, our two-leader model allows one leader to question and probe while the other is available to monitor group process and protect group members) and asked Eileen, "How did you start your career?" Eileen responded, slowly and thoughtfully, "I began as a young head teacher in a day care center." Fran went on, "So you identify with Helen." Again, with great honesty, Eileen said, "I guess I do. I hadn't even thought of that."

Fran's gentle but direct question had invited Eileen to slow down and spend some time reviewing her own feelings and identifications. The major supervisory issue we were looking at as a group involved a supervisor's need, in many situations, to gather facts thoroughly, but also to listen carefully to the supervisee's unspoken dilemma, conflict, or problem. The supervisor must also review and evaluate his or her own circumstances and feelings before making a decision. In this situation, Eileen's personal and professional identification with one of the staff could have resulted in an incomplete or biased analysis of the problem. By intervening while Eileen described the situation as she saw it, Fran invited Eileen to become introspective as she reviewed her own identifications (transferences) with staff. Eileen was momentarily startled and embarrassed, then reflective.

We reminded the group that valuing change intellectually is very different from being faced with personal issues that we are not aware of, that others *are* aware of, and that are impeding our work. The supervisory struggle among Eileen and her two staff members was now taking place between Fran and Eileen. Fran, as consultant, could see Eileen's problem. Her goal was to assist the supervisee (Eileen), within the context of a supportive relationship, so that internal, and later external, changes could occur. Fran acted to help Eileen change her *perspective* so that she could then use a different *strategy* in her supervisory relationship. Fran took the risk, which is inherent in every supervisory practice, of entering and even creating conflict in the present, and of keeping conflict in the spotlight so that learning and change could proceed.

This review and insight brought Eileen closer to a neutral stance. She then shared even more information about Annie's history. Eileen told us that Annie had had a stressful childhood and a troubled adolescence, marked by many losses, which culminated in the birth of her disabled child. Annie also had many strengths, including a will of iron and commitment to her child, her job, and Eileen, who had gone to bat for Annie at the beginning of her employment.

The seminar group began to resist any further disclosure of Annie's history. One member said quite directly, "Talking about Annie makes me feel nervous." Recognizing mounting discomfort in the group, we took time to explain that understanding a person and something of his or her history could help inform supervisory intervention. We introduced the concept of repetition compulsion: the overwhelming urge or need to repeat in the present the same behavior or cycle of behaviors that one constructed in the past in an effort to cope or adapt—regardless of whether these patterns serve the person well in the present. We suggested that a repetition compulsion being played out by Annie and Helen constituted one of the barriers to solving their problem at work. If Eileen could recognize the re-enactment of the past by Annie and/or Helen in the work setting, she could plan a supervisory intervention that would avoid her replaying or being "scripted into an old part" of either Annie's or Helen's enduring issues. We pointed out the difference between a supervisory relationship and a treatment relationship, in which client and therapist contract to work directly on highly personal issues.

As Eileen shared more information about Annie, we could see links between elements of Annie's history that involved acting out, dishonesty, and loss, and her current behavior with Helen. Over and over again, vignettes from Annie's past ended with Annie's "being cut off" or "cutting off." It was this recurrent theme that provided a key to understanding what was needed and that directed our work with Eileen as she moved toward a solution.

We then connected the reality of Annie's job performance to a review of work standards and ethics. We used the group's discussion of work standards in general to move toward a discussion of role boundaries and specific performance standards. The group agreed that Annie was currently unable to act within these parameters, and this time the discussion of her job behavior was based on better knowledge of the people involved. We emphasized that this knowledge was to be used not to "diagnose" or "treat" Annie, but rather to supervise her effectively. But what did this mean to Eileen? She spoke feelingly of her guilt as she once again detailed the many hardships in Annie's life, not the least of which were financial concerns. Plaintively Eileen asked the group, "How do you draw the line between therapist/client, supervisor/supervisee, supervisee/program parent? To what lengths should we go to help?" We pointed out the hazards of replacing the guilt or anger one experiences as a supervisor with the illusion that one can rescue or provide therapy for the supervisee. What is needed, rather, is total respect for the staff member. This is demonstrated by the supervisor's honesty and forthrightness about a problem.

Eileen needed to tell Annie that her current behavior was not acceptable in the workplace, understanding that this behavior was not good for Annie either. Eileen had to realize, believe, and convey to Annie that she was young and could make changes in her life. The Employee Assistance Program was there to help her. Meanwhile, Annie's behavior had to change. If it did not she

**Understanding a person and something of his or her history can help inform supervisory intervention.**

> We do not have the power to "make" people—supervisees, families, or children—function appropriately. To act as if we do is a trap, in any relationship.

could not remain in her job. As supervisor, setting clear limits, clarifying expectations, and giving the struggle and need for change back to Annie, Eileen could perhaps alter the predictable interactions and "endings" set up by this young woman. Eileen would not "cut Annie off" but would rather shift responsibility back to her and give her the opportunity to change her behavior (and interrupt repetition of self-defeating patterns from the past.) Such a respectful and positive supervisory option would both value Annie's potential and, by establishing limits and expectations, protect children and staff.

The group discussed our inability to "make" people function appropriately. We do not have that power with supervisees or with families and their children. To act as if we do is a trap—in any relationship.

### Meanwhile, Polly ......

Polly, another member of the group, was visibly distressed by our focused questioning of Eileen. When we raised this with her at the group's next meeting, she said that she was upset primarily by our questioning of Eileen's motives and identifications within her workplace. She was quite angry at the leaders for taking such an approach. As difficult as this conflict was likely to be for the group so early on, we were pleased to have such strong emotion expressed. We believe that supervisory arenas are an appropriate setting for expressing and considering the range of human emotions—including anger. A quasi-group supervision was now in motion. For not only Polly was angry. Down deep, Eileen was too.

As leaders, we worked to understand the depth of Polly's anger. In our review of this second seminar session, we also reflected on whether we had in fact been too critical, too realistic, too fast. For a little while we too were struggling with self-doubt. (Joint leadership of the seminar, which at first seemed like a luxury, proved important and valuable at every group turning point. Similarly, consultation can offer an administrator/supervisor an arena in which complex and emotion-laden decisions can be processed.) With confidence re-established through our discussion, we made the decision to continue our search with Polly.

When the group met for the third session, Polly's anger was on the table. We asked her why she was so upset by our probing of Eileen's identification with staff. One of the major issues that soon emerged was her fear of being assessed negatively by the people she supervised. Of course assessment goes on all the time on the team (although rarely voiced), between parents and professionals, and between professionals. Polly, a very wise and immensely talented woman, began to get in touch with the connections between her staff's behavior and her own ambivalence about her current job.

The group listened with great interest as the tale of Polly's career history unfolded. Polly had recently made a choice between two jobs, each with its own merits and difficulties. Currently she was struggling with the choice she had made. As the problems involved in taking over her hospital program increased, the job she had rejected looked more appealing. Awash in her ambivalence, Polly was unable to see that her own struggle was affecting her staff. The staff's anger was expressed in a series of unsigned memos that appeared in Polly's mailbox regularly. An example: "There's more trouble here than you will ever know ..." Staff also seemed to be using time as a medium for expressing the lack of cohesion Polly felt: scheduling meetings and team appointments was becoming problematic. Polly was working non-stop to ensure funding for her program and good relationships within the hospital, but nothing she did felt like enough. Staff seemed to show little appreciation for her efforts and certainly no empathy for her predicament.

We suggested that Polly bring up these issues with staff and confront them with the strange variety of indirect communications she was receiving. As our seminar sessions continued, the group became relentless in checking in with Polly at every meeting to see whether she had followed these suggestions. She could not escape! Clearly, to assert herself strongly by announcing that all unsigned memos must stop, and that staff were expected to be on time for meetings, caused Polly considerable anguish. Over time, and with some pain, Polly began to realize that she was having difficulty asserting her expectations because she wasn't sure if, in fact, she did want to "own" the program. We were convinced that until she clarified her expectations with staff she could not be effective or have pleasure in her job, no matter how hard she worked.

Toward the end of the seminar, Polly began to interfere directly with her staff's indirect communication and veiled, if unsubtle, opposition. As she made clear statements about work expectations, staff began to experience Polly's leadership. The norms, guidelines, and limits that she increasingly articulated, first in the seminar and later with staff, were, in essence, the philosophical tenets of a program design that she believed in.

### Eileen, Polly, and company

These two vignettes from the supervision seminar illustrate how issues presented by one member become entwined with the concerns of another. As the nine sessions take place, over the course of about four and one-half months, members continually tell their colleagues about changes or further understandings of their jobs as they occur. At the conclusion of a seminar, members often set a date for a reunion to be held several months later. In Polly's words, "If feelings between people were like strings, the (seminar) room was like a great bowl of spaghetti."

### Reflections on supervision and the seminar for supervisors

In order to work successfully with families, professionals have to be able to establish personal relationships with the people they serve. Not surprisingly, the complexity of professional relationships has emerged as the overriding theme of each of the supervision seminars held over the past three years.

As we saw in the vignettes, difficulties with anger, assertiveness and aggression permeate the seminars. While assertiveness is critical to leadership, people in positions of authority—especially women in the "helping" professions—are clearly not always comfortable with it. While the supervisors who participate in our seminars are generally able to be supportive and empathic to their staff members, they often have trouble recognizing the anger they are experiencing, being clear about expectations, and establishing and enforcing rules so that expectations are met.

Through our comments in the seminar and, most importantly, through the experience of the seminar itself, we offered participants a model of supervision that supports professional growth in staff and furthers the achievement of program goals. Key elements of this model are clear program goals and expectations, an explicit supervisory contract, and an awareness of the purposes and boundaries of the supervisory process.

### *Clear program goals and expectations*

The mission statements of many programs serving infants and their families are framed so broadly that staff cannot hope to meet them. A general goal of "helping families" might be understood variously as involving the transmission of a body of knowledge (or advice) to parents, providing "support" and/or friendship networks, helping to ensure families' well-being during times of stress or crisis, offering job training, or intervening directly to reverse the consequences of maladaptive parenting. Administrators and supervisors must articulate and clarify their program philosophy and goals—and then uphold them. Only when program goals are defined can supervisors help supervisees become more aware of what they really think and believe, and how that squares with program goals. The supervisee is then also in a better position to know

**Through our comments in the seminar and, most importantly, through the experience of the seminar itself, we offer participants a model of supervision that supports professional growth in staff and furthers the achievement of program goals.**

what to expect from program participants. (We should note that when some members of the supervision seminar became aware of the discrepancy between their personal philosophy and the philosophy of their program, they chose to leave their jobs.)

### The supervisory contract

The seminar group spends its first session listening to what seminar members want to accomplish. We, as leaders, share our philosophy, goals, and procedures for the group. This mutual sharing of expectations is the first, necessary step in any supervisory experience. This process is what the social work literature refers to as "contracting" in supervision.

A contract is a binding agreement made between two or more parties. The contract between supervisor and supervisee clarifies the boundaries and responsibilities of this unique relationship. The supervisory contract is the vehicle through which the work of the supervisee is examined, explored, reviewed, pursued, and changed. The supervisor also continually examines, explores, and changes herself. The supervisee is responsible for "bringing in" her work and sharing her ideas and feelings about it. The supervisor is responsible for creating an environment in which such "risky" sharing can take place; she pursues and focuses on conflict, rather than avoiding it. The supervisor thus helps the supervisee achieve new levels of mastery, both of personal conflicts aroused by the work and of skills needed to accomplish the work itself.

We use the construct of the mutual contract throughout the seminar for supervisors at two levels. First, we invite group members to clarify what contractual arrangements they have or have not made with their staff; second, we use the contract model to establish parameters for what goes on in the seminar itself. As we have suggested, many people in supervisory positions in programs serving very young children and families have not themselves had a supervisory experience in which the powerful feelings evoked (and the personal psychological issues *re*-evoked) by such work were addressed. Our seminar offers this experience. And just as a child learns to comfort and regulate himself through a relationship with someone who has regulated and comforted him, supervisors can be more effective if they themselves have experienced a supervisory process that promotes mastery of conflict.

### Purposes and boundaries of the supervisory process

The distinctions between supervision and therapy and between supervision and consultation arose as issues in our group. While at times the seminar took on a therapeutic character, we remained cognizant of the different purposes of supervision and therapy. The therapeutic contract suggests the need to address underlying personality problems; therefore, the therapist may need to make conjectures about underlying dynamics. The purpose of supervision is helping the supervisee to learn how to be her best professional self, in order to provide the best possible service to children and families. While supervision sometimes includes dealing with the supervisee's personality and unconscious dynamics, they are not the focus of supervision. The worker's dynamics are addressed only when they interfere with the work.

When a supervisor makes a psychological interpretation to a supervisee, one must question whether or not the comment is an angry attack disguised as psychotherapeutic "help." A supervisor who is clear about program goals and expectations should be able to set appropriate limits for the supervisee and wonder aloud with the supervisee how to help her within the terms of their contract. The supervisor then brings the problem back into the supervisory situation and thus provides an opportunity for helpful change through the interaction between herself and the supervisee.

This is very different from trying to meet the supervisee's possible need for psycho-

> Only when program goals are defined can supervisors help supervisees become more aware of what they really think and believe, and how that squares with program goals.

therapy. While supervision is designed to help effect "inner" changes in the supervisee, these are limited to changes in skill and in the use of the professional self. Of course, professional growth is likely to have an impact on other aspects of life and on other relationships, but these areas are not themselves an appropriate focus of supervision. Like the therapist, however, the supervisor must find a "stance"—some proper distance from which she can be genuinely empathic yet not over-involved. The supervisor must be able herself to experience strong emotions and to resolve conflicts, so that the supervisory relationship she offers will be able to address the complex and difficult issues with which staff—and families—struggle.

Just as supervision differs from therapy, so it differs from consultation as well. One of the major tasks of the supervisor is to make judgments and evaluate the supervisee's job performance. Consultation, on the other hand, is a voluntary relationship. The consultant does not have the supervisor's evaluative responsibility.

As leaders of the supervision seminar, our role is that of consultants who *model* the supervisory process. In the time-limited nine-session format, the process raises participants' personal issues so quickly and intensely that two leaders are necessary. One leader is free to pursue content issues, while the other is always available to monitor the process. The leaders take turns with these roles, depending on the particular expertise required and the relationships that evolve in the group. The leader who questions, probes, and uncovers conflicts can be forthright and single-minded, knowing that her partner is taking the role of protecting group members. As the leaders review the process of each seminar session together, they are better able themselves to reach a stance toward the group that is empathic but not over-involved. The entire process is designed to allow problems to be pursued, not avoided. Because leaders are open to, and accept, the whole range of feelings, the group members are helped to accept their own feelings, those of their supervisees, and those of the families with whom they work.

We have found that it works well to have as leaders of the seminar an administrator and an academic, both of whom are also clinicians. The administrator brings a working knowledge of service systems and experience supervising staff in a setting where the major goal is providing the best possible service to the client. The academic brings theoretical knowledge and experience supervising students, where the major goal is promoting their learning, including self-knowledge. This combination has helped us to balance our attention in the seminar between administrative concerns and problematic aspects of relationships.

### The supervision seminar as a model for the field

We think that the supervision seminar offers a promising model for the field of work with young children and their families. In their evaluations of the seminar, participants say that the group serves as a needed and valued support. Feelings of anguish and insecurity about making difficult decisions are illuminated and normalized for supervisors by the experience of sharing problems and discovering the commonality of both systemic and personal difficulties.

Obviously each participant takes something different away from the seminar. Some feel validated as supervisors and/or administrators. One member remarked, "The leaders gave me the nerve to change—to assert myself. It's not too much to say this has changed my professional life." Other members use the seminar to take a closer look at their expectations of themselves and of those with whom, and for whom, they work. Still others come to new understandings of the supervisory process as a relationship, rather than simply a mechanism for evaluation; they realize the need to examine what lies underneath behavior.

Many participants pursue continued consultation for themselves once the

> **The purpose of supervision is helping the supervisee to learn how to be her best professional self, in order to provide the best possible service to children and families. The worker's dynamics are addressed only when they interfere with the work.**

seminar is over. One member said, "I wouldn't dream of not providing supervision for my staff, yet it never occurred to me that I needed it for myself." Another concluded, "Before the seminar I didn't think I could afford to pay for consultation. Now I know I can't afford *not* to."

People who work with infants and their families face multiple levels of difficulty. We believe in and respect the desires of these professionals to do meaningful and effective work—and their capacity to grow and change in order to do so.

*The authors would like to thank Linda Gilkerson not only for having a wonderful idea but also for her insightful comments on an earlier draft of this article.*

# Appendixes

# Appendix A

# Supervision and Mentorship

## A Qualitative Study of Early Intervention Practitioners, Child Care Professionals and Public Agency Supervisors in Maryland

### EDK Associates

### Learning through supervision and mentorship

The effectiveness of programs designed to improve developmental outcomes for very young children and their families depends heavily on the competence of front-line staff. In recognition of this, **ZERO TO THREE/** National Center for Clinical Infant Programs has made training of practitioners who work in a variety of roles with infants, toddlers, and their families one of the chief priorities of their organization.

**ZERO TO THREE** is currently involved in a project designed to improve the quality of supervision and mentorship arrangements in the development of practitioners in the field. As part of that project they commissioned EDK Associates to conduct focus group research to deepen our understanding of the meaning of supervision and mentorship for practitioners in the field and assess how these training mechanisms are used in different professional settings.

### Methodology

Focus group discussions are used in communications research to explore how people approach issues and problems. They provide the texture, language, and psychological understanding needed in the development of materials to communicate ideas in a way that will be receptive to the audience you are trying to reach.

Using an open, unstructured format allowed us to see how people think and talk about mentorship and supervision without framing the issue for them. It also provided an opportunity to see if **ZERO TO THREE**'s preliminary analysis of supervision, which identifies reflection, collaboration, and regularity as central dimensions of supervision, is shared by practitioners in the field.

The study was designed to explore similarities and differences in the meaning and value of supervision and mentorship across four different groups in the infant/family field:

1) Early intervention practitioners (I), working in programs for infants and toddlers with disabilities or at risk of developmental problems, who have had some social work, clinical psychology, or other "mental health" training;

2) Early intervention practitioners (II) who have not had "mental health" training;

3) Infant/toddler child care professionals—lead teachers working in licensed day care facilities;

4) Public agency supervisors of employees working with multirisk families.

All four groups were conducted in Maryland to assure that the social and political context was held constant. The average group size was eight participants. The groups were recruited by **ZERO TO THREE** staff.

## I. Setting the context

### A. Agreement on basic principles

A consensus has been developing around principles believed to lead to quality in infant/family programs. **ZERO TO THREE** pulled together a list of convictions reflected, among other places, in the accreditation standards for child care programs of the National Association for the Education of Young Children and in the specifications of requests for proposals issued by federal and state agencies serving diverse populations.

Each focus group began work by evaluating the following six goals/principles that define the context for what leads to quality in infant and family programs, to determine whether there was agreement with these goals and the extent to which these principles are actually applied.

## Basic principles

1. Services for infants, toddlers and their families must be specially designed for this population in order to be developmentally appropriate. They cannot be scaled-down versions of programs for older children.

2. Infants and toddlers must be understood and served within the context of their families.

3. Families are the constants in a child's life; the job of the professional is to assist families in supporting children's development.

4. Services to infants, toddlers and their families must be individualized to respect (and build on) unique constitutional, developmental, and cultural differences.

5. Service coordination should be available to ease families' access to the range of services they require.

6. Policy and practice should recognize and build on the capacities, resilience, and resourcefulness of children and families.

Basically all four focus groups acknowledged that these six principles were important in theory, but they had some reservations when it came to practice. The first concern revolved around the role of parents and family and signalled an undercurrent of ambivalence toward parents that would characterize later discussions. The second concern had to do with the lack of resources to implement these principles.

Support for serving infants within the context of their families (statement #2) depended on whether one subscribed to a "medical model" or a "family-centered" model. This difference in perspective was strongest within the group of public agency supervisors.

*"Well it depends on the service that you are providing for them. . . .[Moderator: Can you think of an example?] Okay let me think of something medical, Down syndrome. I look at it from the perspective of what may be available for that child."* **Social service supervisor**

*"I'm not going to pick on the health department . . . the infant or toddler was seen as the patient and they were taken out of the context of their families, and as social workers we came in, and were looking at a broader picture. There was this communication [problem] between workers because of the difference of perspective".* **Social service supervisor, child services.**

*"Agree but it isn't always practical . . . Should be, I agree with that part but context isn't always that apparent. [later] One of the things I don't like about my job is being powerless to bring the main players [the parents] into the picture. [Moderator: "Are you powerless?"] At the moment."* **MSW working in a therapeutic nursery.**

*"I try to learn about the family from the social worker but I rarely see the family."* **Ph.D., Clinical psychology**

Participants who were in agreement with the principle of serving infants within the context of their families expressed frustration that it was increasingly unrealistic since it required resources. Many participants working in early intervention said that home visits are discouraged because they are very costly. Some people try to work around that, but it is an uphill battle.

There was also strong sentiment for the recognition that the statement "Families are the constants in a child's life" (#3) was not completely accurate—the family is not always the constant in a child's life. **In addition to questioning the accuracy of the statement, objections were voiced in a way indicating the speaker might feel that her role was being diminished by this assertion.**

*"The family of an infant isn't always the 'family'—the primary context is often nurses and therapists."* M.D., psychiatric needs assessment of infants and toddlers

*"Some families aren't the constant of a child's life. The children I see in protective services, the parents aren't there emotionally and sometimes physically. They aren't there for them. In theory they should be, and obviously the professional would have an easier time dealing with the child and the child's problem, and helping the parent to handle it."* Supervisor in child protective services

*"Working with children with AIDS you see other people need to step in. Family members die or become too ill to take care of the children. Family context is shifting all the time. The thing that remains constant is the care provider."* MSW working with chronically ill children

*"School is often the constant for emotionally disturbed children—my school lost 11 of its teachers, so the predictable environment is now chaos and very difficult." (Several people nod in agreement).* MSW, play therapist

Most focus group participants acknowledged that individualized care that respects developmental and cultural differences (Statement #4) is ideal but unrealistic. Six out of eight participants in the early intervention group with some mental health training said individualized care was very hard to deliver. One woman in the child care group said "This shoots pretty high," and the rest of the group agreed. The public agency supervisors stressed that there are few resources to make this principle real.

*"It's the ideal. I wish that every child could be guaranteed that but I don't see how society can do it."* Community health nurse, supervisor in Department of Health

*"If you're going to provide services to as many infants and toddlers as you can, the very basic area that needs to be addressed I would imagine would be language. Beyond that I don't know how far any group can go, as far as the money will allow, but given that restraint I would imagine that at least language would be an area that would have to be addressed."* Supervisor, child services

### B. The joys and hardships of working with infants, toddlers and their families

Most of the participants had planned to work with children but the focus on very young children—infants and toddlers—happened by accident. Most enjoyed their jobs. The complains they expressed focused on too heavy caseloads, administrative overload, and lack of resources.

When asked what was the hardest thing about working with infants, toddlers and their families, group members focused on parents. Supervisors in public agencies and day care workers were more likely to see themselves in potential conflict with parents than early intervention practitioners. Some participants were disgusted with the parents' lack of responsibility. Others focused on the parents' neediness, lack of concern, or demands. Some were hostile.

*"Some of us really do have no use for parents."* MSW, hospital children's center

*"Meeting parents' expectations. Every parent would like to have special attention given to every baby. We can't do it."* Infant worker in child development center

*"They become your children. You sometimes see these children differently than the parents. When you need to come together to work for the good of the child sometimes it's very stressful for the parents to deal with the things you see they don't want to see."* Day care worker in toddler program

*"I get really upset when I hear about a drug mother who's having her fifth baby. I don't see any reason for it, I mean that's just my personal opinion."* Supervisor, public agency

*"I know a lot of parents who don't see anything wrong with their kids. If their kids are having developmental delays or even some physical problems, y'know they'll think, it'll all just kind of work itself out."* Supervisor, public agency

Early intervention practitioners also expressed frustration but showed more understanding and tolerance for the parent's behavior. When the moderator indicated any criticism of parents these two groups (especially those with mental health training) were quick to come to the parents' defense.

They asserted that the parents were ultimately the best therapists for their children and that it would be hard to make progress without their involvement. They pointed out that their job was to figure out how to make this happen. The goal of intervention was to build on the parents' strengths, and their task was to determine how to get parents to see they could help their child.

The participants refused to describe this part of their job as a "challenge" or a "hardship" and preferred to call it a goal. They did not deny that this goal was not always easy to achieve but they did express understanding for why this was so.

*"Hardest cases I have are usually where the parent is so needy and clearly the parent never got what he or she needed growing up . . . they can't really begin to reach out and give to the child."* MSW, hospital children's center

*"One of the hardest things is coming in at such a crucial point. The children are so young that a lot of families haven't accepted the child's diagnosis of disability yet, so you are coming in at a time when it is very new, so I think support [for parents] is very important."* Masters in special education, homebased teaching with children with disabilities

*"Parents really are the best therapists for their child if you can uncover what their strengths are."* MSW, play therapist

*"A lot of what you are doing with parents is selling them on their kids (and on themselves). It's not so hard to do."* MSW/occupational therapist working with children with disabilities

Perhaps these practitioners were more sensitive to parents' lack of emotional development because their intervention is aimed at not repeating the cycle of emotional or physical neglect.

*"What could go wrong is what caused their parents to be where they are right now so it makes it easier to connect with the parents."* MSW working in a therapeutic nursery

They have experience with seeing parents labeled "hopeless" by other institutions turn around.

*"I learned this from experience seeing parents who I was told by social services cannot parent, for a variety of reasons, abuse, whatever. Given the kind of services we could provide at that time because we had the money . . . we were able to get some families really functioning in a way that they would respond to their child, the child could respond to them."* MSW, play therapist

There is also a lot of joy in working with infants, toddlers, and their families. The joy comes from seeing growth in *both* the children and their parents. When asked about the joys of working with this population they became animated. They told of recent cases that went well or focused on the importance of little steps leading to long term change. They clearly felt that what they did made a difference and that after a rough start the parents thanked them for their efforts.

## C. The joys of working with infant/family programs

### Early Intervention Group (I)

*"Seeing them enjoy themselves, each other"*

*"The kids we work with are very physically handicapped and watching the parents being able to accept the child as they are; being able to appreciate the small things."* MSW/occupational therapist

### Early Intervention Group (II)

Get a lot back

See them grow

Getting resources to family

Seeing a family get a little less dysfunctional

Establishing a relationship with the family

Succeeding

*Child Care Group*

Children are honest, open and loving

Seeing them grow developmentally, come in crawling and leave walking

See parents grow

The discussion on the *joys* of working with this population underscored how much personal satisfaction the participants get from helping children and families grow. They recognize that what they do is valuable.

## D. Strategic lessons

There are **three key strategic lessons** to be learned from this discussion. First, the move toward a family-centered model of intervention may meet resistance because it does not allow for the acknowledgement that the family can also be the source of the child's problem. The discussion of principles and hardships of working in this field seemed to trigger an underlying anger towards parents, especially among public agency supervisors and child care professionals. There is also a subsidiary problem that these statements of principles may be meeting with resistance because they may be perceived to diminish the role of the professional.

Second, there is an element of dismissal in addressing the basic principles because they deal with ideals more than reality. The products developed out of this project must address the issue of resources and priorities, otherwise they will be dismissed as "shooting pretty high." Supervision and mentorship will have to be sold in the context of how they help deal with heavy caseloads, growing demands for administrative reporting, and lack of resources.

Third, people in this field take great pride in how hard they work. The joy they take in their work stems from the consequences of their success—*people's lives get better.* That needs to be a part of the context of the overall message in the materials developed. Don't forget the value of some cheerleading.

## II. Supervision and mentorship

Supervision and mentorship are relationships for learning. While they take on many forms and build on many traditions in work with infants, toddlers, and their families, **ZERO TO THREE** has identified three important dimensions—reflection, collaboration, and regularity—that characterize virtually all effective supervisory and mentorship relationships in this diverse field.

**Reflection** refers to teaching and learning perspective. It emphasizes the ability to understand and explain the reasons for how we do our work. As part of this process there is an effort to address feelings as well as ideas as central to understanding. There is also a need for an examination of the values we bring into the situation, how we balance competing priorities or tradition and innovation, and how we value ourselves and what we bring into the situation.

**Collaboration** presents the field of work with infants, toddlers and their families as a frontier that cannot be traveled alone. It builds on a model of shared power where the supervisor respects the supervisee's knowledge of the clients and appreciates the pooling of expertise and cultural experiences. It builds on ongoing self-evaluation for both parties rather than the traditional "review" or "evaluation" periodically scheduled to monitor (read, "grade") the person being supervised. It requires clear and mutual expectations based on agreement on logistics, confidentiality, and open communications.

**Regularity** means that time must be allocated to these relationships and that time must be protected in spite of the pressures to spend time in direct services, time consuming administrative reporting requirements, and very little personal "down time." Practitioners in this field are often reluctant to invest in their own professional development and regularly scheduled meetings make that a part of the job rather than a personal luxury.

## A. Free association: What do these words mean?

The goal of this section of the research was to see how participants defined supervision and mentorship and see how close their understanding matched these critical dimensions. There was some concern that in too many work experiences supervision means, at worst, "checking up on people," at best, measuring the adequacy of performance against some fixed list of competencies. Neither of these views fits the interactive model of learning that characterizes good supervision.

Participants in all four groups saw clear distinctions between a supervisor and a mentor. Supervision was seen as a more professional relationship while mentorship was seen as more personal. Supervision was described in words focusing on getting the job done with an emphasis on administration and evaluation. It was characterized by words like learning, feedback, boss, teacher, and rules.

Mentorship was described in much more personal terms from "Mentorship is inspirational" to "Mentorship provides more guidance." A mentor focuses on the person's development. Mentors are described in words such as role model, teacher, advisor, and friend. They offer challenge, encouragement, empowerment, and stimulation.

There is a recognition that both supervision and mentorship are relationships for learning, evidenced by the use of teacher in describing both roles. Supervision is not necessarily punitive. Three of the groups used positive terms like "support" or "care" to describe supervision.

When asked to describe the difference between these two words, groups noted that mentorship was a more personal relationship and a more voluntary one as well. A supervisor could be a mentor but did not have to be. In several cases participants voiced the desire to keep them separate.

"*Mentor—more a friend than a supervisor*" MSW, play therapist

"*Supervisor focused on what it is I am doing. Supervision can be much more administrative. Evaluations for purposes of career not necessarily supportive of my development.*" MS in clinical psychology working with children under six

"*Mentor more a coworker with more experience. Supervisor more administrative.*" MSW/occupational therapist

"*You have a choice whether you want to be a mentor or a supervisor.*" Supervisor in public agency

"*Supervision is checking in and watching over you but mentorship is more sitting down with the person and helping guide them.*" Child care worker

"*You may not necessarily want to identify supervisor as mentor.*" Child care worker in toddler/two program

Supervisors in the infant/family field tend to be promoted to their jobs rather than trained for them. When asked how they learned to be supervisors they said they did not know, or by trial and error. Many found themselves drawing, quite consciously, on their own experiences of being supervised to figure out what to do.

When asked to describe what makes for a good supervisor all four groups chose descriptions of recognition, mutual respect, knowledge, and support.

"*Fosters development of someone without pulling your punches about what they need to work on, what they have as a real strength, what they can build on.*"

"*Knowing to be directive and when to give a free hand.*"

"*I listen to what people have to say and I try to motivate my staff to try to get them to remember to be compassionate, focus on the best interest of the child.*"

Many of the descriptions associated with good supervision had dimensions of *reflection* (Someone who explains things, sensitivity, good listening skills), *collaboration* (Mutual respect, treat your staff as professional and give them autonomy, handle conflict constructively, and someone willing to work along side of you), and, to a lesser degree, *regularity* (availability).

The free association discussion of what makes for good supervision suggests that participants in the infant/family field subscribe to and value the dimensions being promoted by this project. **It means there is an opportunity for people to listen, because at some level they already want the characteristics associated with reflection, collaboration, and regularlity and believe that they are a valuable part of good supervision.**

## B. What makes for good supervision?

Broad knowledge base

Sensitivity

Availability

Good listening skills

Treat your staff as professional and give them autonomy

Can handle conflict constructively

Feedback

Someone who explains things

Mutual respect

Someone willing to work alongside of you

### A good supervisor:

Is a sounding board

Never gives criticism without giving help along with it

Helps person come up with alternatives

Inspires confidence

### A bad supervisor:

Belittles person in front of others

Resists confronting problems

Not being available

One who does not have a lot of knowledge

## C. Reflection, collaboration, and regularity

The connection between supervision and reflection, collaboration, and regularity was pursued later in the group discussion through another series of word associations. The purpose of the exercise was to see whether these words by themselves triggered images that we usually use when we apply them to supervision.

First, the participants were told to forget about supervision and mentorship for a moment and asked to clear their toughts and say the first thing that came to mind when they heard each word: reflection, collaboration and regularity.

This was followed by another word association exercise asking what these words meant when applied to supervision. For example, what does reflection mean in relation to supervision? **All three concepts were validated as important dimensions of supervision.**

Collaboration had the most central association as participants clearly expressed their desire for reciprocity, recognition and respect. The value of collaboration to the client and to the young professional was commented upon by several people in every group.

*"Working together to maximize the quality of care the client receives and maximizes your growth as a professional"*

*"If you have cooperation you wind up with a greater product"*

Reflection was seen as a time for self assessment and an opportunity to think about what you are doing. Public agency supervisors did not respond well to reflection. Child care workers paused for quite a bit when asked to apply reflection to supervision but they did offer "Lets you work through something," and the ability to "pick things apart." The result of reflection is "better work."

Regularity was the weakest of the three. There were giggles or comments in every group when the word was used. It was easier to come up with synonyms like consistency, predictability, and dependability than a clear understanding of the concept. They liked regularity but wanted to insure access at other times. This dimension triggered concerns about their own time pressures. While they all wanted supervision they were less willing to embrace regularly scheduled meetings. The majority of participants did not have weekly meetings to review their work.

## III. Supervision and mentorship: Just how important are they?

### A. Importance to working in infant/family field

Everyone acknowledged that supervision was important, especially in a field where so little is really known and a lot of the learning comes through experience. Working with infants and their families is very stressful. The cultural and value divisions between the practitioner and the family exacerbates this tension.

*"You have to get rid of your own value system and listen to what the parents are saying and what the kids are saying and it gets very difficult and that's when you need to go back and tell everyone what your thoughts are and get the support not only in what to do with the child but what to do with the parents and what to do with yourself."* Masters in special education, works with infants and toddlers

Participants agree with the assertion that they are front-line workers in a frontier field. In fact a clinical psychiatrist said so in almost exactly those words:

*"Psychology and social work are pretty much the last frontiers for understanding infants ... Babies don't come out and tell other people 'Oh, I just had a really good session.' I have had the medical director ask me countless times 'Besides assessments just how would you work with an infant?' It is literally beyond what he can see."*

Almost everyone expressed the desire to have people to bounce ideas around with but that was not necessarily their supervisor. The early intervention practitioners with allied health training spoke of being isolated. They wanted peer supervision to help them review their work.

Child care workers and the second group of early intervention practitioners did not really see their supervisor as a partner. Some complained that their supervisors did not have the necessary knowledge base. Others saw them as administrators evaluating their work and were hesitant to reveal their weakness. For these two groups, coworkers were the key to working out problems and bouncing around ideas.

*"A lot of times I'm going to my director asking her questions: 'What about this? What about that?' But she can't always answer my questions so I have stopped asking. I'm just now trying to figure things out between myself and a coworker and we just kind of come up with something that works for us. We don't even ask anymore."* Senior teacher for toddler room, child care center

**In reviewing the conversation I think it is noteworthy that the participants focused largely on their experience with being supervised. There was little voluntary discussion of their roles as supervisors. The day care workers, all lead teachers, did not see themselves as supervising other teachers or aides.**

Many of the early intervention practitioners resented the time constraints supervision placed on them or hated supervising because they did not know how to do it well. Some felt over their head and worried about the consequences:

*"I did it this summer. I did not like it. There is so much to teach and I just needed a lot more training. I don't know how to supervise, that's for sure."* MS, clinical psychology

*"I am supervising a student. It is time consuming. More time consuming than I thought, especially in the beginning."* MSW working in hospital

*"I absolutely hate it. It is the worst part of my job because I don't like the conflict and I find it very difficult ... I had one class on supervision and administration and most of it was on budgeting and policies and contracts ... You just learn through experience."* Early intervention practitioner working with homeless families

The value of supervision was best expressed by an early intervention practitioner (without "mental health" training) who liked being a supervisor:

*"I have had positive experiences as a supervising teacher. I had three student teachers. All three were wonderful. Open to constructive criticism and implementing suggestions. I have also been able to learn from them."*

**The ZERO TO THREE project has found that people who have had positive experiences being supervised become advocates for**

quality supervision. On the whole, these focus group discussions tend to support that finding. However, the fact that many of these participants either do not think of themselves as supervisors in the sense that the project is promoting or they do not like the role (largely because they do not have any training for it) means it will be harder to get them to be advocates for supervision.

## B. The consequences of inadequate supervision

The participants in both early intervention groups and the group of child care professionals were asked what happens when there is no supervision or inadequate supervision. "Chaos" and "panic" were the instant responses in all three groups. It is a serious impediment to doing the work. People told stories of past experiences with bad supervision that meant they did not know what to do to help their clients. This frustration and anger ultimately led several participants to look for a different job.

### [Moderator: "What happens to your ability to do your work?"]

*"Extremely difficult. I have to seek help elsewhere and it is frustrating. When I come across a problem that I can't solve and I can't find somebody to talk about it then I am stuck ..."* MSW working in a therapeutic nursery

*"It is a bad feeling to see another growing professional not getting the kind of help he or she needs, especially in clinical psychology where the tests have a lot of impact on that child. When you know the results that this unsupervised student or intern is putting out are not accurate then that bothers you and it adds a lot of stress to the job."* MS in clinical psychology working with children under six

*"I wanted someone to help me. I was floundering, fresh out of school with little confidence in my own ability outside the classroom and wanted to know what to do."* Early intervention (II)

*"The time when I had an inadequate supervisor, I felt there were very few resources available. What happened to me was I started looking for another job."* Early intervention (II)

*"Where I got from the professional I worked with good supervision and support, I felt confident and I was happy in what I was doing. In the areas where I was not getting it, I was much more insecure and unsure what I was doing for the child."* Child care professional working with toddler/two program

*"[Starting out teaching children with learning disabilities] I was frustrated and stressed because I had no support. I had parents that really did not care enough about their children to really stick to the things that needed to be done to help. My principal—it was her first year—she wasn't giving the support that her teachers needed, that I needed. After my first year I resigned."* Child care professional

### [Moderator: "What did you need?"]

*"I just needed some guidance to tell me: Is this right? No one ever spent time in my room or asked to see my lesson plans. [Would you have wanted her to?] Yes, because it would have given me reinforcement or she could have told me that's not the way to do that, that's not the right idea."*

The conversation about the consequences of inadequate supervision focused on the consequences for the professional—how it made their ability to do the work much more difficult. The absence of any reference to the potential harm to the client was significant. So much so that the moderator probed further by asking who suffers when there is bad supervision. The initial reaction was "everyone" and then, after some silence, "the client" or "the kids suffer". The tone of the response differed by group.

The early intervention group with some "mental health" training was most sensitive to the issue of actually doing harm. They not only worried about not doing the best job possible to push their clients to their potential but they also worried about doing harm.

*"Painful to think that there are times when you could have delivered better service. It may not be your fault that you did not get good supervision but you still feel helpless and responsible like the agent of the damage. Our mistakes could be the death sentences for some of our kids."* MSW working in therapeutic nursery

*"My first reaction when I wasn't getting good supervision was 'I am going to hurt someone by mistake!'"* MSW, play therapist

The second group of early intervention practitioners without "mental health" training acknowledged that bad supervision means not pushing clients to potential but resisted/resented the idea that they might cause harm because they "know what not to do." What they need help in is to push clients to their potential. For them, the consequence of bad supervision was not being able to do their job.

*"I was hired to help children and I wasn't doing anything."* MS in special education, homebased teacher of children with disabilities

*"We want to have someone say 'Yes, you are doing the right thing' and give you that reinforcement to make sure you are performing your job."* Occupational therapist

The child care professionals said inadequate supervision leads to chaos, but for them chaos meant the children get out of control. Inadequate supervision of the teachers becomes harmful to the children when the child care professional does not do a good job. There was not that much discussion because they thought it self-evident that "not watching children" will lead to some harm. They, like the first early intervention group, felt personally responsible for the safety and security of the children. This was not just a matter of not doing the best job possible.

There was an underlying current of denial in the discussion of the value of supervision which forced the moderator to ask whether the absence of good supervision does harm. Most participants in the infant/family field have a very strong sense of responsibility for their clients. It is hard for them to acknowledge that real harm can come about from inadequate supervision. Resistance may be magnified by the fact that they perceive inadequate supervision as a pervasive problem that they don't see as changing, so why confront it.

When forced to confront the issue there was a lot of discomfort but an acknowledgment that inadequate supervision, at best, means not doing a good job, and, at worst doing real harm. The challenge to increasing the salience of supervision is not a matter of emphasizing its importance but rather addressing the pervasive sense of acceptance of uneven supervision that makes it hard to both acknowledge and attack this problem.

## C. The bottom line

Having acknowledged the importance of supervision, the participants were **not ready to allocate scare resources to improve the delivery of supervision.** In a world of heavy caseloads, reduced services and administrative overload, supervision is seen as too removed from these more pressing problems.

The participants in both early intervention groups and child care professionals were asked how they would spend $50,000 if it were given to their program. "Personnel" and "more services" were the most common answers in each of the groups.

Most of the early intervention practitioners with "mental health" training gave the supervision provided in their institutions a low grade (two-thirds got less than a B). Yet supervision was not a high priority for this group. Services was the number one priority for allocating new money, followed by more personnel. Two people in this group did volunteer supervision after some discussion by the moderator. But they would allocate hundreds, not thousands of dollars to this effort.

All the participants in the second early intervention group gave their institutions high rating on supervision. They would put new money in personnel and equipment. When asked why they would not spend money on supervision it became clear that it was not seen as something that directly impacts on the clients. One participant who talked about how supervision was critical in helping her cope with the cultural differences in values between herself and the families she works with and who left a job because of bad supervision said:

*"I would not put much value on supervision. I know that sounds harsh but I think the value is in the program and let's try to beef it up."*

Another woman who had been a strong advocate of supervision and championed the family-centered approach over the medical approach to working in this field said:

*"I see as a priority the people that we are serving and the people we are serving are the children. So I guess when somebody says, 'Here I'm going to give you this money,' that's where your first thoughts go. Ultimately, I guess better supervision is important but it just seems so far away, so far removed."*

The child care group didn't believe they were being supervised. At best they had monthly staff meetings. They did not think this was willful but rather a matter of scarce resources. With increasing ratios and decreasing profit margins most said supervision was a luxury. They would, however, spend the money on training. Training was seen as a way to help cope with increasing demands.

**The bottom line of this discussion is that while practitioners in the infant/family field recognize the benefits of supervision to themselves they do not see it as a priority when it comes to helping their clients. They do not feel entitled to spend money on themselves because they are there to serve their clients. It is unclear to the participants in all three groups how supervision helps their clients. How does one weigh that help in comparison to more personnel and access to services?**

There was a strong sense of working harder to help the client. Supervision was something that would help them. While they wanted and knew they needed this help, it was seen as at the expense of the client rather than to their benefit.

## Conclusion

The findings of this study point to some important validation of **ZERO TO THREE's** work in defining and designing a model for supervision and mentorship and suggests some challenges that the development of such a model may face.

The discussion of what makes for good supervision and the word association exercises underscored that participants in the infant/family field subscribe to and value reflection, collaboration, and regularity as central dimensions to supervision and mentorship. This means that the new "language" to capture these dimensions will be understood and accepted by the audience.

The most salient challenge to selling the saliency of supervision is the lack of entitlement many of these practitioners feel. They see supervision as something for them rather than their clients and they are not as important as the people they serve. In order to really institutionalize good supervision and mentorship programs, the project will have to do some education on how supervision translates to better care for the client so that the practitioners feel entitled to ask for this help.

The second most important challenge (linked to the first) is that supervision and mentorship cannot be discussed in a vacuum, independent of the restraints on resources and growing caseloads that everyone is experiencing. There has to be some discussion beyond the value of supervision to how one does it in a world of limited resources.

The men and women working in this field get a tremendous amount of self-satisfaction in doing this work but they get very little validation from the world outside their workplace. The participants in these groups felt terrific about being asked for their opinions, and the process of going through this collective conversation helped clear their thoughts on supervision and mentorship. Several said they actually learned a lot and would now be better supervisors. This learning underscores why there needs to be an effort to improve the quality of supervision and mentorship arrangements in the development of practitioners in the field.

# Appendix B
# Selected Readings on Supervision and Mentorship

Publications that specifically address supervision and mentorship in infant/family training and practice are scarce indeed. The following articles, books, and other materials were recommended by members of **ZERO TO THREE**/National Center for Clinical Infant Programs' Work Group on Learning through Supervision and Mentorship or discovered by project staff in the course of a limited review of the supervision/mentorship literature of a number of professional disciplines and the field of business and organizational management. As the findings of the Learning through Supervision and Mentorship Work Group suggest, the conceptualization and practice of supervision and mentorship vary greatly with discipline and context. We hope that readers interested in supervision and mentorship in the infant/family field will find themselves informed, stimulated, and challenged by a look at perspectives offered by writers both within and beyond their own area of specialization.

American Speech-Language-Hearing Association. 1989. *Language, Speech and Hearing Services in Schools.* 20:3.—*special clinical forum on the supervisory process, with articles by Kathryn J. Smith, Judith Brasseur, Ann Johnson Gloser and Carole Donnelly, Brenda Mawdsley and Rosalind Scudder, and David Shapiro and Nelson Moss.*

Anderson, EM. & Shannon, AL. 1988. Toward a Conceptualization of Mentoring. *Journal of Teacher Education.* (January-February) 38-42.

Austin, LN. 1952. Basic Principles of Supervision. *Social Casework* 33. (December) 411-419.

Bailey, DB, Jr., Palsha, SA, & Simeonsson, RJ. 1991. Professional Skills, Concerns, and Perceived Importance of Work with Families in Early Intervention. *Exceptional Children.* Vol. 58, No.2.

Bernstein, VJ, Hans, SL & Percansky, C. 1991. Advocating for the Young Child in Need Through Strengthening the Parent-Child Relationship. *Journal of Clinical Child Psychology.* 20:1, 28-41.

Bloom, PJ, Sheerer, M & Britz, J. 1991. *Blueprint for Action: Achieving Center-Based Change Through Staff Development.* Lake Forest, IL: New Horizons Educational Consultants and Learning Resources.

Bullough, RV. 1990. Supervision, Mentoring and Self-Discovery: A Case Study of a First-year Teacher. *Journal of Curriculum and Supervision.* 5:4, 338-360.

Catalyst. 1991. Mentoring-What Makes it Work? *Catalyst Perspective.* (December). (Catalyst, 250 Park Avenue South, New York, NY 10003 1459.)

Child Care Employee Project and Chabot College Early Childhood Development Department. 1990. Child Care Mentor Teacher Pilot Program: Final Report. Berkeley, CA and Hayward, CA: Authors.

Clark, RW & Zimmmer, BP. 1989. Mentoring: Does it work? *Lifelong learning: An omnibus of practice and research.* 12:7, 26-28.

Cogan, ML. 1976. Rationale for Clinical Supervision. *Journal of Research and Development in Education.* 9:2, 3-19.

Dreher, GF & Ash, RA. 1990. A Comparative Study of Mentoring Among Men and Women in Managerial, Professional, and Technical Positions. *Journal of Applied Psychology.* 75:5, 539-546.

Ekstein, R & Wallerstein, RS. 1980. The Supervisor Meets the Student. *The Teaching and Learning of Psychotherapy.* New York: International Universities Press.

Fawcett, MT. 1986. *Supervision in Early Childhood Education; A Developmental Perspective*. New York: Teachers' College Press.

Gardner, J. 1990. *Community*. Stanford, CA: Graduate School of Business, Stanford University.

Gehrke, NJ. 1988. On Preserving the Essence of Mentoring as One Form of Teacher Leadership. *Journal of Teacher Education*. (January February) 43-45).

Greenspan, SI & Wieder, S. 1984. Dimensions and Levels of the Therapeutic Process. *Psychotherapy*. 21, No. 1.

Hawthorne, L. 1975. Games Supervisors Play. *Social Work*. (May).

Holusha, J. 1991. Grace Pastiak's "Web of Inclusion." *The New York Times: Business*. (May 5) Sec. 3 & pg. 6.

Howey, K. 1988. Mentor-Teachers As Inquiring Professionals. *The Education Digest*. (December) 19-22.

Hurley, D. 1988. The Mentor Mystique. *Psychology Today*. (May) 41 43.

Jones, E. 1986. *Teaching Adults: An Active Learning Approach*. Washington, DC: NAEYC.

Kagan, DM. 1988. Research on the Supervision of Counselors- and Teachers-in-Training: Linking Two Bodies of Literature. *Review of Educational Research* 58:1, 1-24.

Kaplan, M & Buescher, T. 1986. Inservice Training for Urban Day Care Centers: An Evaluation of Training Strategies. *Child Care Quarterly*. 15:1, 38-49.

Mackey, R. 1980. Developmental Process in Growth-Oriented Groups. *Social Work*. (January) 26-30.

Manis, F. 1979. *Openness in Social Work Field Instruction*. Goleta, CA: Kimberly Press, Inc.

Mead, DE. 1990. *Effective Supervision: A Task-Oriented Model for the Mental Health Professions*. New York: Brunner/Mazel, Inc.'

Musick, JS. & Stott, FM. 1989. Paraprofessionals, Parenting and Child Development: Understanding the Problems and Seeking Solutions. In S. Meisels and J. Shonkoff (Eds.). *Handbook of Early Intervention*. New York: Cambridge University Press.

Neugebauer, R. 1984. Assessing Team Performance. *Child Care Information Exchange*. (November) (published by Exchange Press, Inc., PO Box 2890, Redmond, WA 98073)

Neugebauer, R. 1984. Step by Step Guide to Team Building. *Child Care Information Exchange*. (June)

Neugebauer, R. 1984. Who's Responsible for Making Your Team Work? *Child Care Information Exchange*. (January)

The Program for Infant/Toddler Caregivers. 1988. *Visions for Infant/Toddler Care: Guidelines for Professional Caregiving*. Sacramento, CA: California State Department of Education.

Provence S & Naylor, A. 1983. *Working with Disadvantaged Parents and Their Children*. New Haven and London: Yale University Press.

Public/Private Ventures. 1992. Mapping the Mentoring Phenomenon. *Public/Private Ventures News*. xx. (Winter) (published by Public/Private Ventures, 399 Market Street, Philadelphia, PA 19106)

Public/Private Ventures. 1992. Intergenerational Mentoring Gets Test in Two Cities. *Public/Private Ventures News*. xx. (Winter)

Rein, M & White, SH. 1982. Practice Worries in the Helping Professions. *Society*. (Sept./Oct.).

Rothman, P & van der Zande, I. 1990. *Parent/Toddler Group: A Model for Effective Intervention to Facilitate Normal Growth and Development*. Los Angeles, CA: The Early Childhood Center, Cedars Sinai Medical Center.

Rowe, W & Sheilds, R. 1985. A Supervisory Model for Child Care. *Child Care Quarterly*. 14:4. (Winter) 262-272.

Schaefer, AB. 1982. Clinical Supervision. *Counseling Psychologist*. 10.

Scherz, FB. 1958. A Concept of Supervision Based on Definitions of Job Responsibility. *Social Casework*. (October) 70-82.

Schowalter, JE & Pruett, K. 1974. The Supervision Process for Individual Child Psychotherapy. Paper presented at the 21st annual meeting of the American Academy of Child Psychiatry, October 26. Abstracted in *Psychiatric Spectator*. (Fall, 1975). 9:12, 8-9.

Sergiovanni, TJ. 1976. Toward a Theory of Clinical Supervision. *Journal of Research and Development in Education*. 9:2, 20-29.

Sheafor, B and Jenkins L. 1982. *Quality Field Instruction in Social Work*. New York: Longman.

Shulman, J. 1988. Look to a Colleague. *Instructor*. (January) 32-34.

Shulman, J. 1986. *The Mentor Teacher Casebook*. San Francisco, CA: Far West Laboratory.

Walker, JA. 1978. The Practicum Supervisor Inches Toward Competence: Preliminary Thoughts on a Process. *TEASE*. 1:2, 14-27.

Wasik, BH., Bryant, DM. & Lyons, CM. 1990. *Home Visiting: Procedures for Helping Families*. Newbury Park, CA: Sage Publications.

Winton, PJ. 1991. *Working with Families in Early Intervention: An Interdisciplinary Preservice Curriculum*, Second Edition. Chapel Hill, NC: Carolina Institute for Research on Infant Personnel Preparation, Frank Porter Graham Child Development Center, University of North Carolina.

Young-Holt, CL. 1983. Participatory Management: A Supportive Leadership Model for the 80s. *Child Care Information Exchange.* (January/February)

Zimpher, NL. 1988. A Design for the Professional Development of Teacher Leaders: Leadership. *Journal of Teacher Education.* (January-February) 53-60.

# Contributors

*Kelley Bateman* - Manassas, Virginia

*Judith Bertacchi* - Virginia Frank Child Development Center, Jewish Family and Community Service, Chicago, Illinois

*Carole W. Brown* - George Washington University, Washington, D.C.

*Julie Coplon* - Virginia Frank Child Development Center, Jewish Family and Community Service, Chicago, Illinois

*Tippie DeLeo* - Prince George's County Health Department, Maryland

*Robert Drachman* - Prince George's Hospital Center, Cheverly, Maryland

*Linda Eggbeer* - **ZERO TO THREE**/National Center for Clinical Infant Programs, Arlington, Virginia

*Emily Fenichel* - **ZERO TO THREE**/National Center for Clinical Infant Programs, Arlington, Virginia

*Barbara Fields* - New York, New York

*Linda Gilkerson* - Erikson Institute, Chicago, Illinois

*Robert Halpern* - Erikson Institute, Chicago, Illinois

*Barbara Ivins* - Children's Hospital, Oakland, California

*Mary Larner* - National Center for Children in Poverty, New York City

*Judith Pekarsky* - San Francisco General Hospital, University of California, San Francisco

*Jane Perry* - Child Care Employee Project, Oakland, California

*Kyle Pruett* - Yale Child Study Center, New Haven, Connecticut

*Madie Robinson* - Healthy Start, Florence, South Carolina

*William M. Schafer* - Ann Arbor, Michigan

*Rebecca Shahmoon Shanok* - Jewish Board of Family and Children's Services, New York City

*Frances M. Stott* - Erikson Institute, Chicago, Illinois

*Nancy Sweet* - Children's Hospital, Oakland, California

*Eva K. Thorp* - George Mason University, Fairfax, Virginia

*Serena Wieder* - Silver Spring, Maryland

*Carol Lou Young-Holt* - Far West Laboratory for Educational Research and Development, Sausalito, California